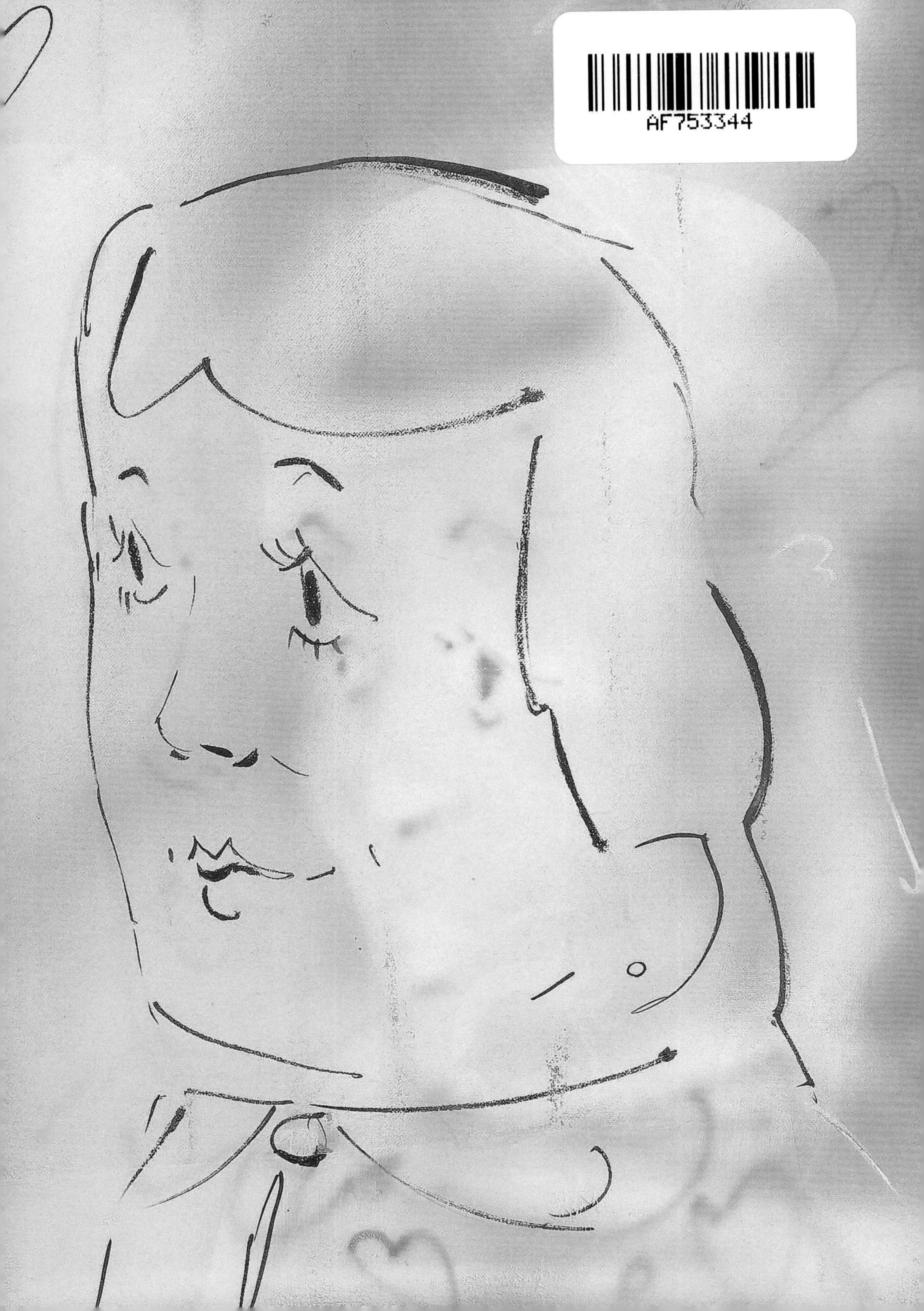

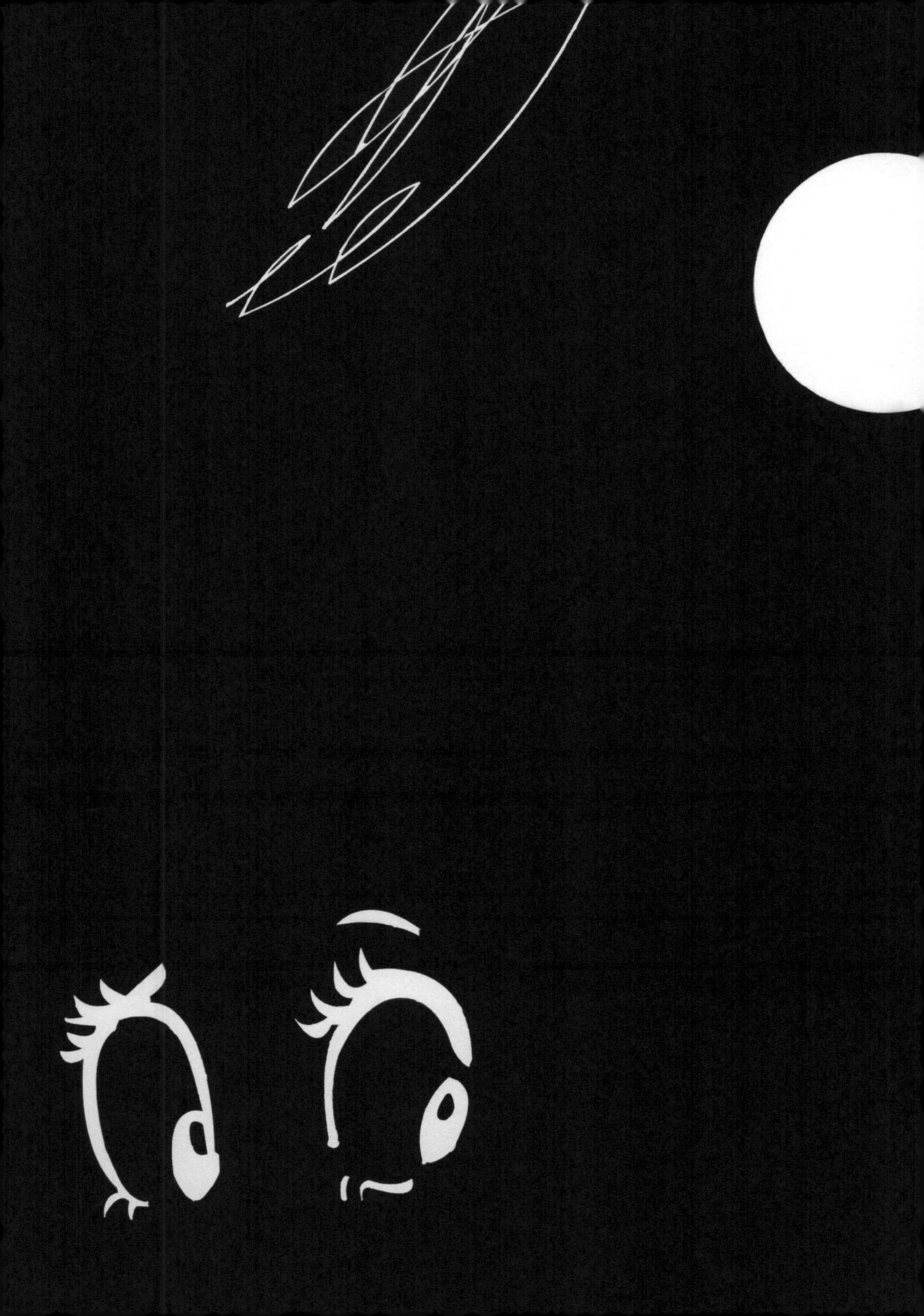

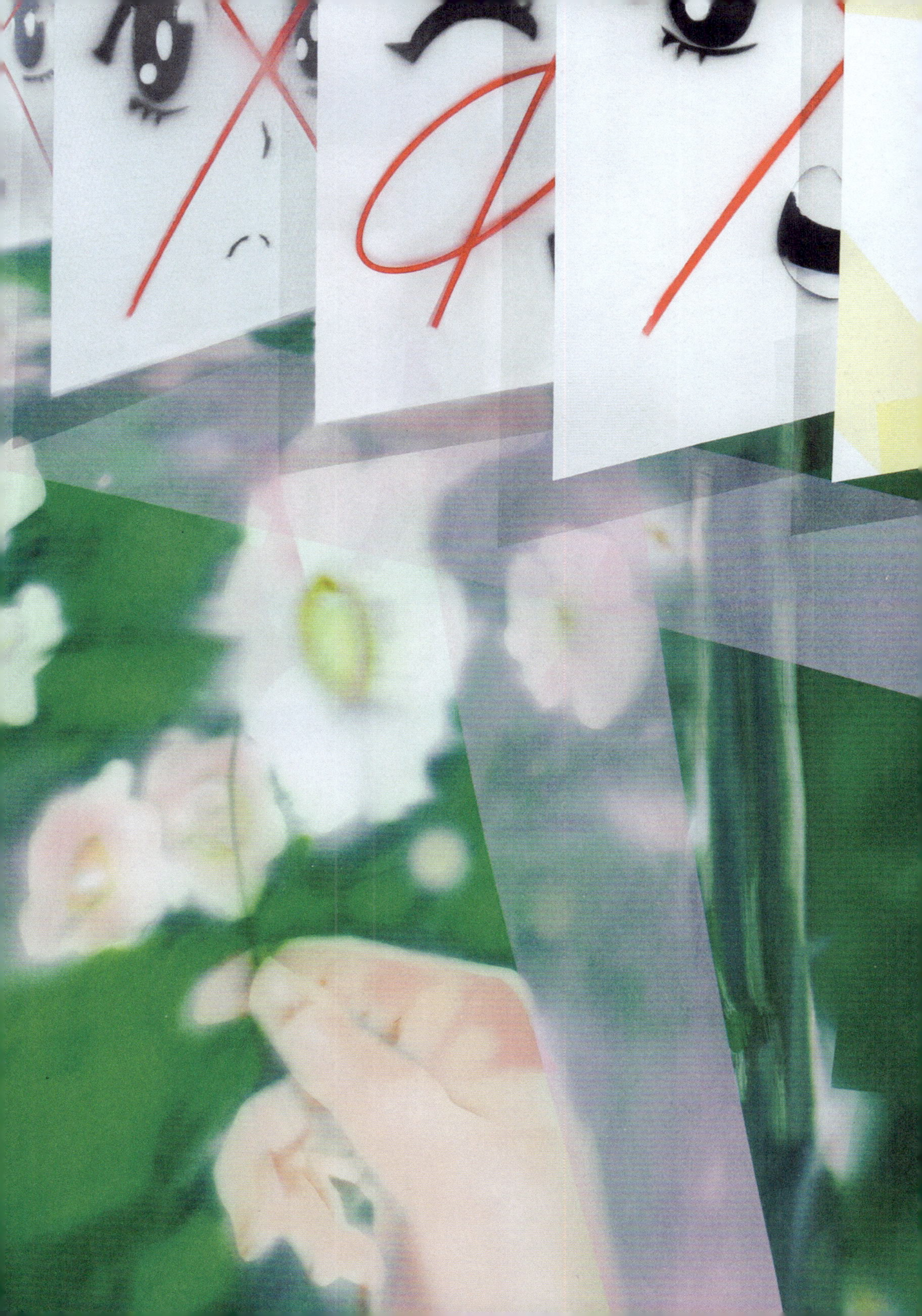

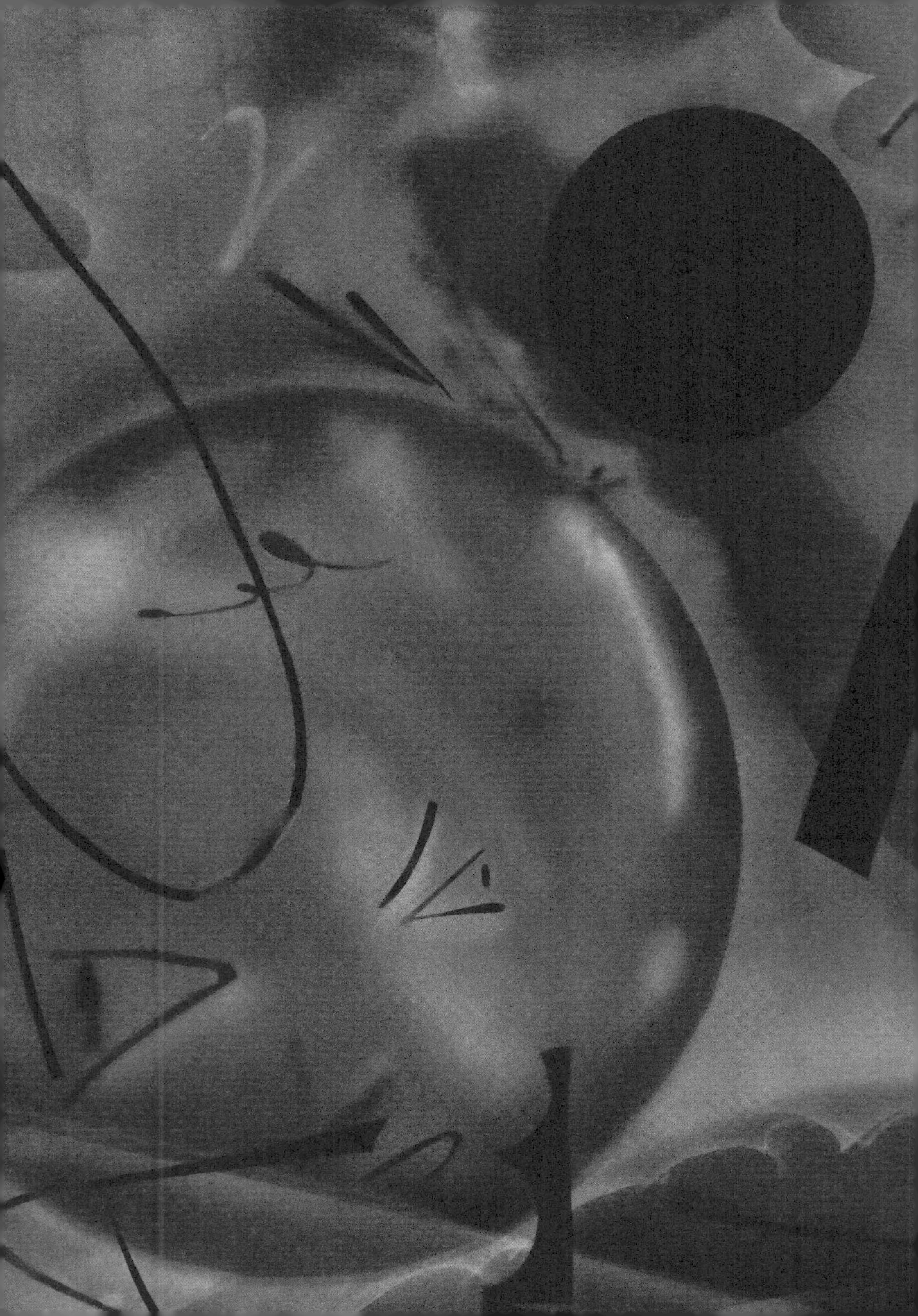

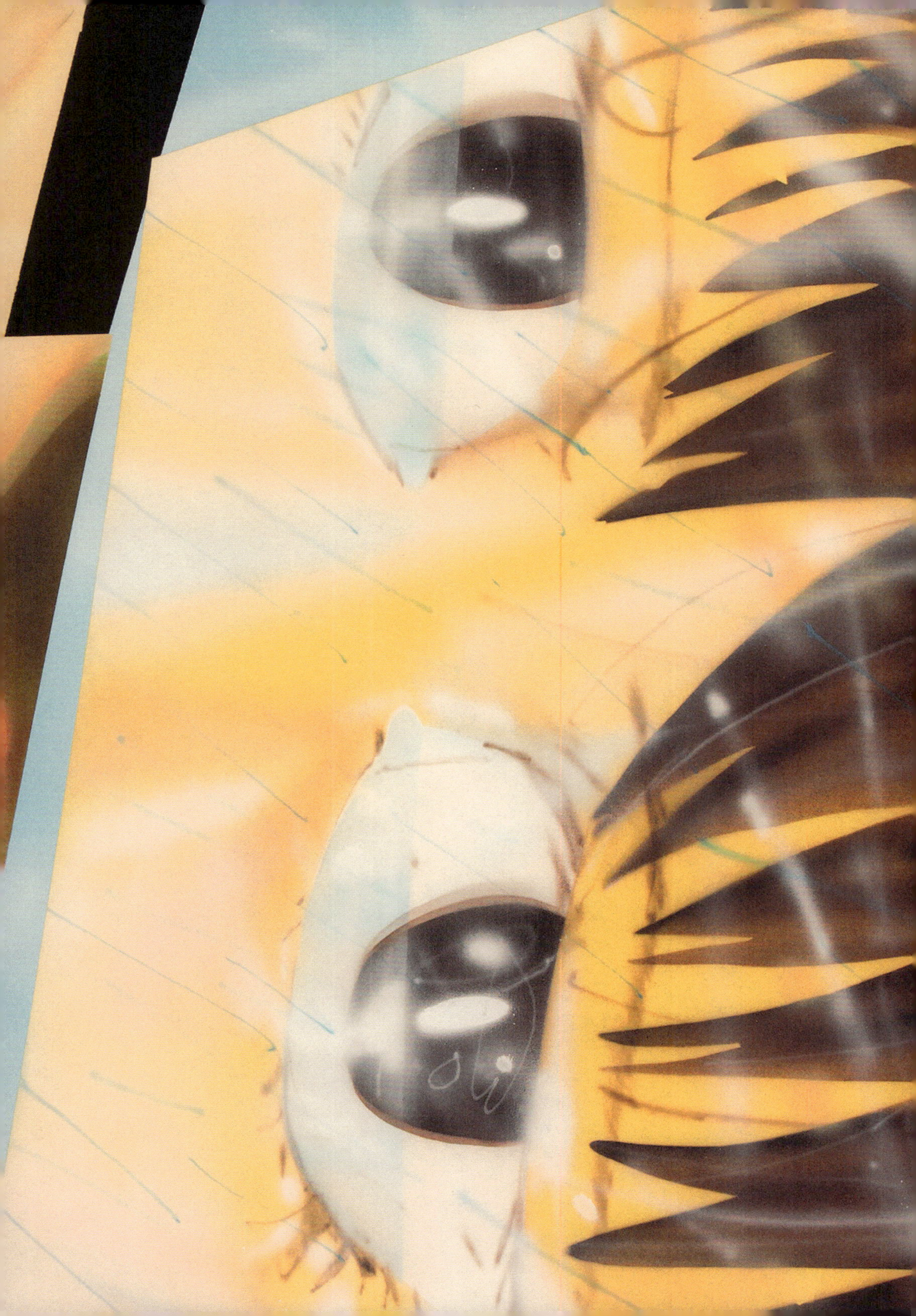

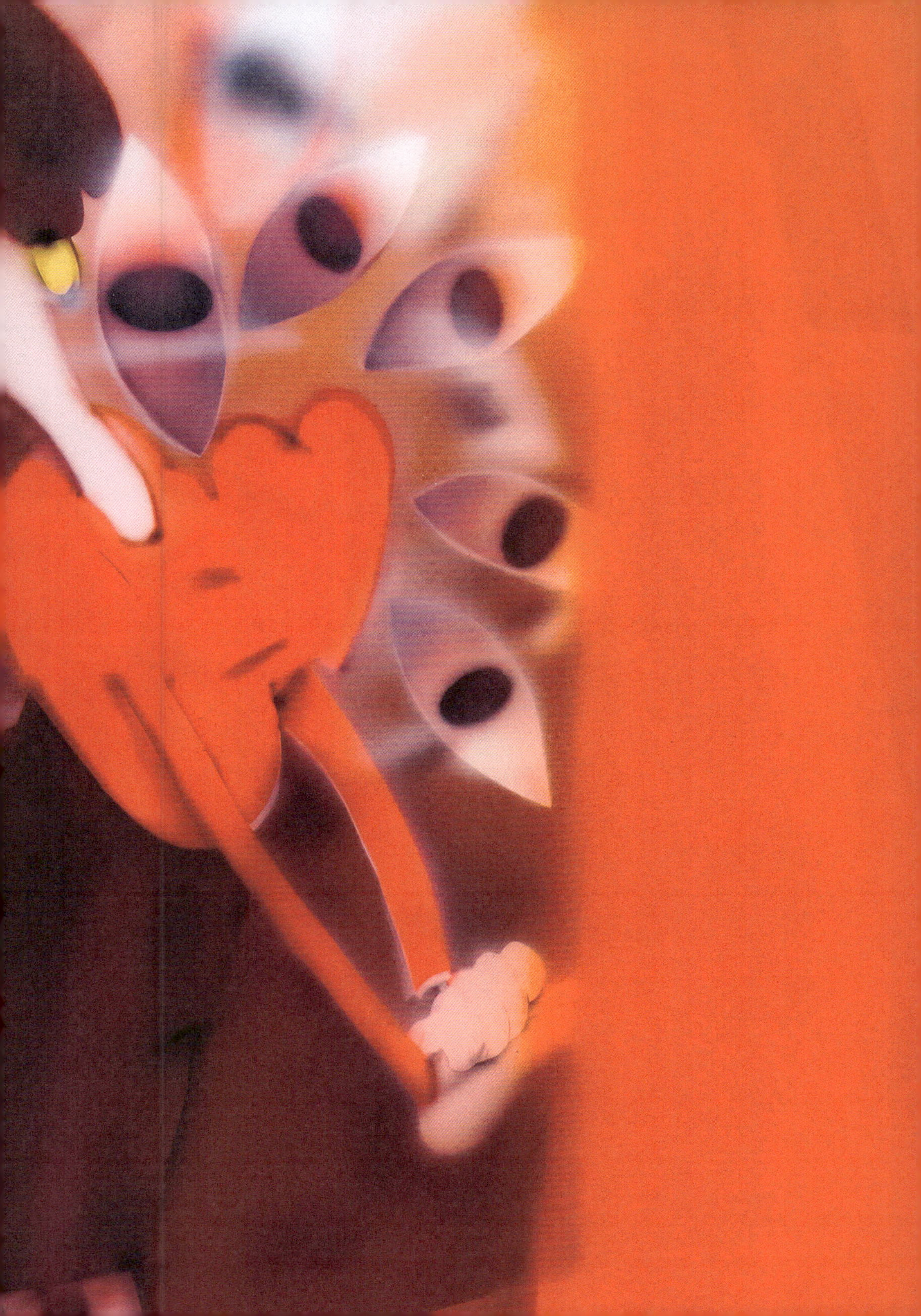

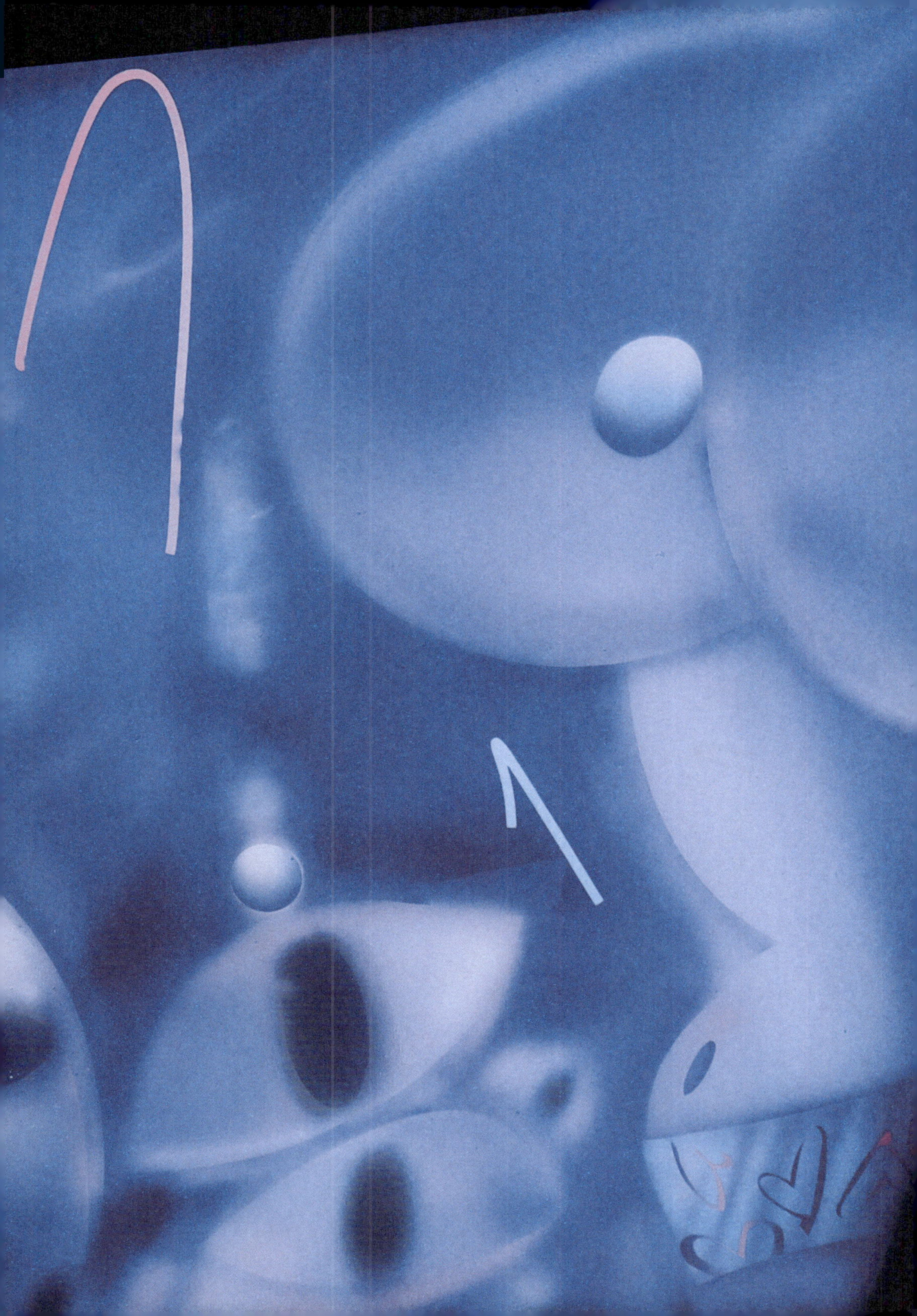

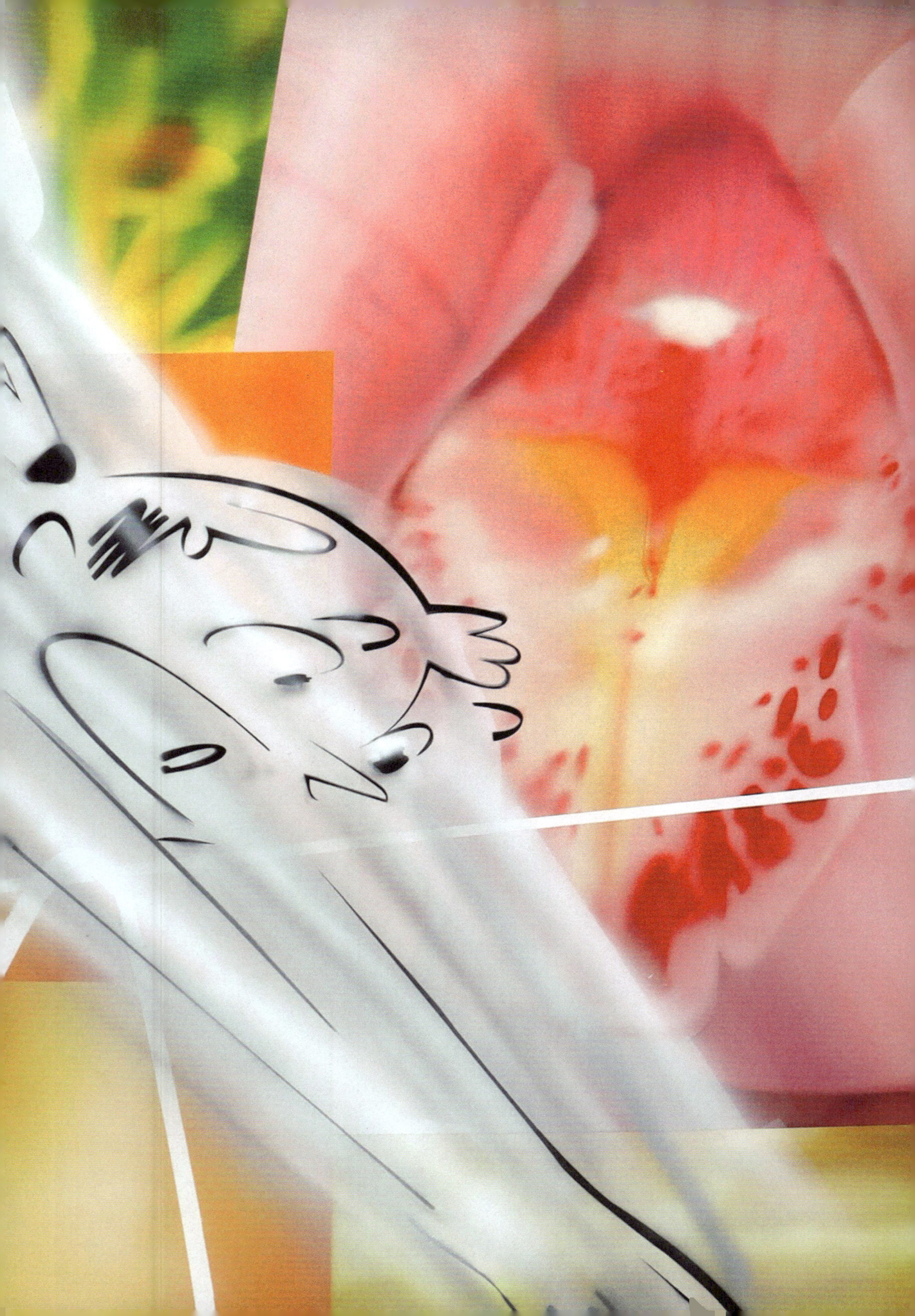

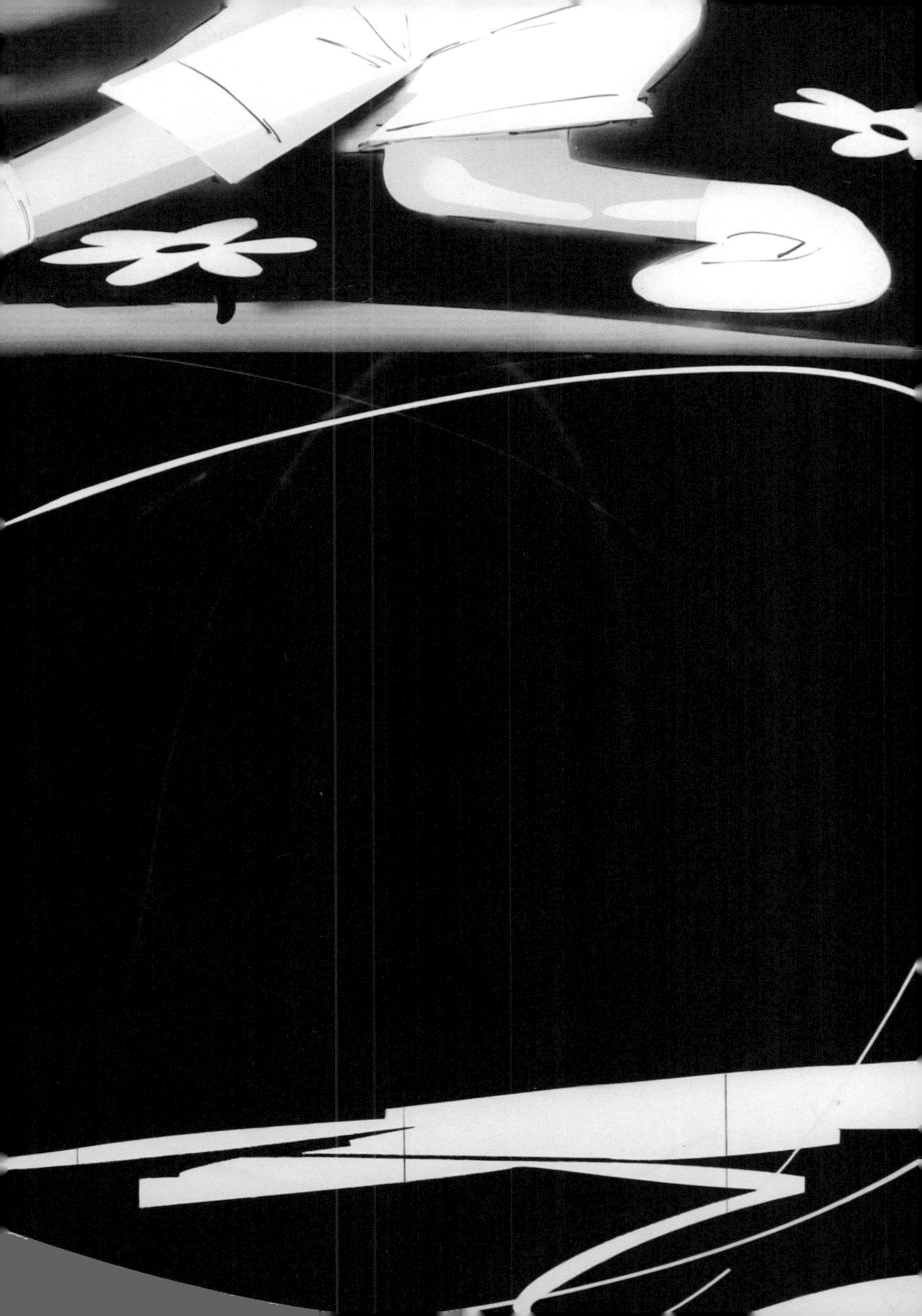

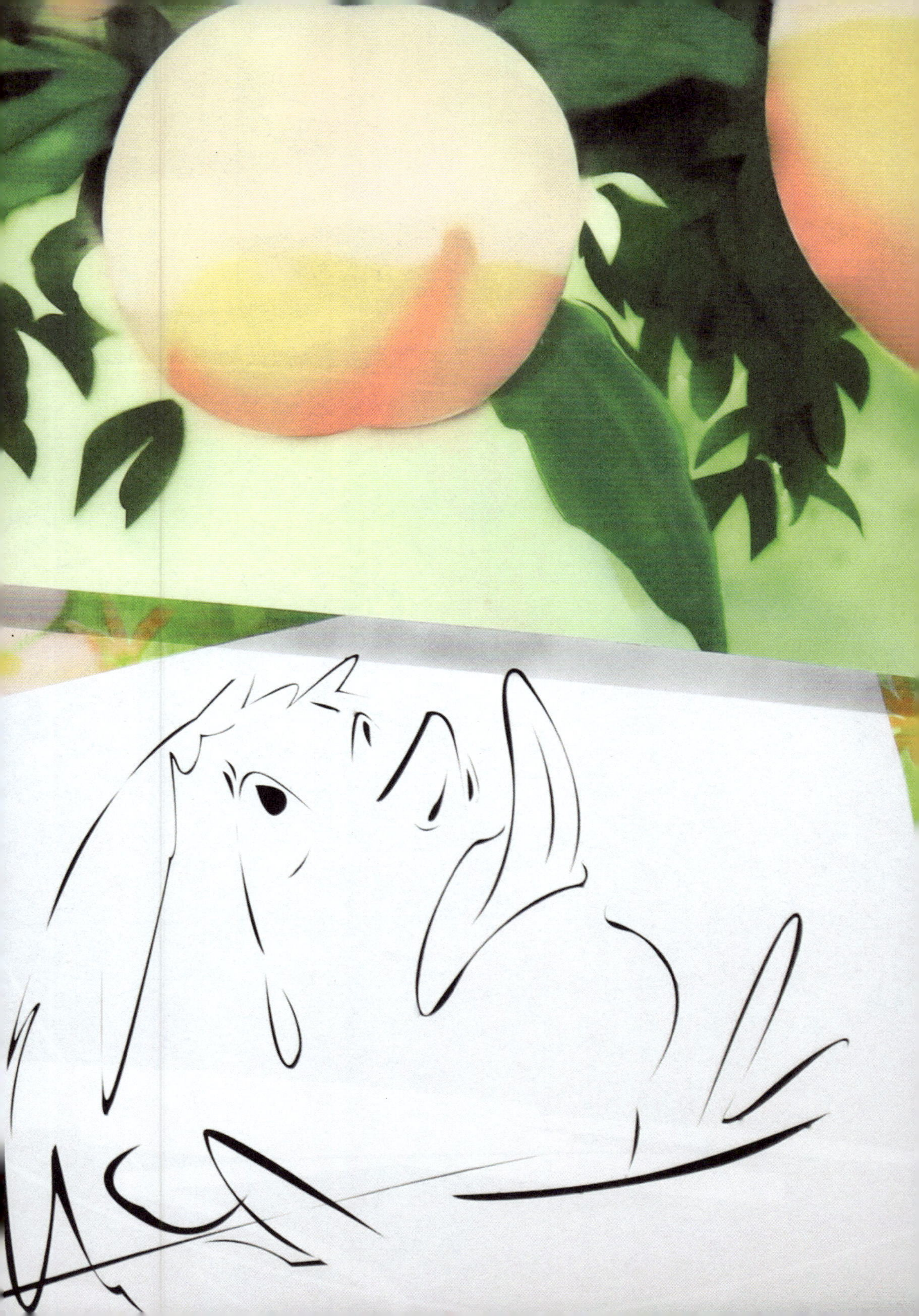

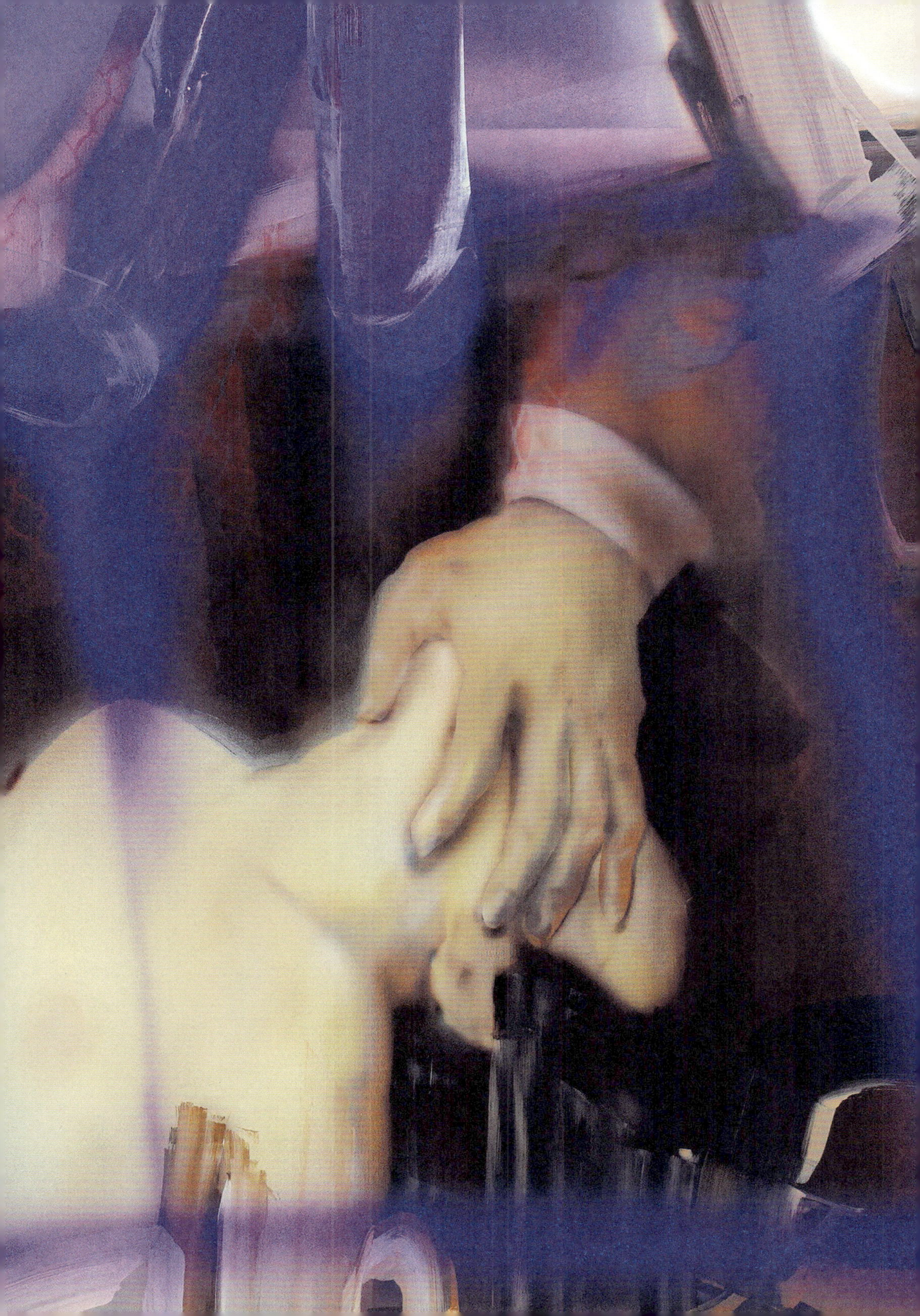

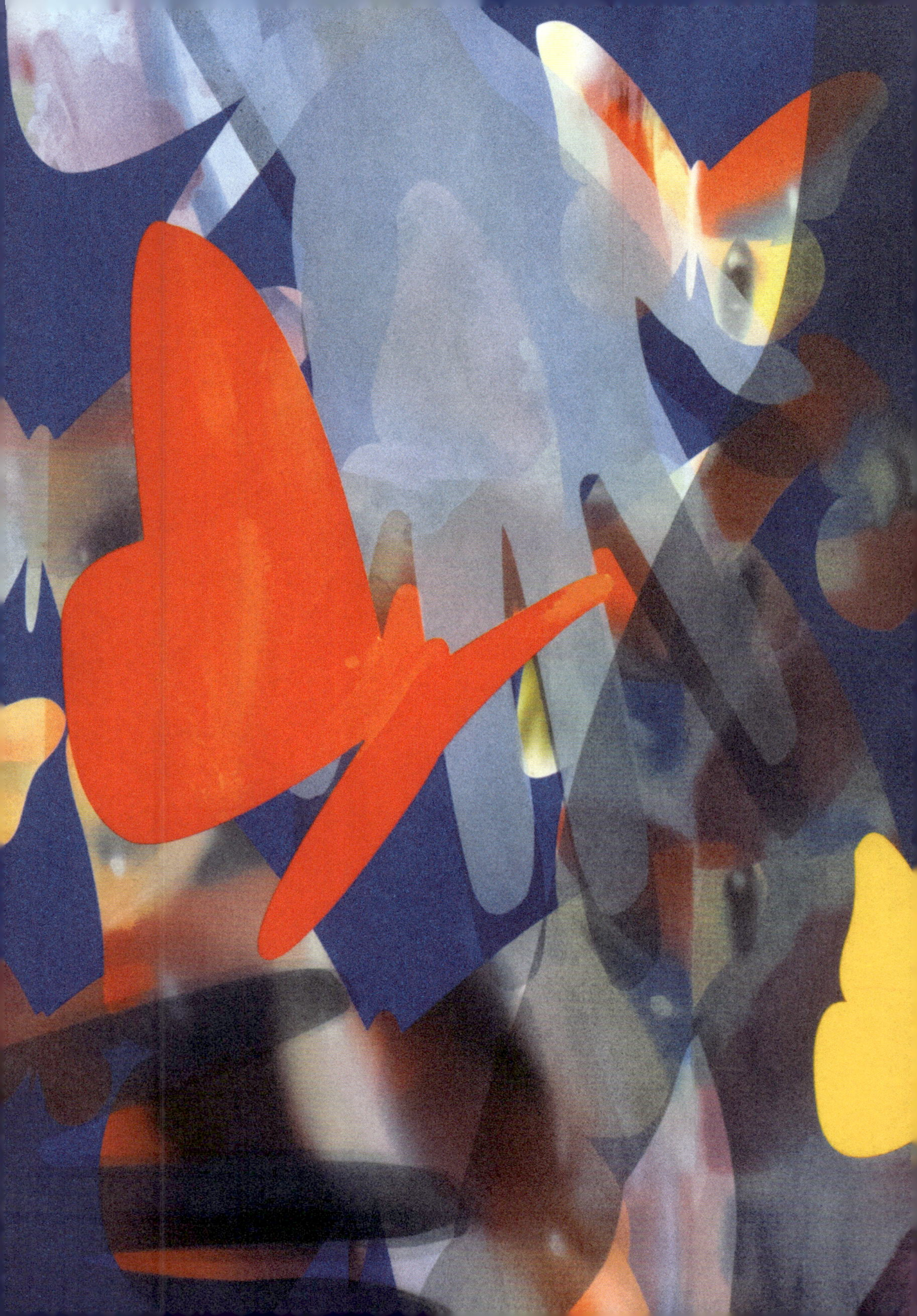

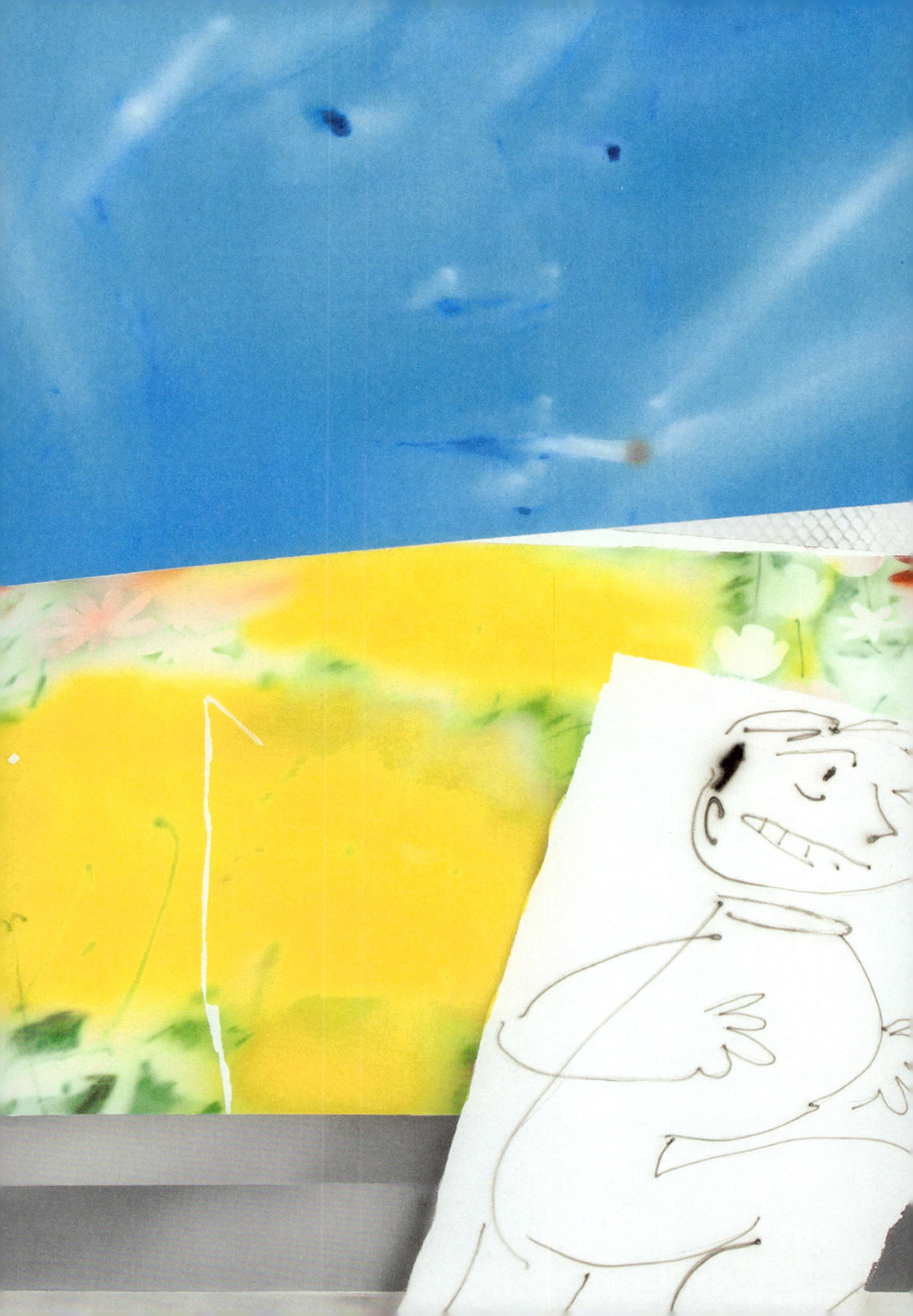

*Where Is the Flower Gone?* (detail), 2019. Acrylic on canvas, 150 × 100 cm
*How to Make Vertical Sky* (detail), 2021. Acrylic and modeling paste on canvas, 150 × 120 cm
*I Died but I still Love You* (detail), 2019. Acrylic on canvas, 139 × 107 cm
*The Darkness Reveals the Eyes* (detail), 2020. Acrylic on canvas, 180 × 150 cm
*Flowers Are Picked One by One* (detail), 2022. Acrylic on canvas, 170 × 200 cm
*Untitled* (detail), 2019. Acrylic on suede canvas, 100 × 70 cm
*Dear St. Agatha I Am Witness of Your Tears, In the Land of Tulips* (detail), 2020. Acrylic on canvas, 150 × 130 cm
*The Love Fire* (detail), 2021. Acrylic on canvas, 180 × 150 cm
*The Chill Fighter Can Scatter the Eyes* (detail), 2021. Acrylic on canvas, 150 × 180 cm
*There Is a Brick Wall, Bricks Are Broken and She Falls, So Happy Birthday to All* (detail), 2021. Acrylic on canvas, 210 × 175 cm
*I Am Here, I Am Not Here* (detail), 2021. Acrylic on canvas, 150 × 120 cm
*Tantalus Punishment* (detail), 2021. Acrylic and silkscreen print on canvas, 210 × 175 cm
*Purple Is Healing the Wound Between Sword and Neck* (detail), 2022. Acrylic on canvas, 180 × 150 cm
*Oh! Butterflies* (detail), 2023. Acrylic on canvas, 210 × 175 cm
*All Beautiful Lives Start Floating when Dark Falls, Maybe I Am Somewhere Else Above Skies* (detail), 2019. Acrylic on canvas, 185 × 151 cm

*Black as Black*, 2021. Acrylic on canvas, 210 × 175 cm

*Last Sunset, Last Dive*, 2021. Acrylic on canvas, 210 × 175 cm

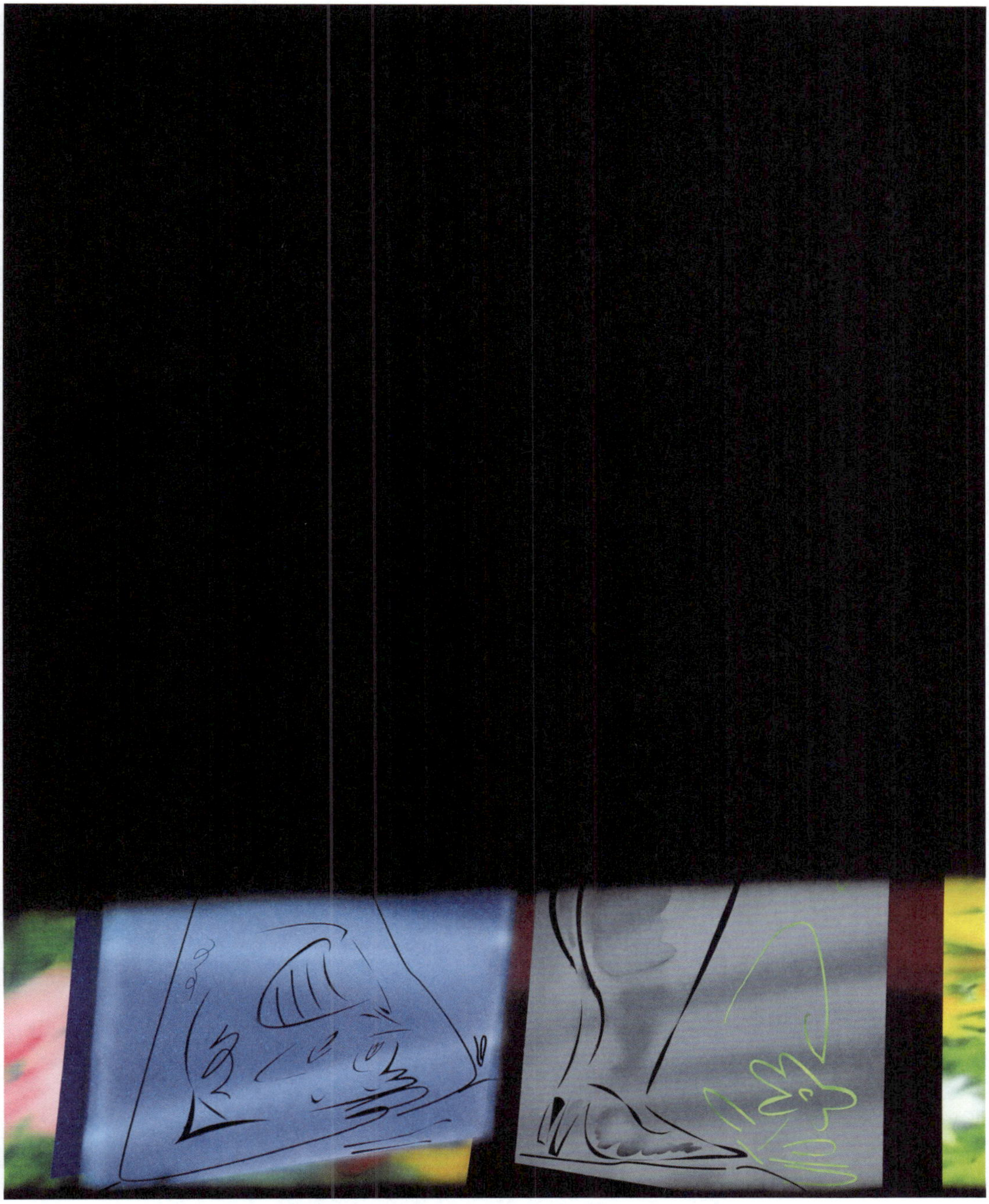

*The Top Secret*, 2021. Acrylic on canvas, 210 × 175 cm

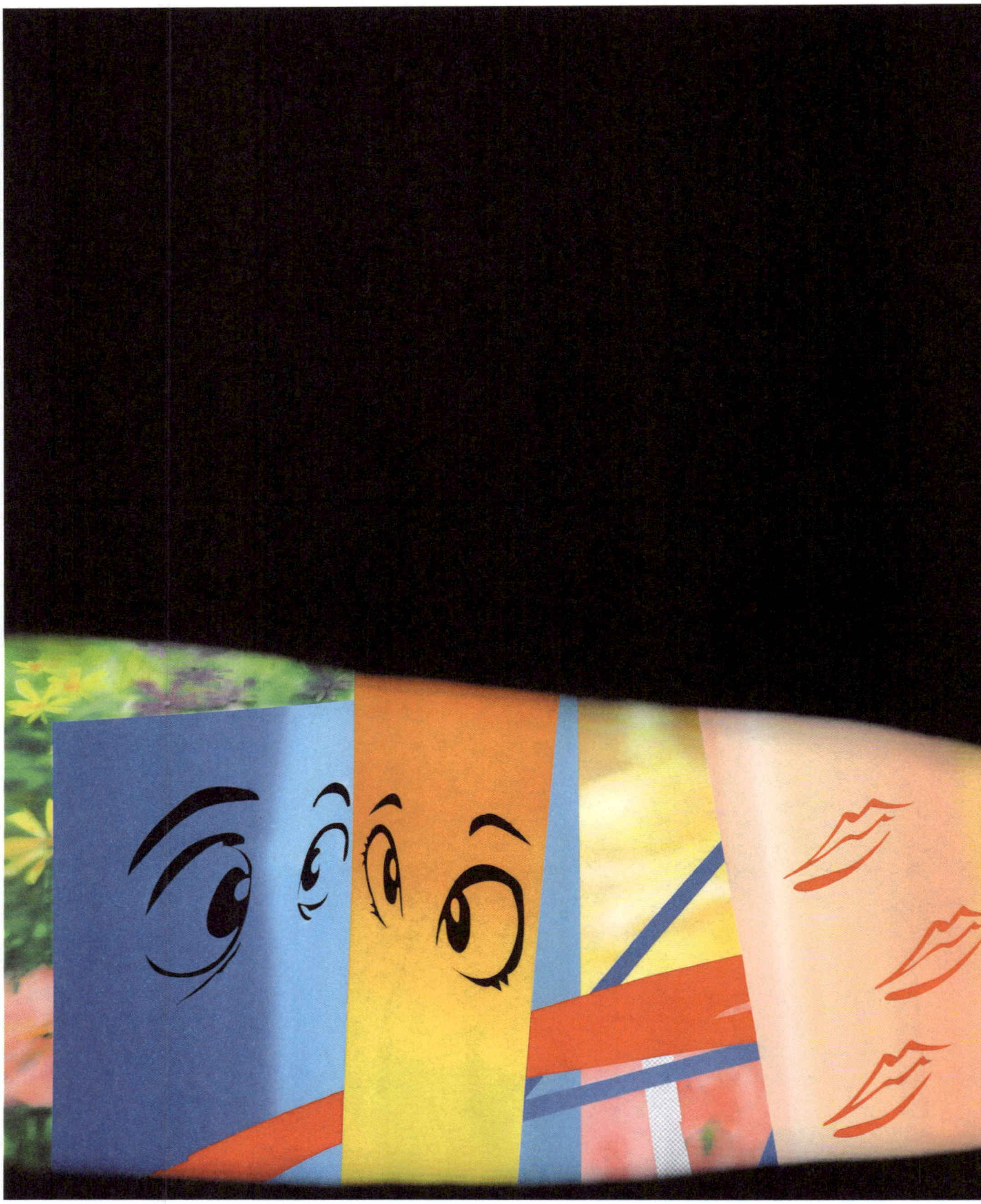

*Along Evening*, 2021. Acrylic on canvas, 210 × 175 cm

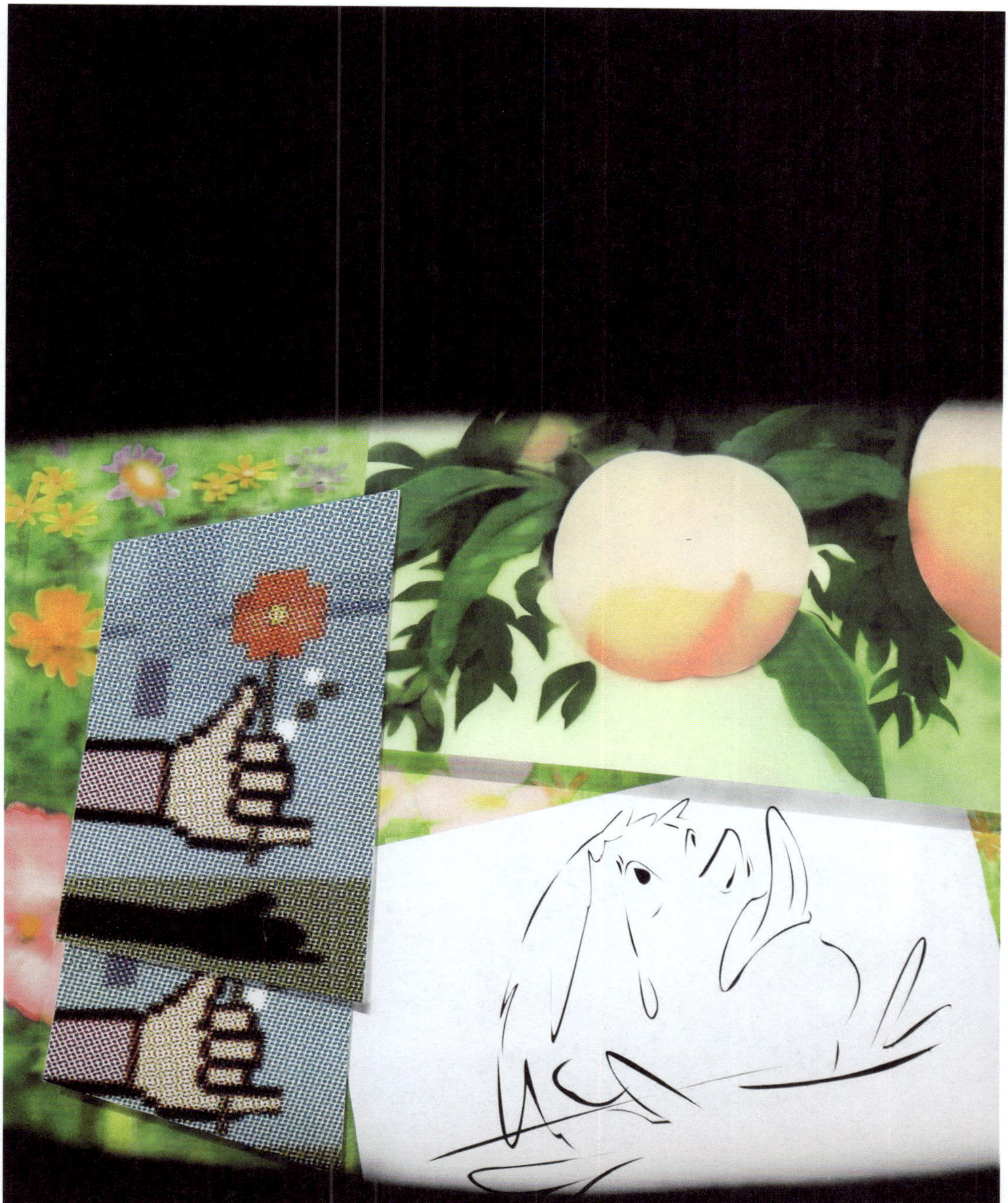

*Tantalus Punishment*, 2021. Acrylic and silkscreen print on canvas, 210 × 175 cm

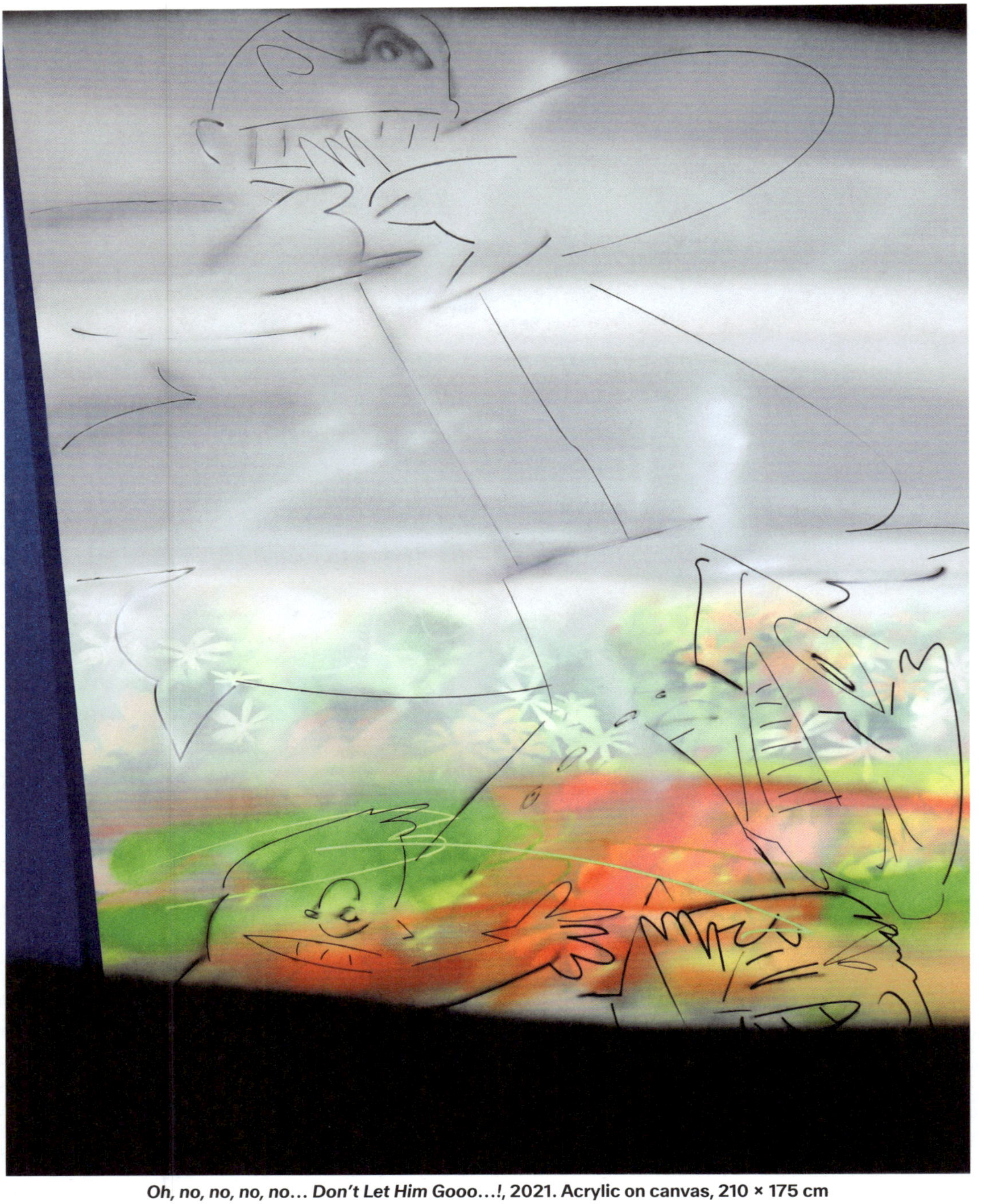

*Oh, no, no, no, no… Don't Let Him Gooo…!*, 2021. Acrylic on canvas, 210 × 175 cm

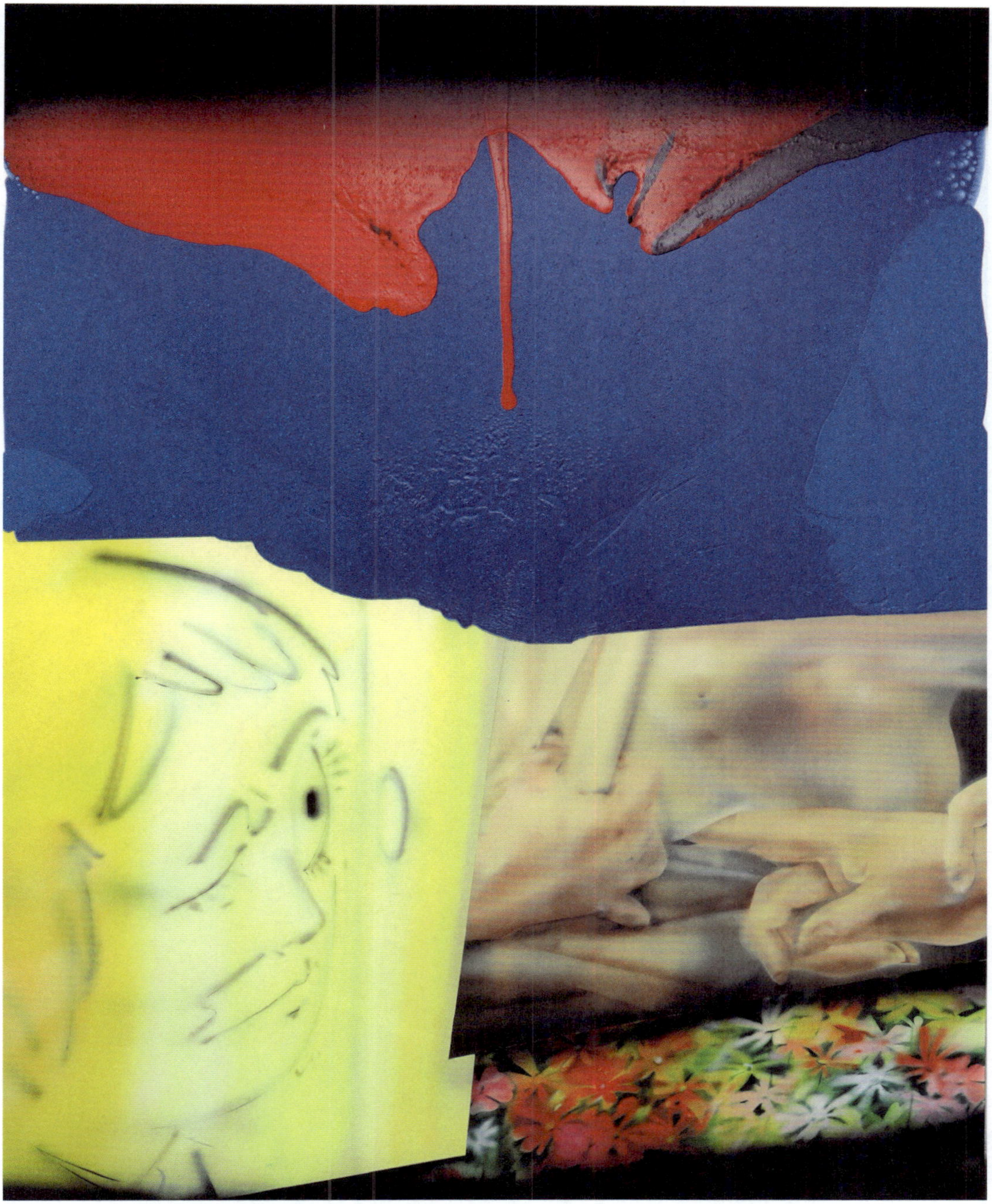

*The Curiosity of St. Thomas Made the Hole, as the Holes Make the Eyeholes*, 2021.
Acrylic and wood glue on canvas, 210 × 175 cm

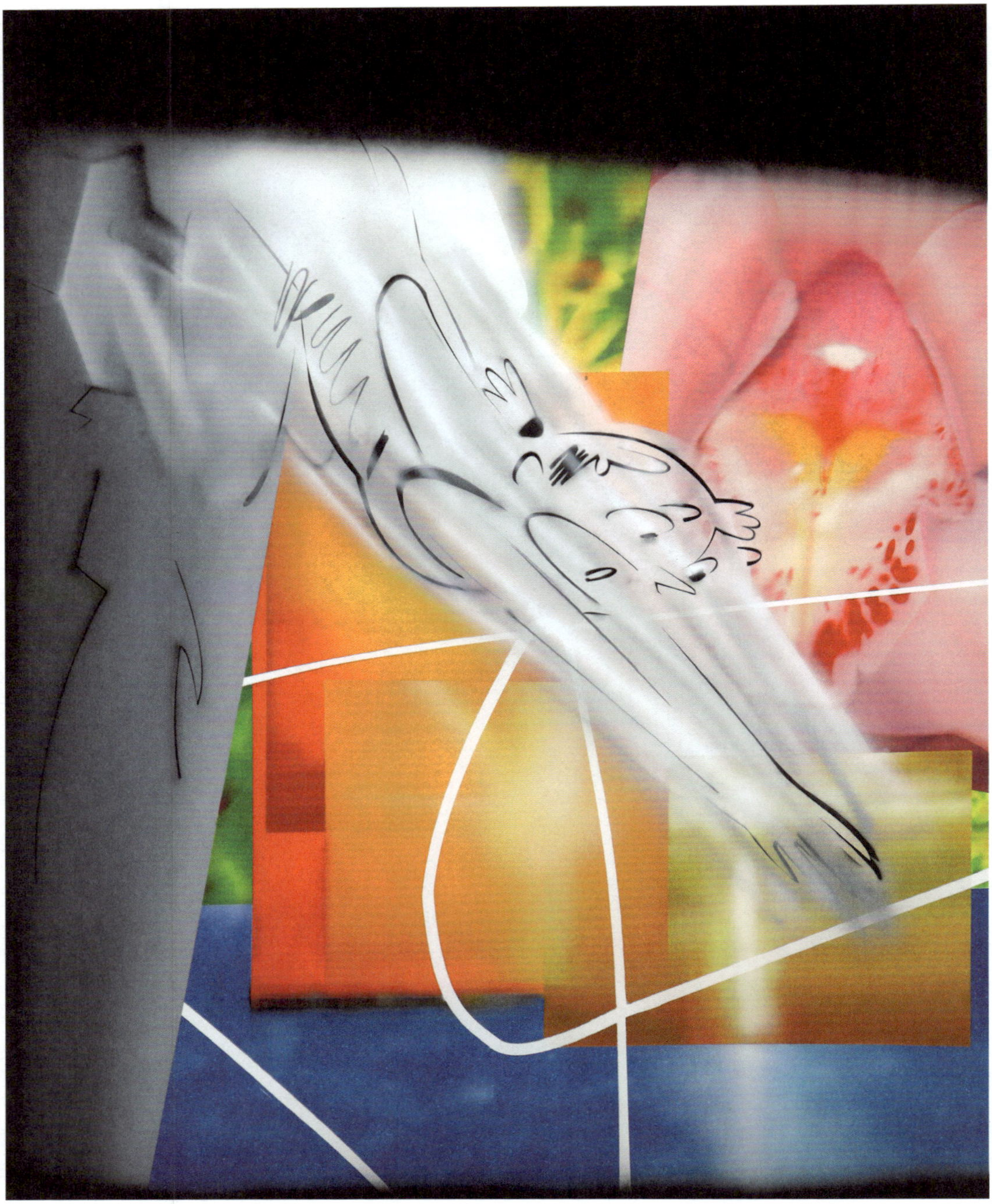

*There Is a Brick Wall, Bricks Are Broken and She Falls, So Happy Birthday to All*, 2021.
Acrylic on canvas, 210 × 175 cm

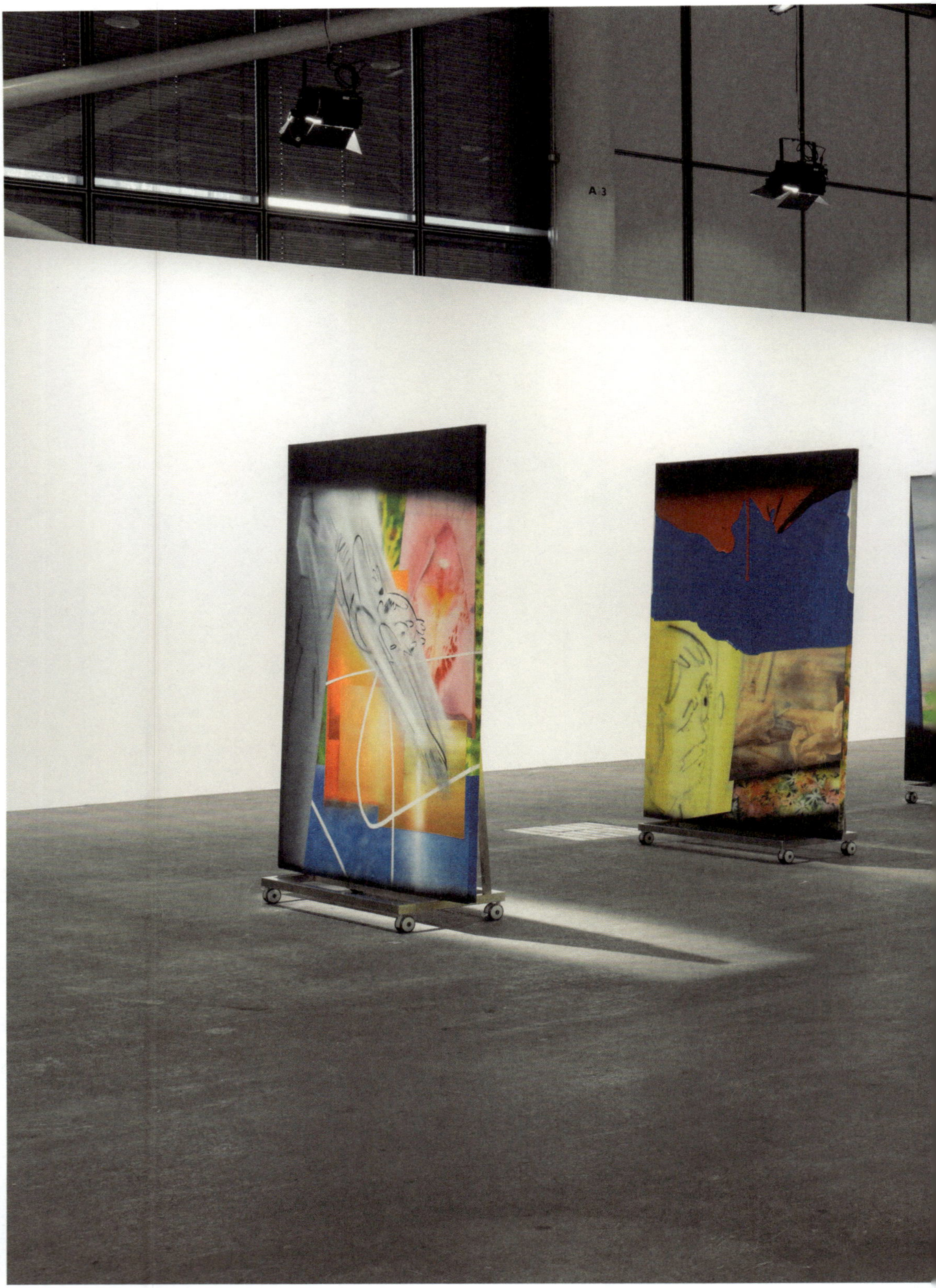

***In Appreciation of Blinking*, 2021, installation view at Unlimited/Art Basel, 2023**

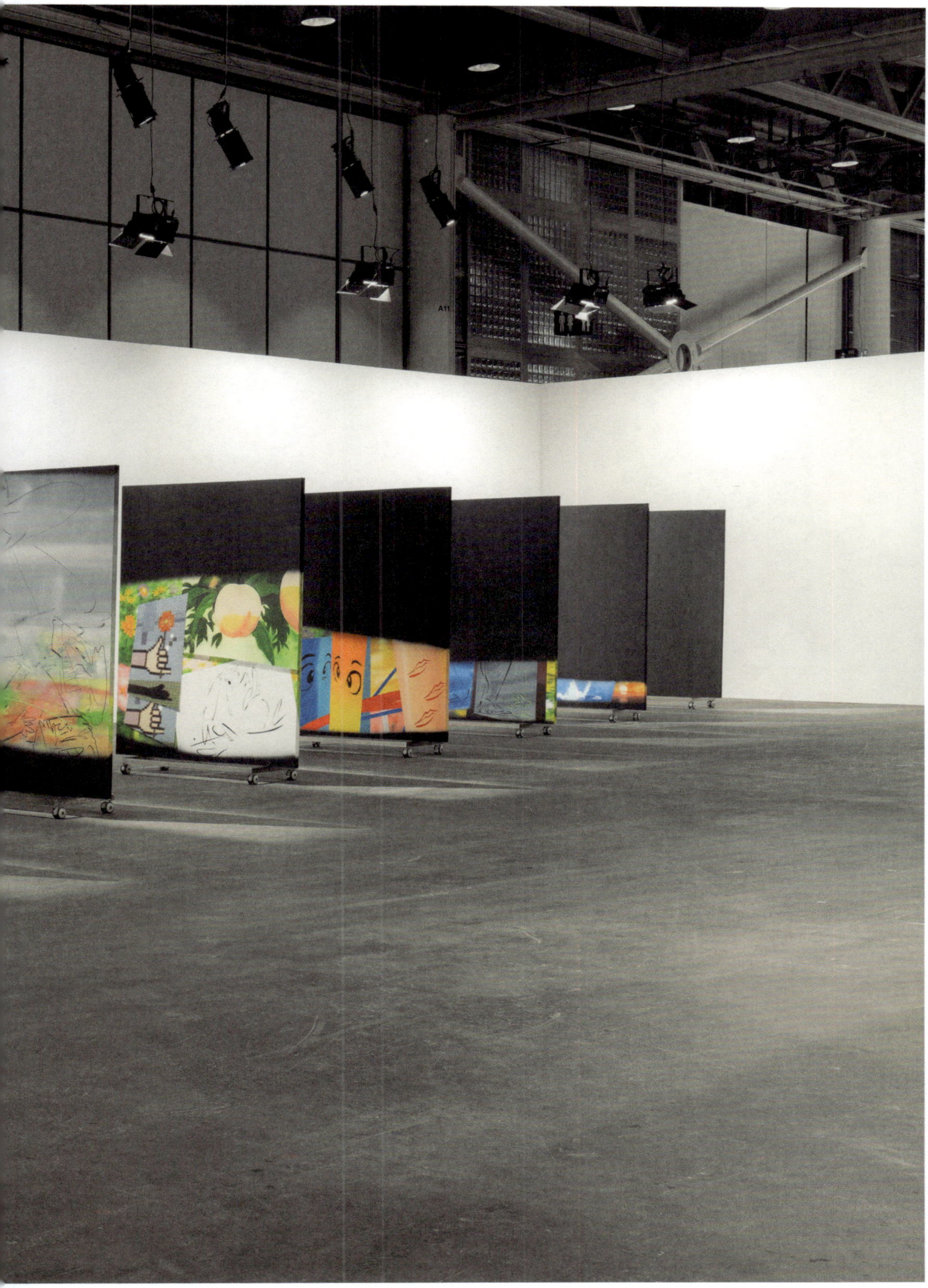

Set of 8 paintings: 210 × 175 cm (each)

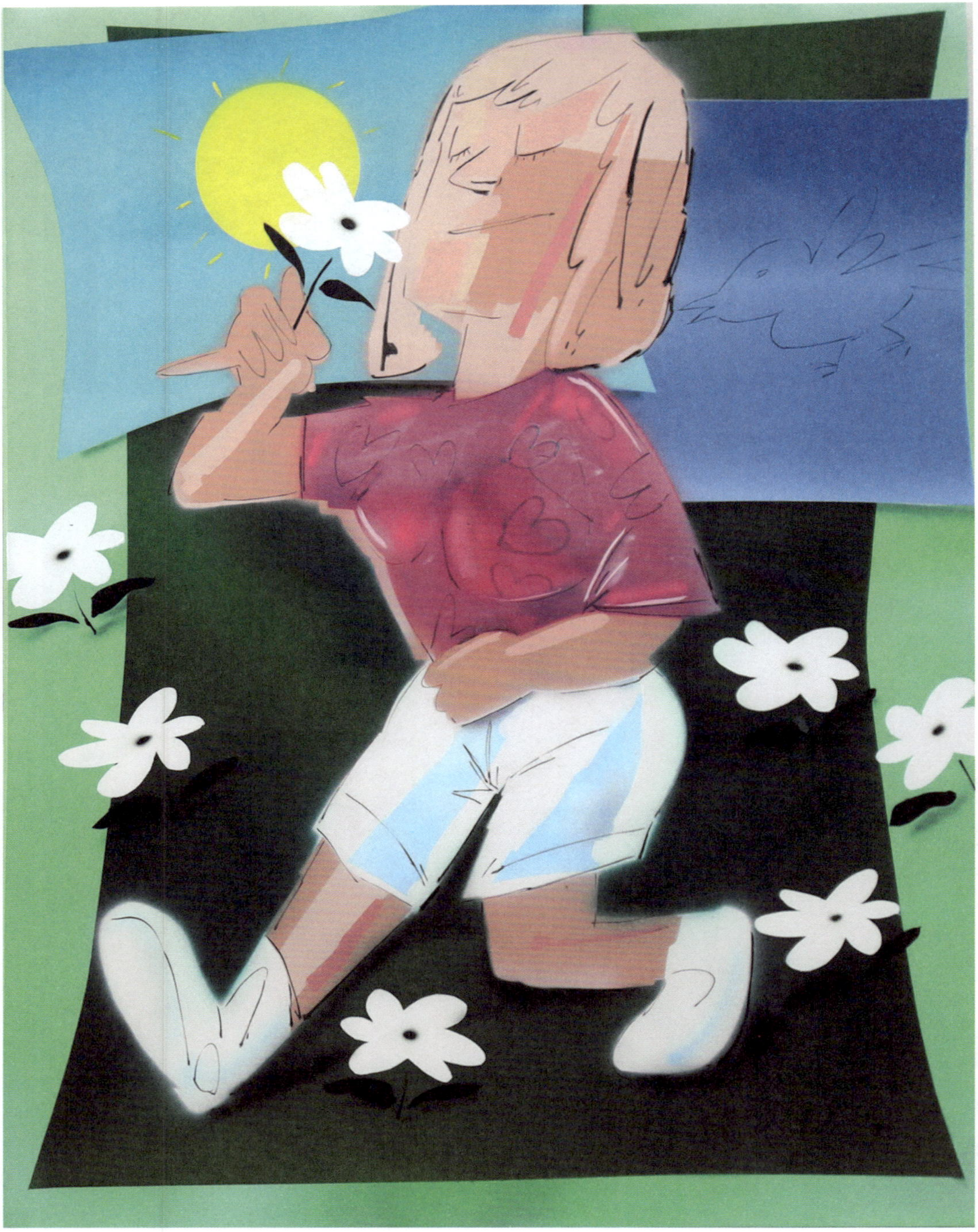

*I Am Here, I Am Not Here* (diptych), 2020. Acrylic on canvas, 150 × 120 cm (each)

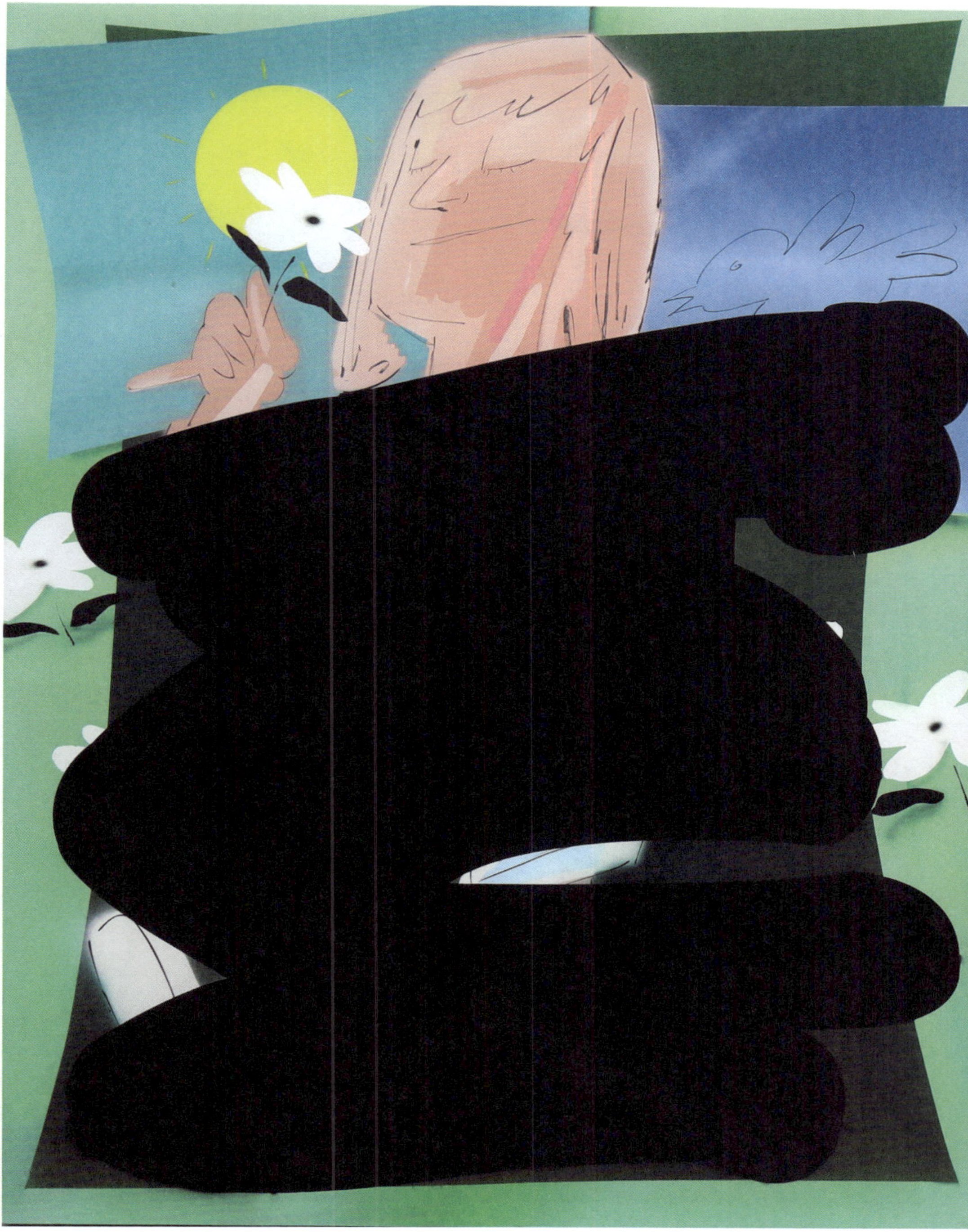

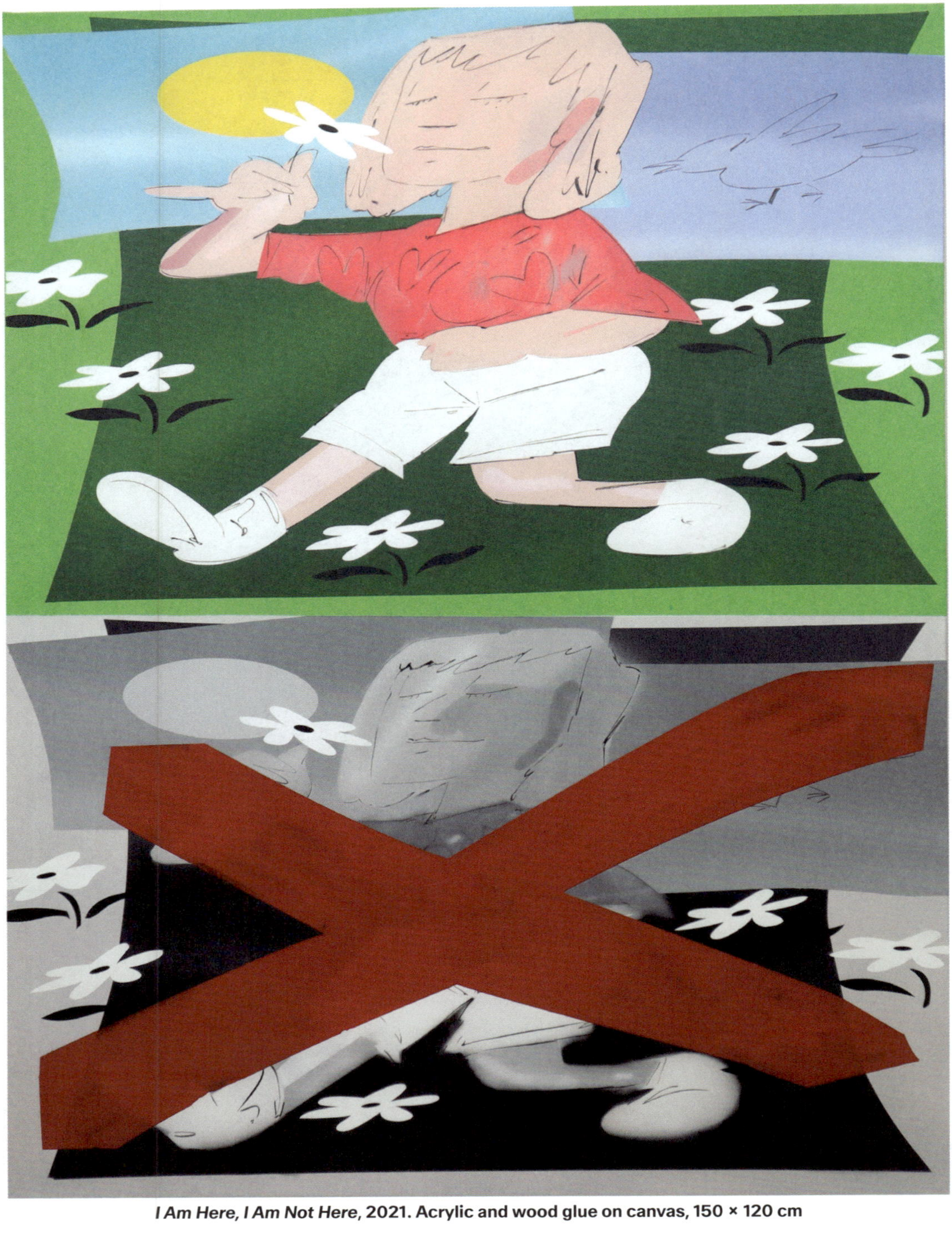

*I Am Here, I Am Not Here*, 2021. Acrylic and wood glue on canvas, 150 × 120 cm

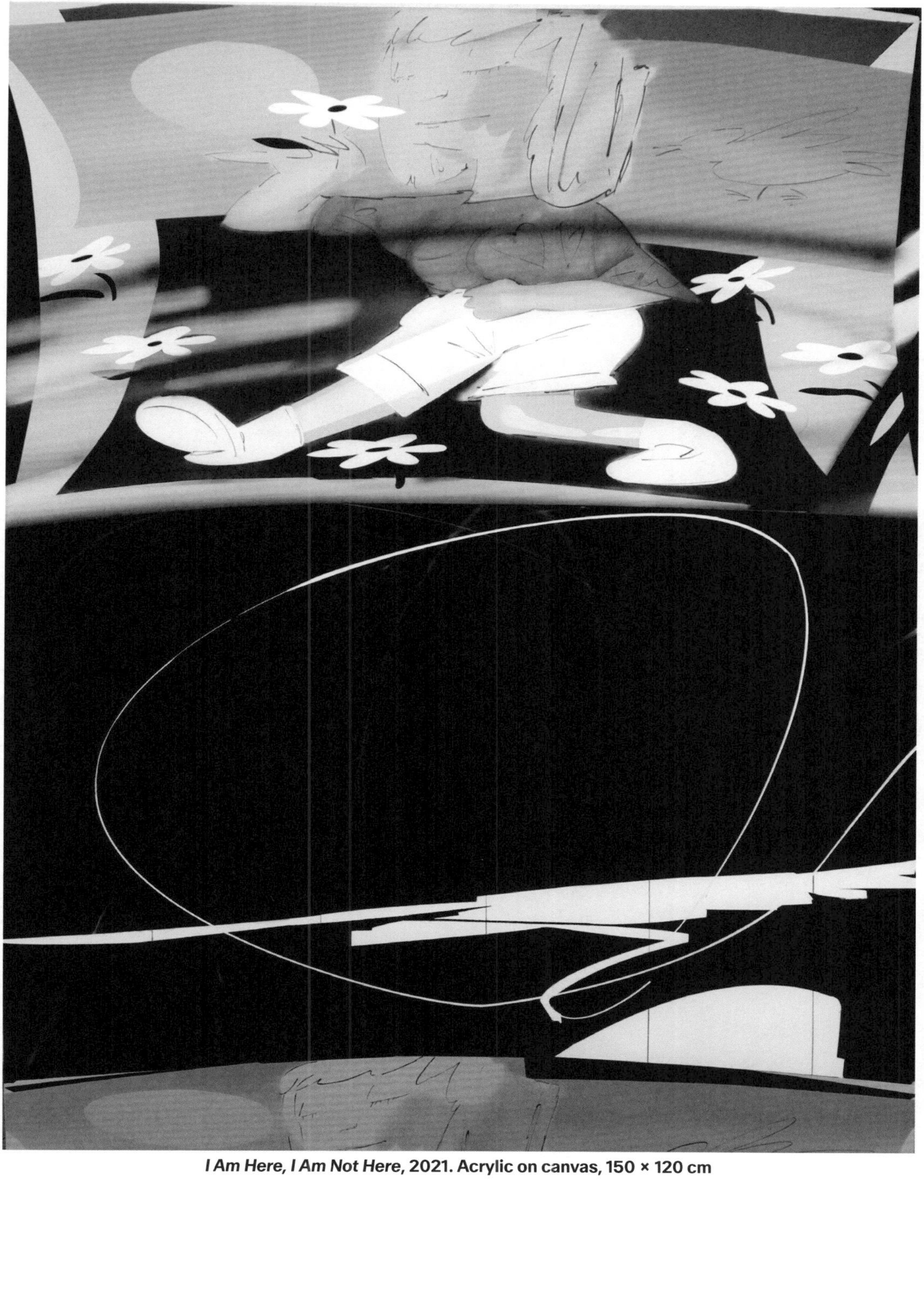

*I Am Here, I Am Not Here*, 2021. Acrylic on canvas, 150 × 120 cm

*I Am Here, I Am Not Here*, 2021.
Acrylic, modeling paste, and Plexiglas on printed canvas, 150 × 120 cm

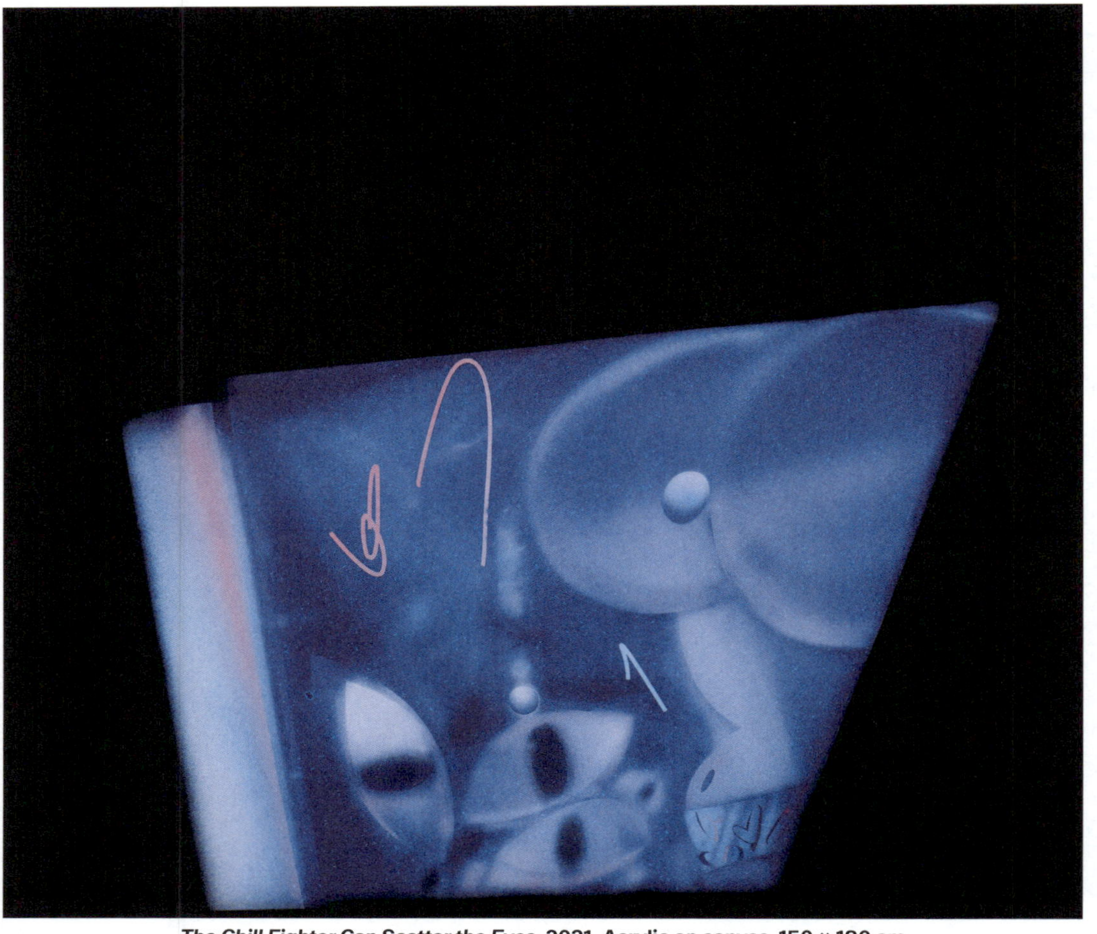

*The Chill Fighter Can Scatter the Eyes*, 2021. Acrylic on canvas, 150 × 180 cm

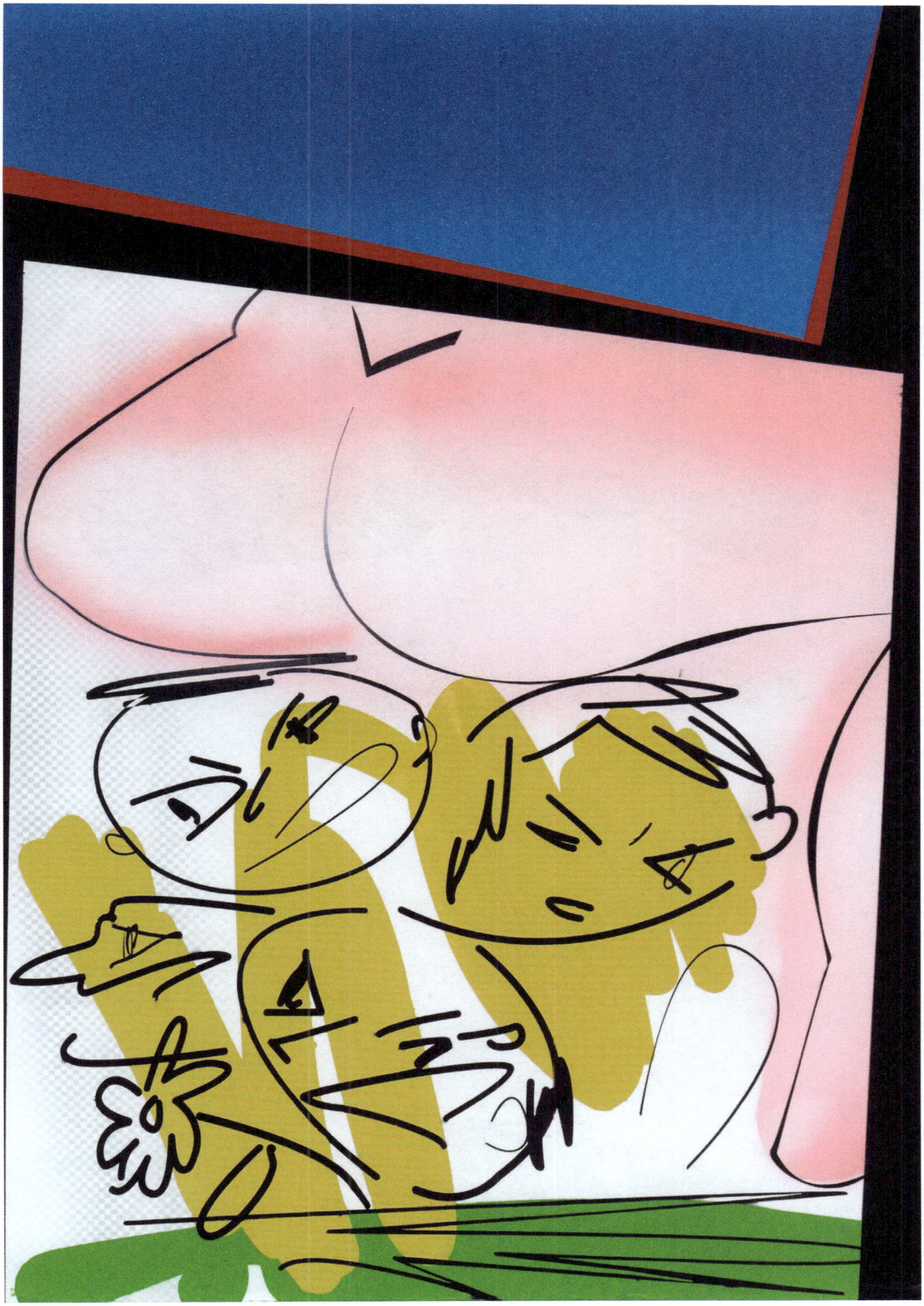

*Untitled*, 2021. Acrylic on canvas, 100 × 70 cm

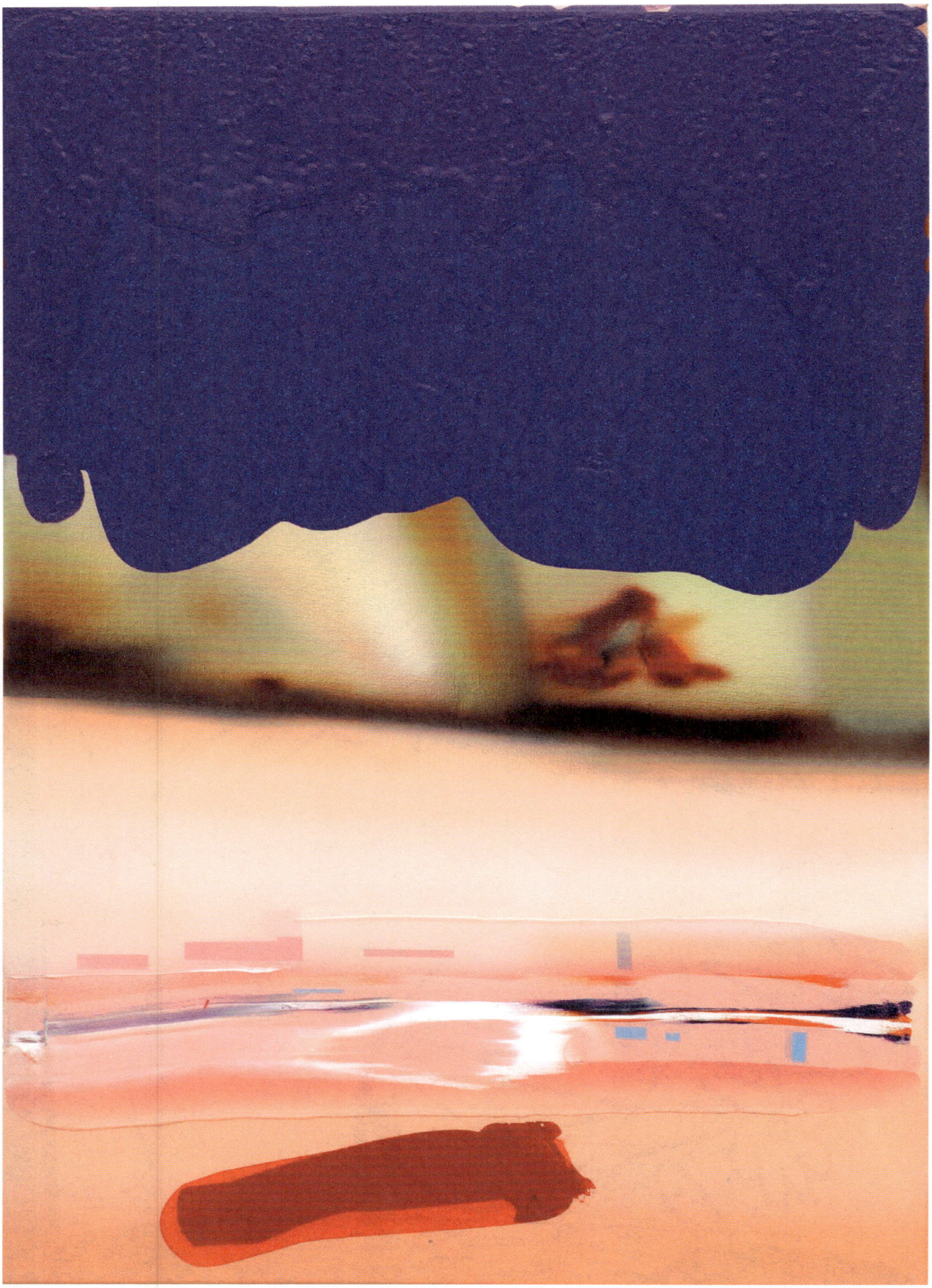

*Between Lips and Lipstick*, 2022. Acrylic and wood glue on canvas, 70 × 50 cm

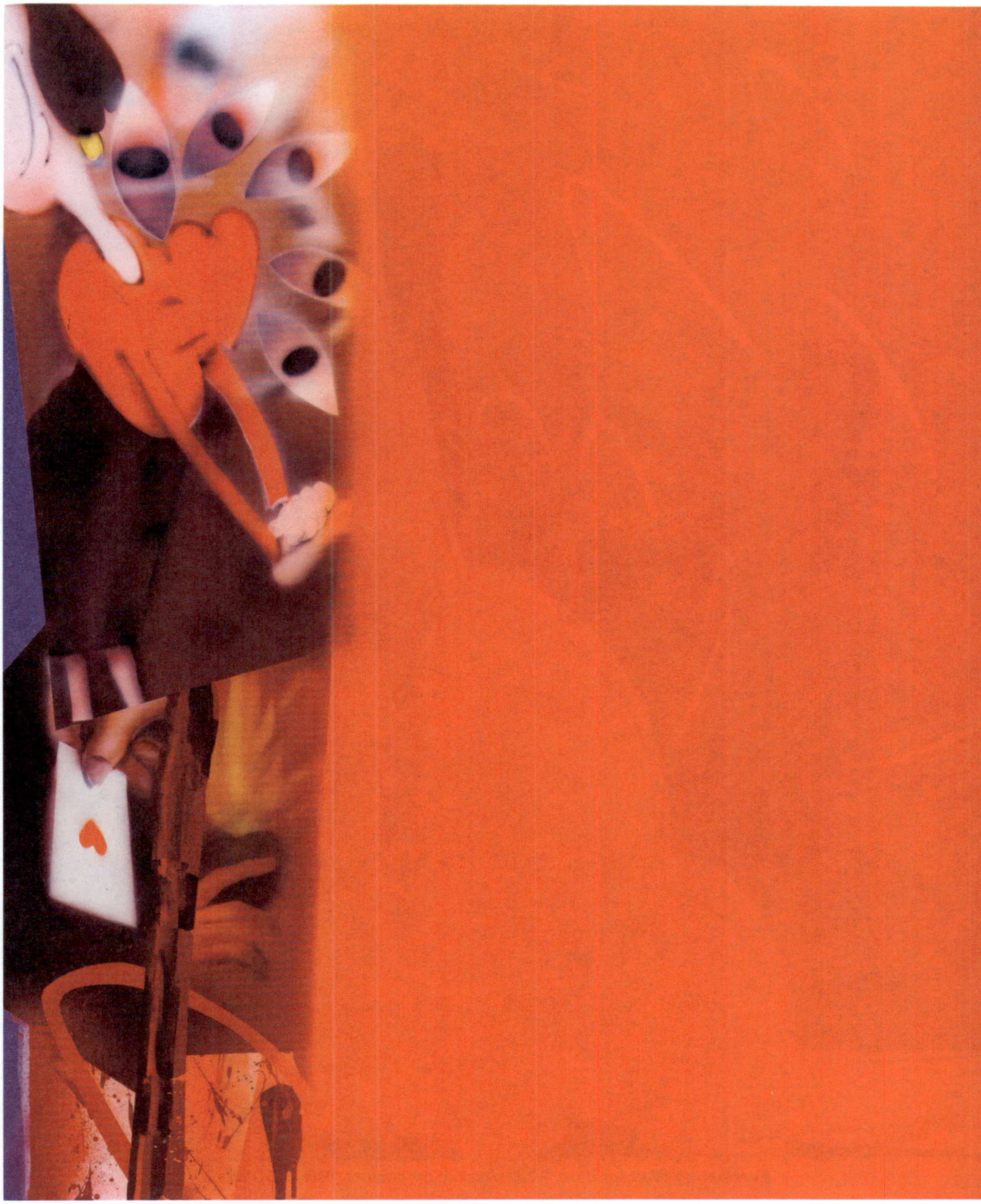

*The Love Fire*, 2021. Acrylic on canvas, 180 × 150 cm

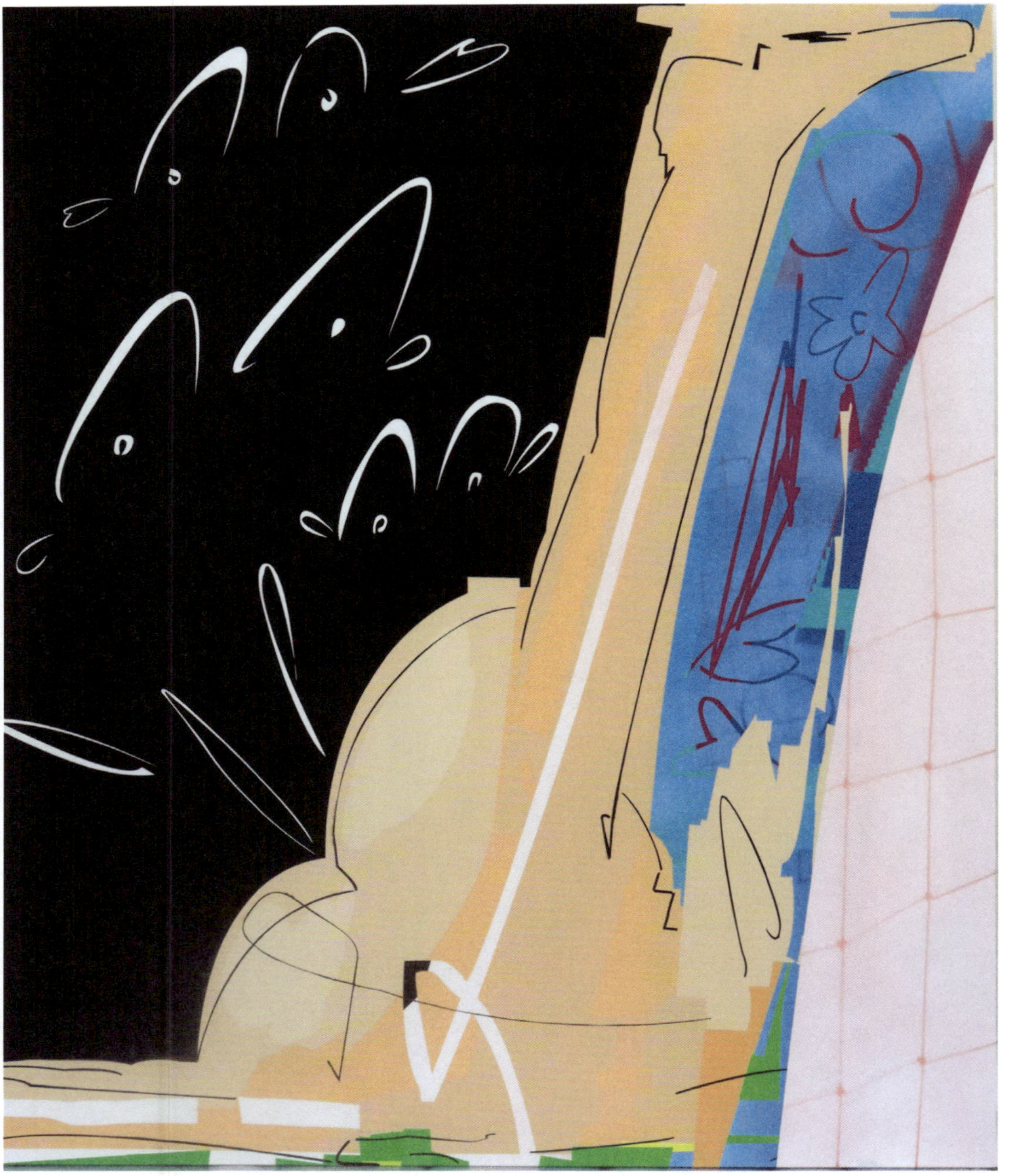

*Everlasting Wait for Blue*, 2021. Acrylic on canvas, 180 × 150 cm

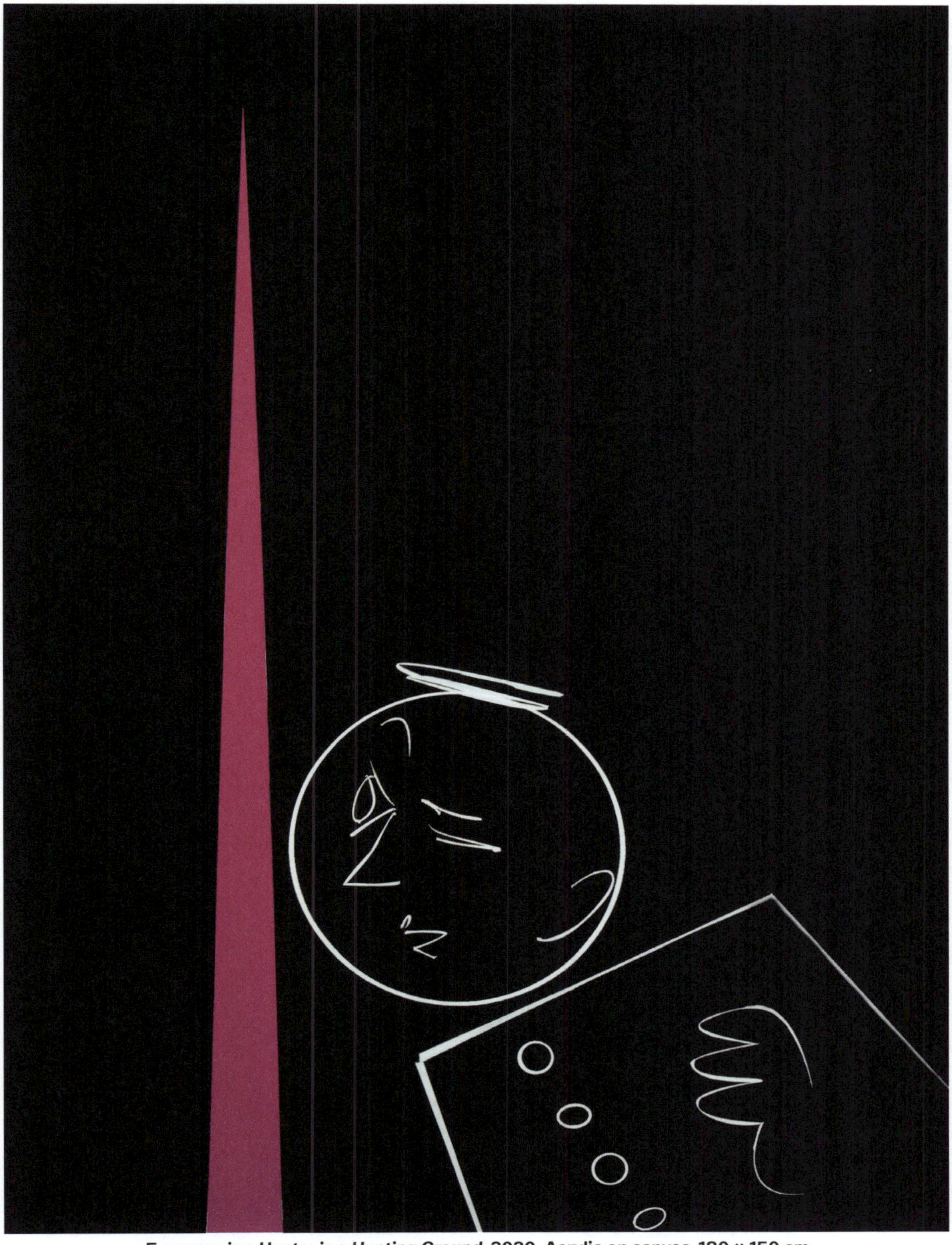

*Everyone is a Hunter in a Hunting Ground*, 2020. Acrylic on canvas, 180 × 150 cm

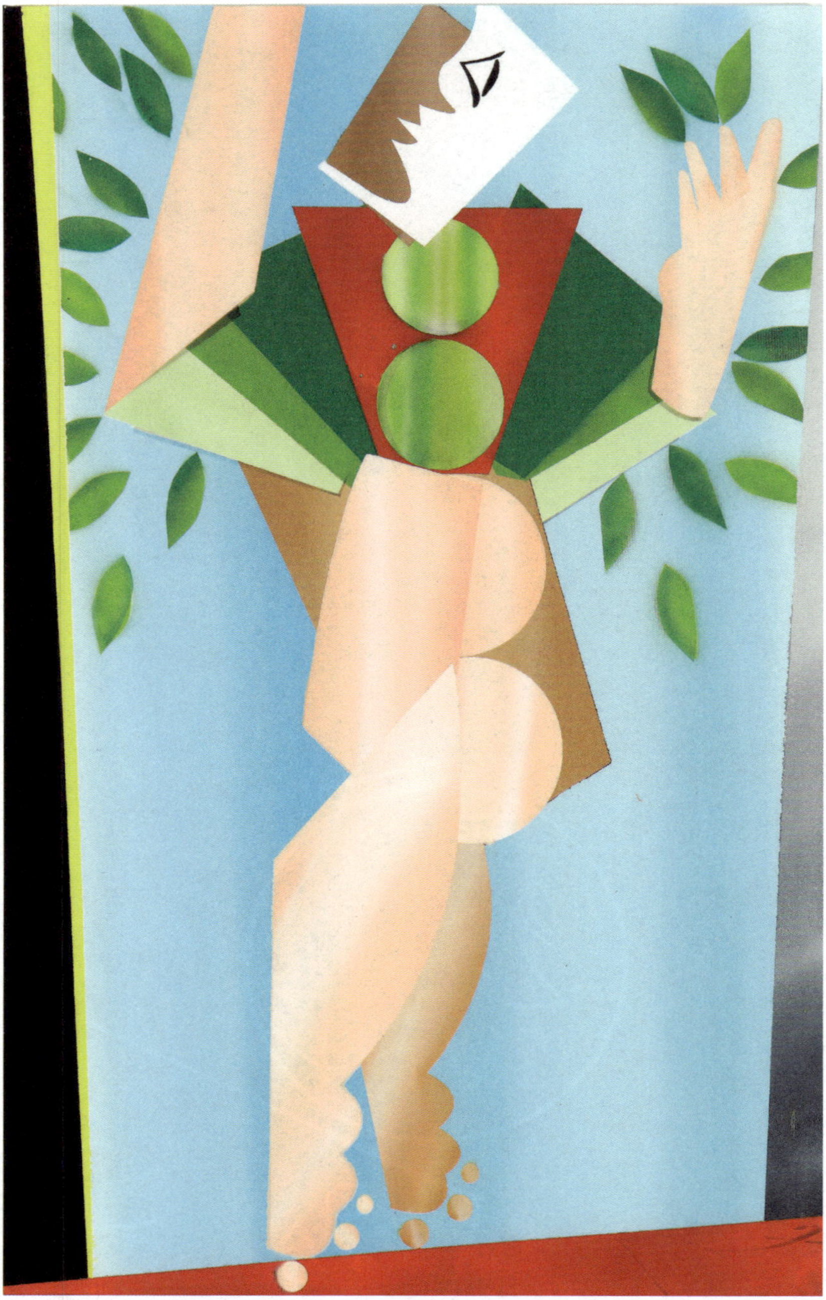

*Apollo Pursuing Daphne* (diptych), 2020. Acrylic on canvas, 140 × 90 cm, 150 × 120 cm

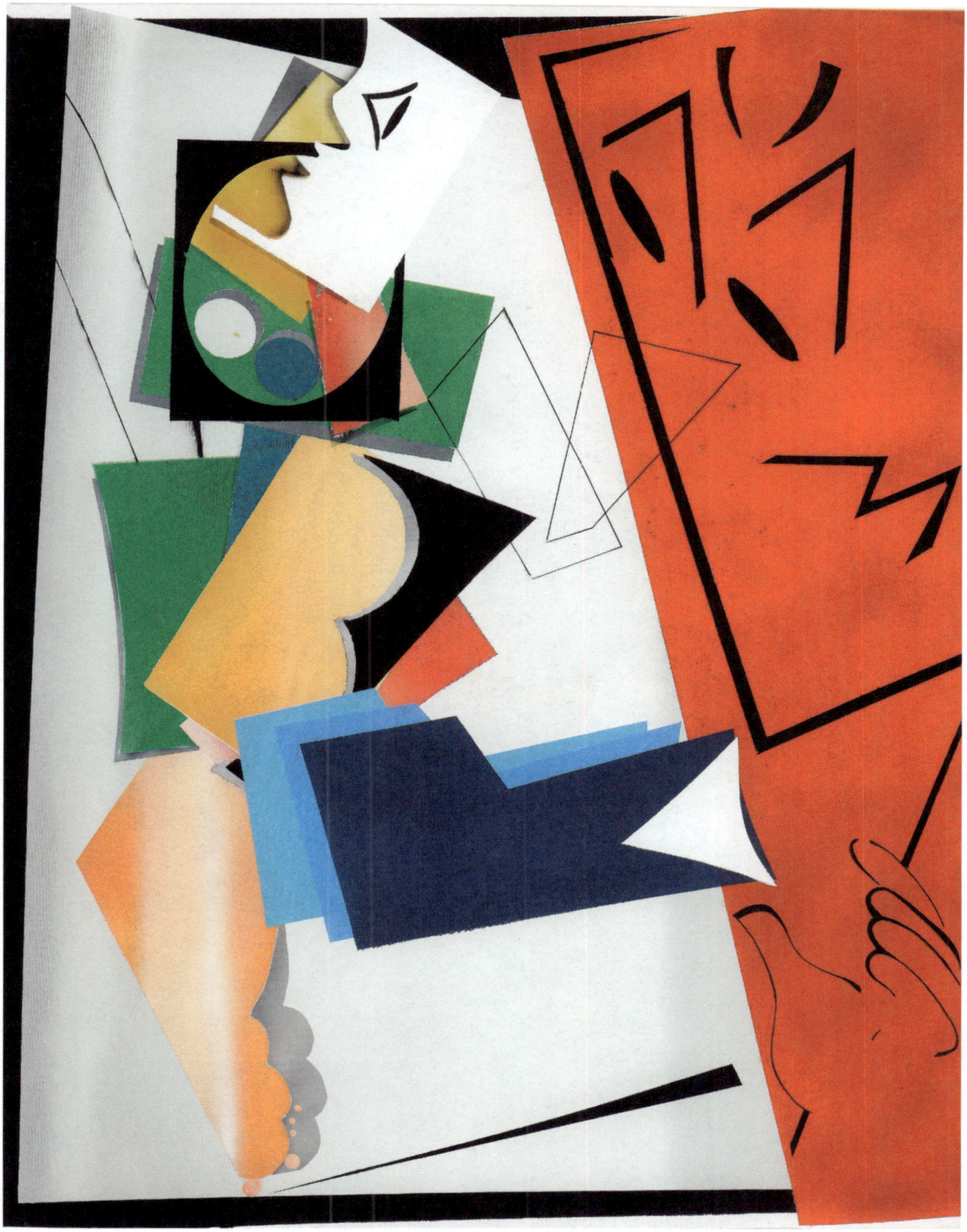

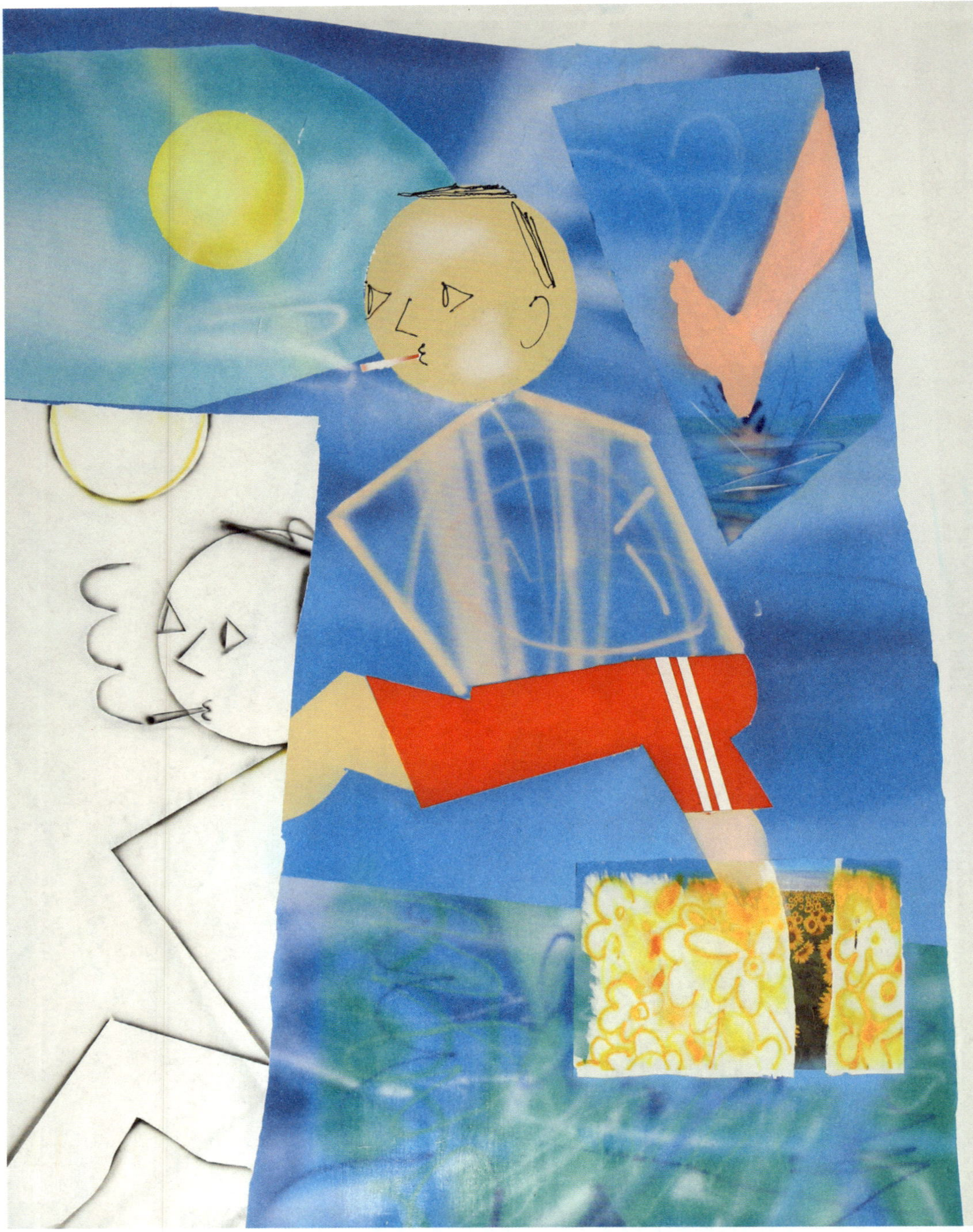

*I Am Walkin While I Am Walkin*, 2019. Acrylic on canvas, 150 × 130 cm

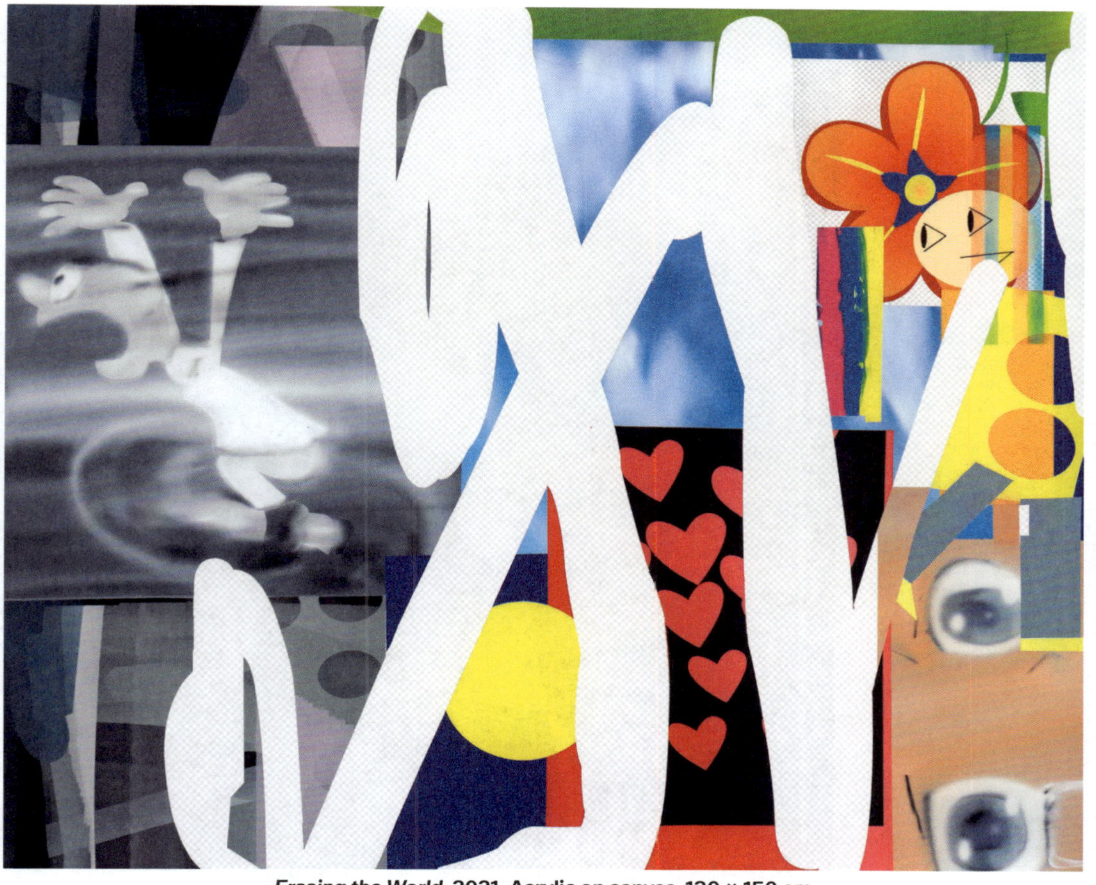

*Erasing the World*, 2021. Acrylic on canvas, 130 × 150 cm

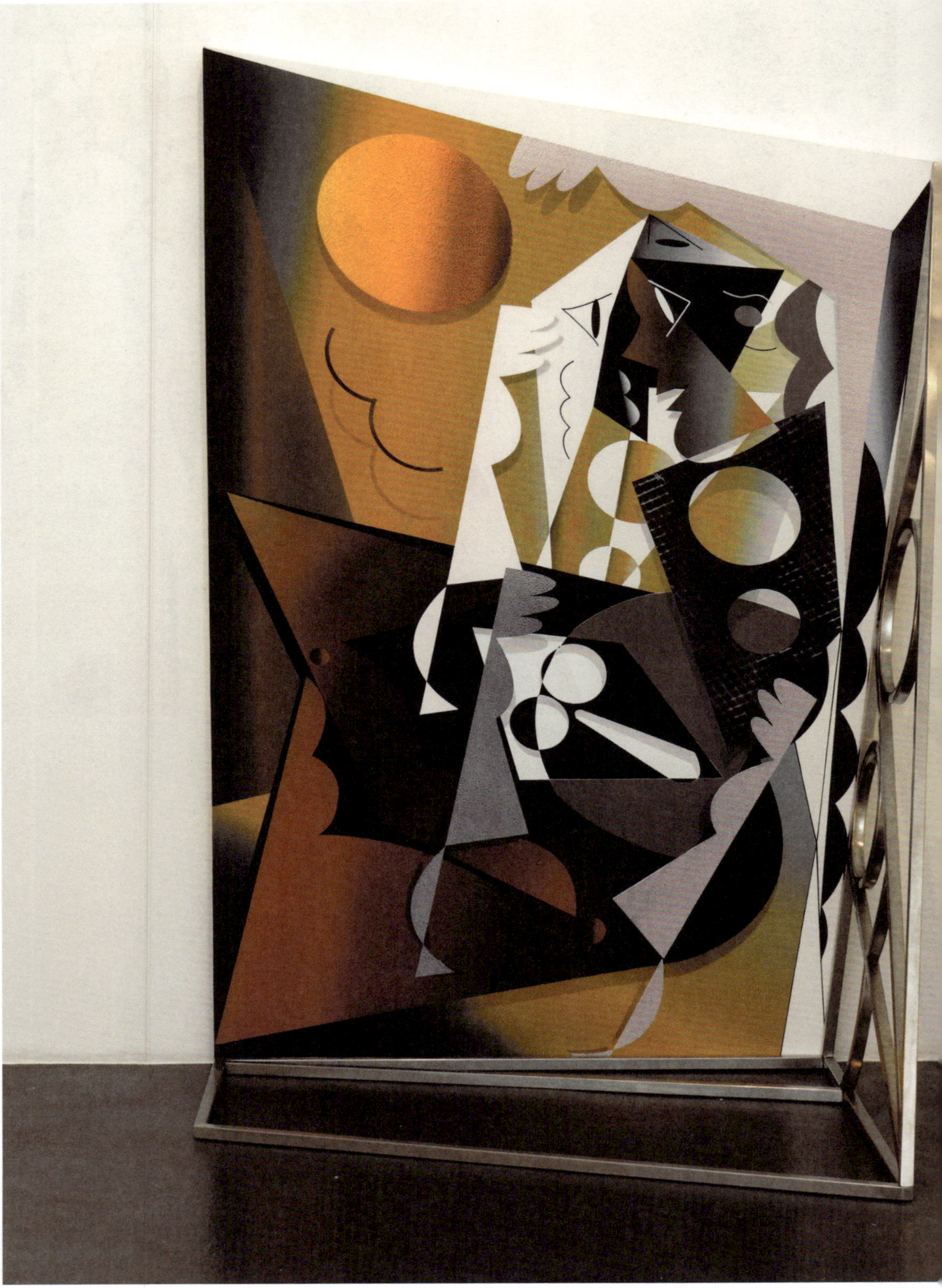

*I Am Here, I Am Not Here* at Galerie Nathalie Obadia, Paris, 2022

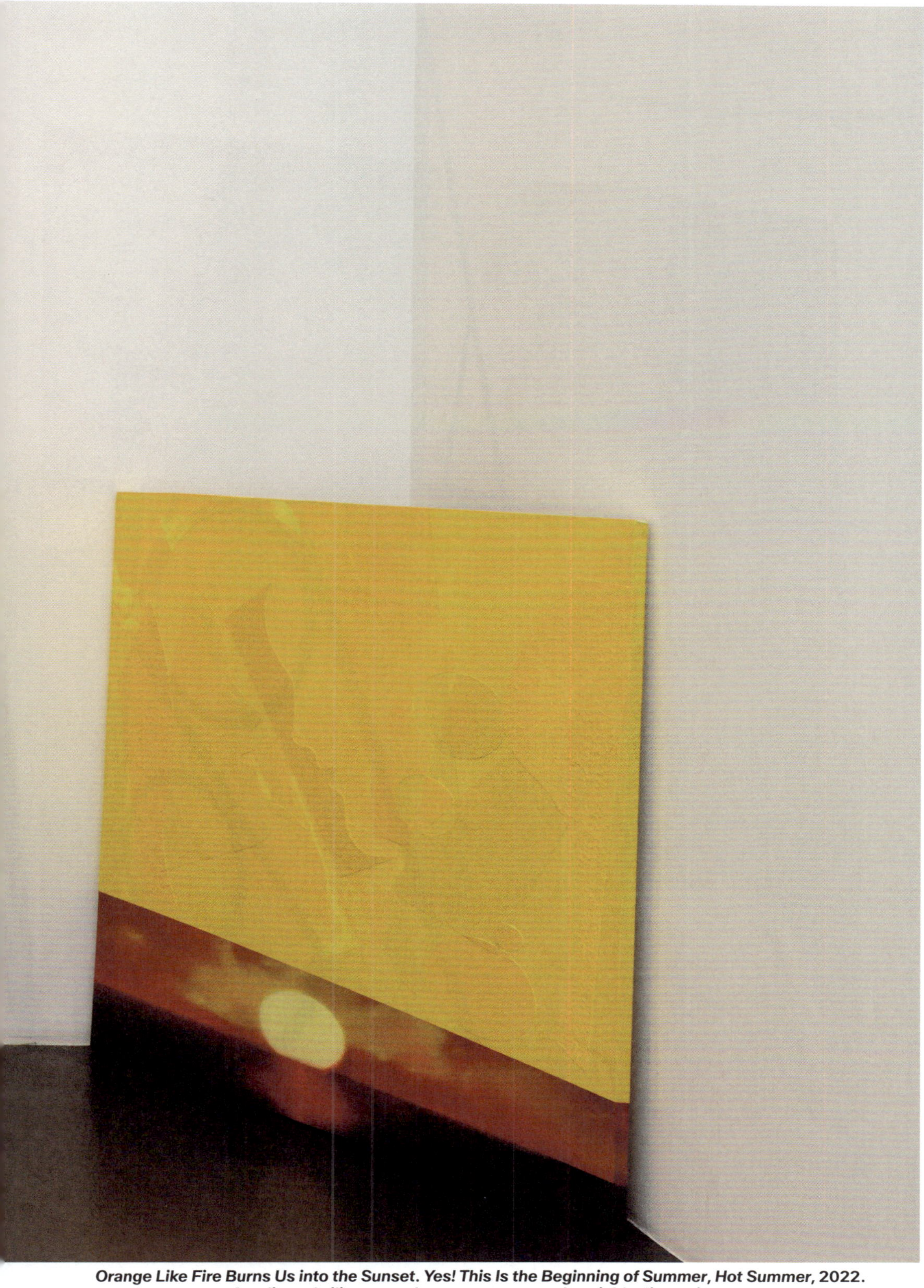

*Orange Like Fire Burns Us into the Sunset. Yes! This Is the Beginning of Summer, Hot Summer*, 2022.
Acrylic and silicon powder on canvas, metal, variable dimensions

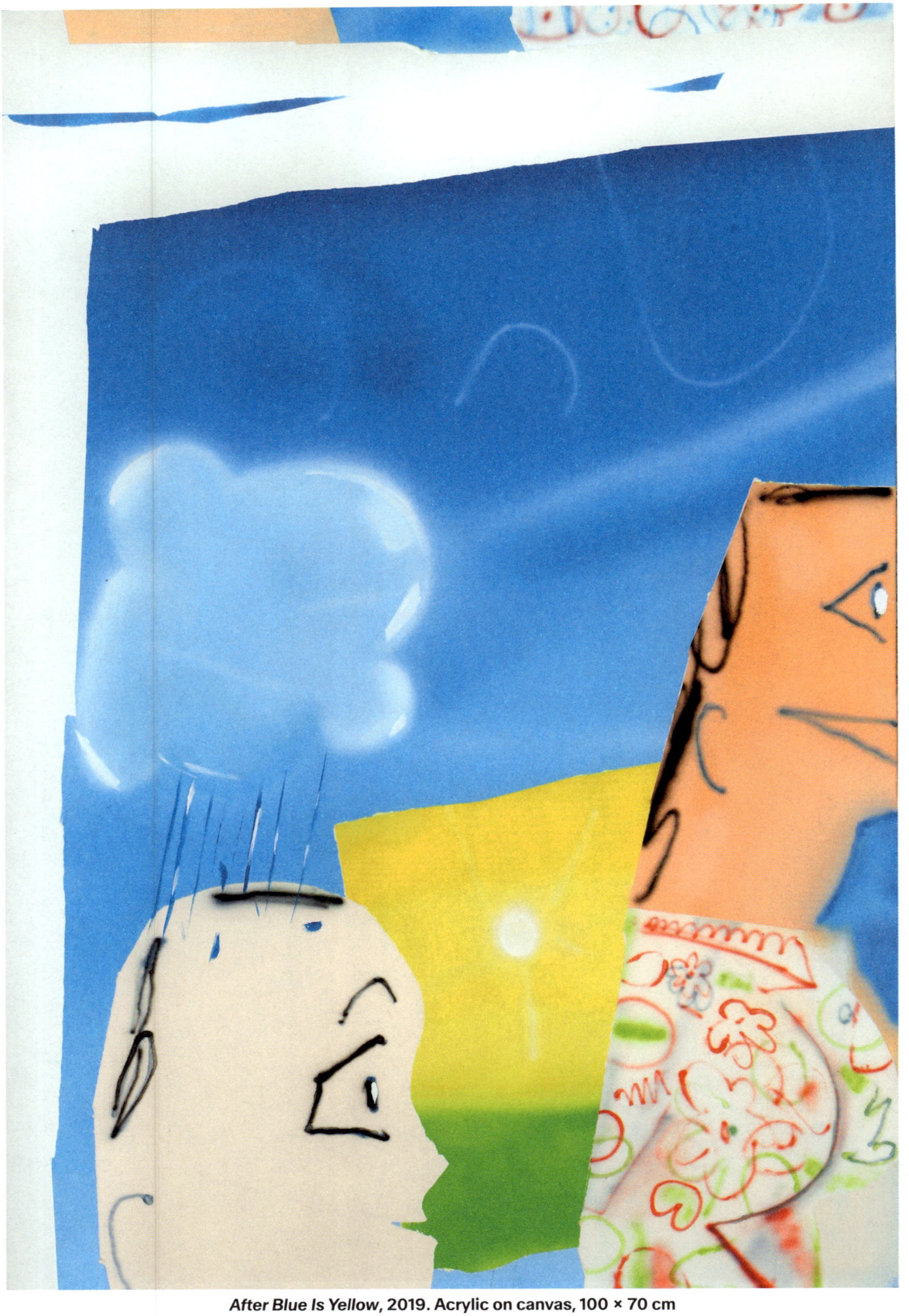

*After Blue Is Yellow*, 2019. Acrylic on canvas, 100 × 70 cm

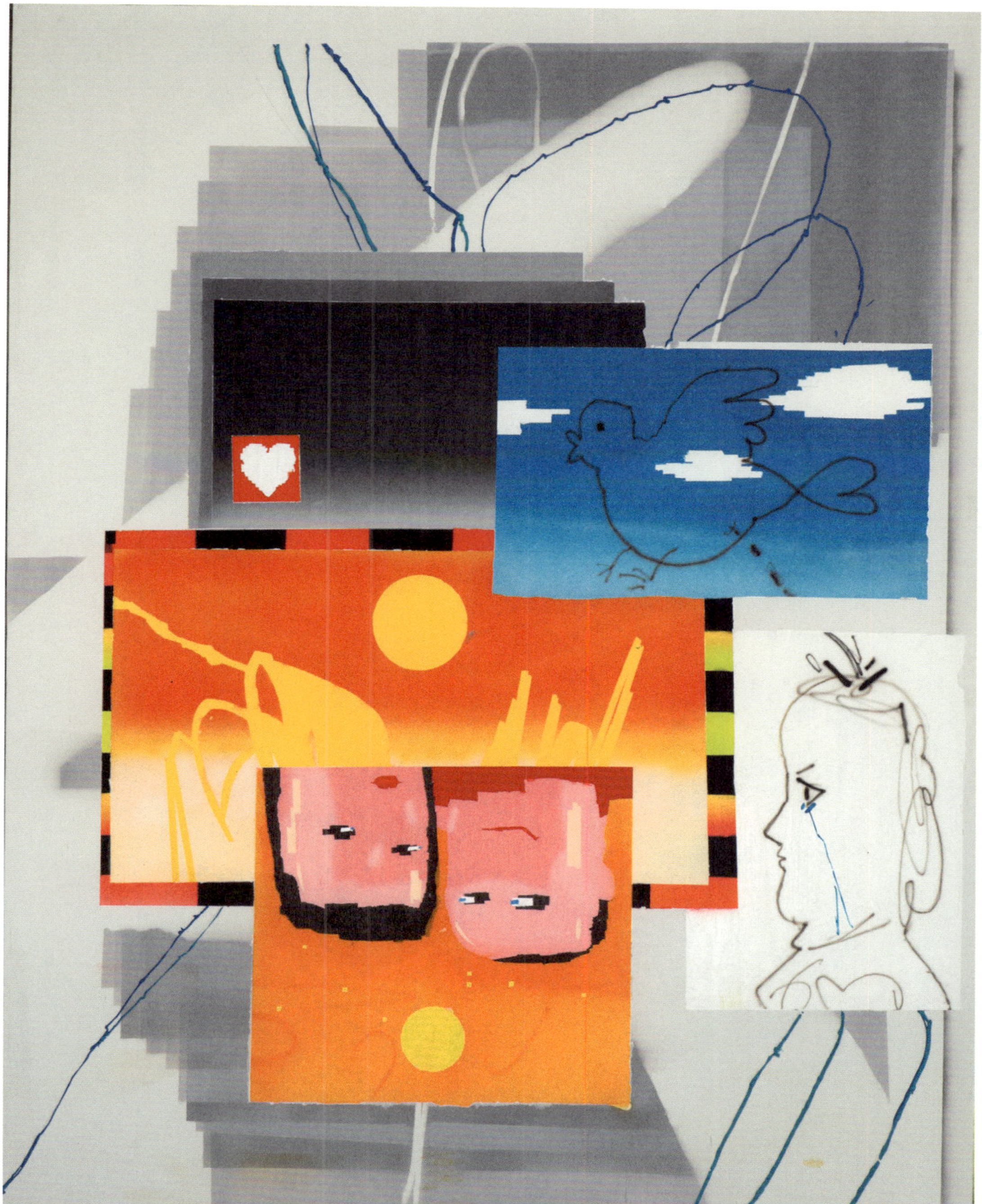

*Bird Sings from Orange Which Is About Majesty*, 2019. Acrylic on canvas, 180 × 150 cm

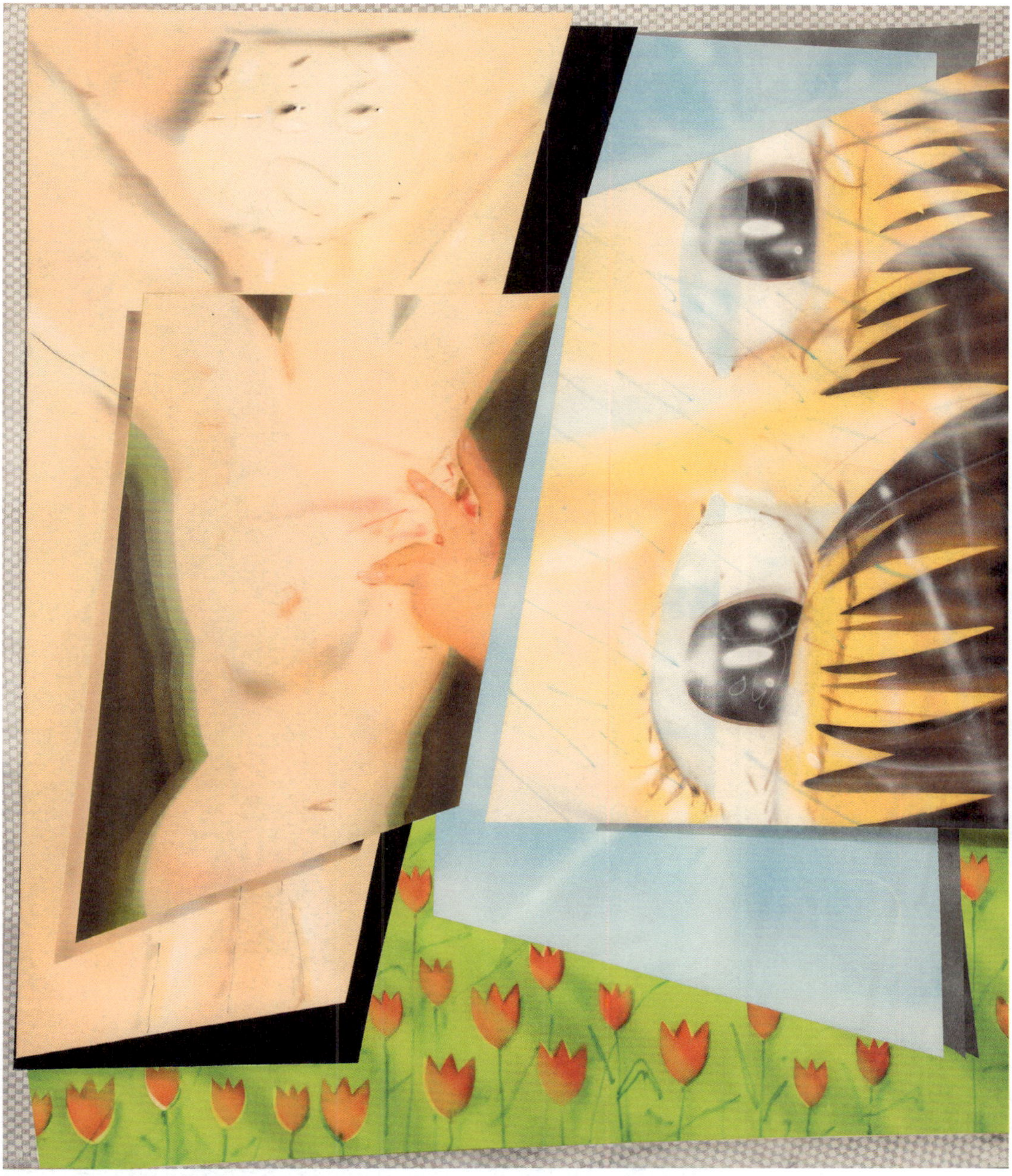

***Dear St. Agatha I Am Witness of Your Tears in the Land of Tulips*, 2020. Acrylic on canvas, 150 × 130 cm**

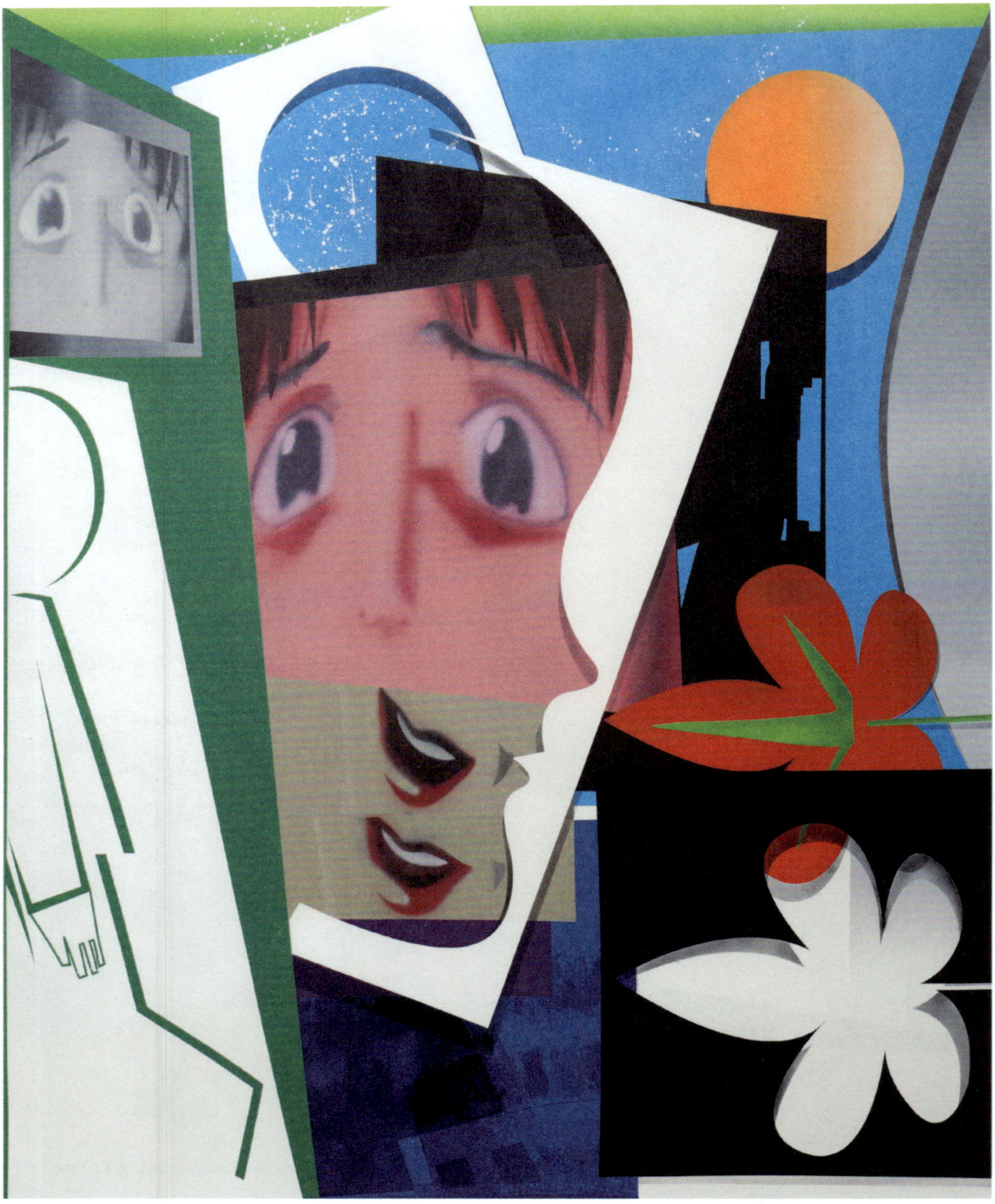

*The Time He Left His Shadow*, 2021. Acrylic on canvas, 180 × 150 cm

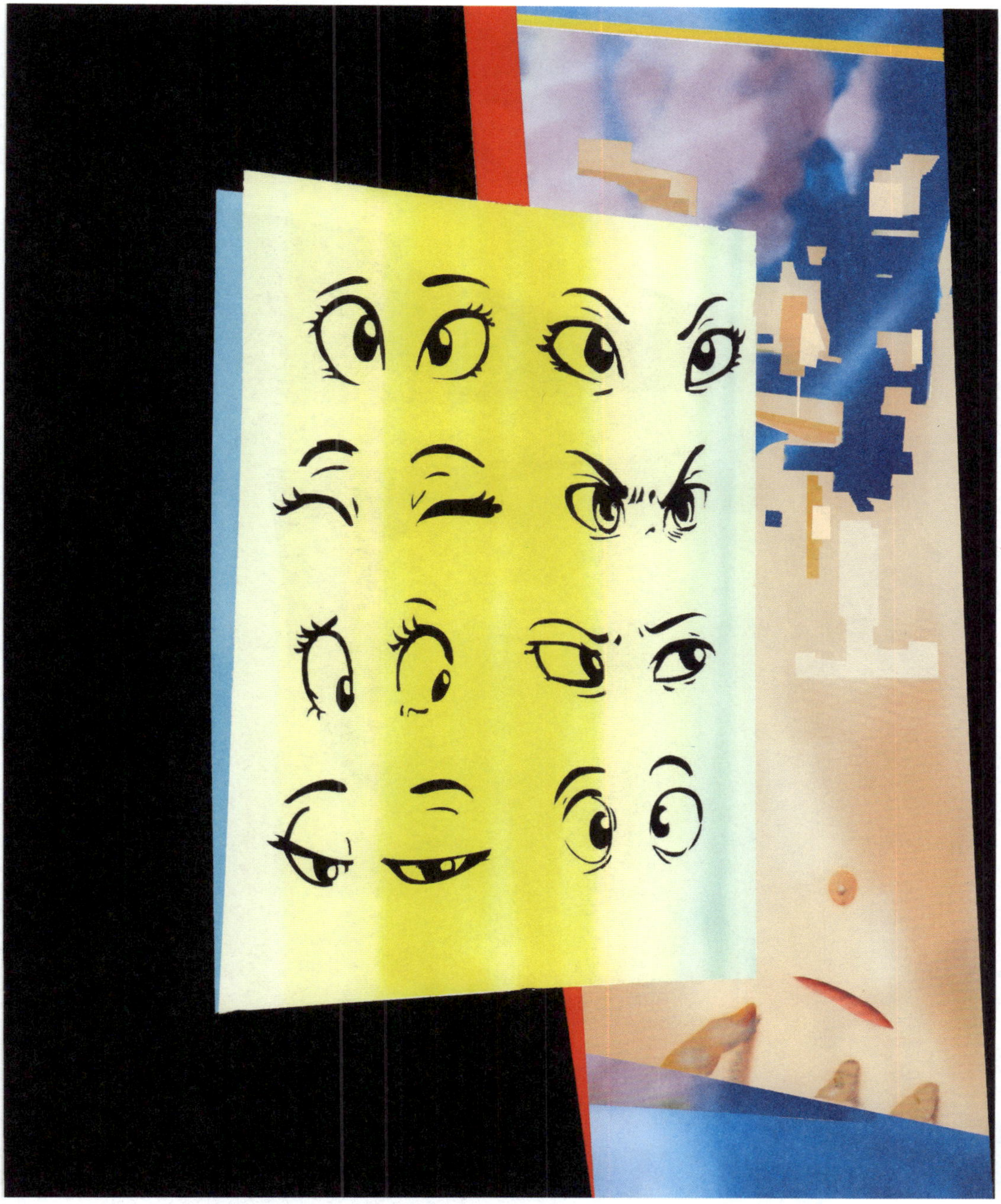

*Eyes Never Stop Seeing All Things*, 2020. Acrylic on canvas, 180 × 150 cm

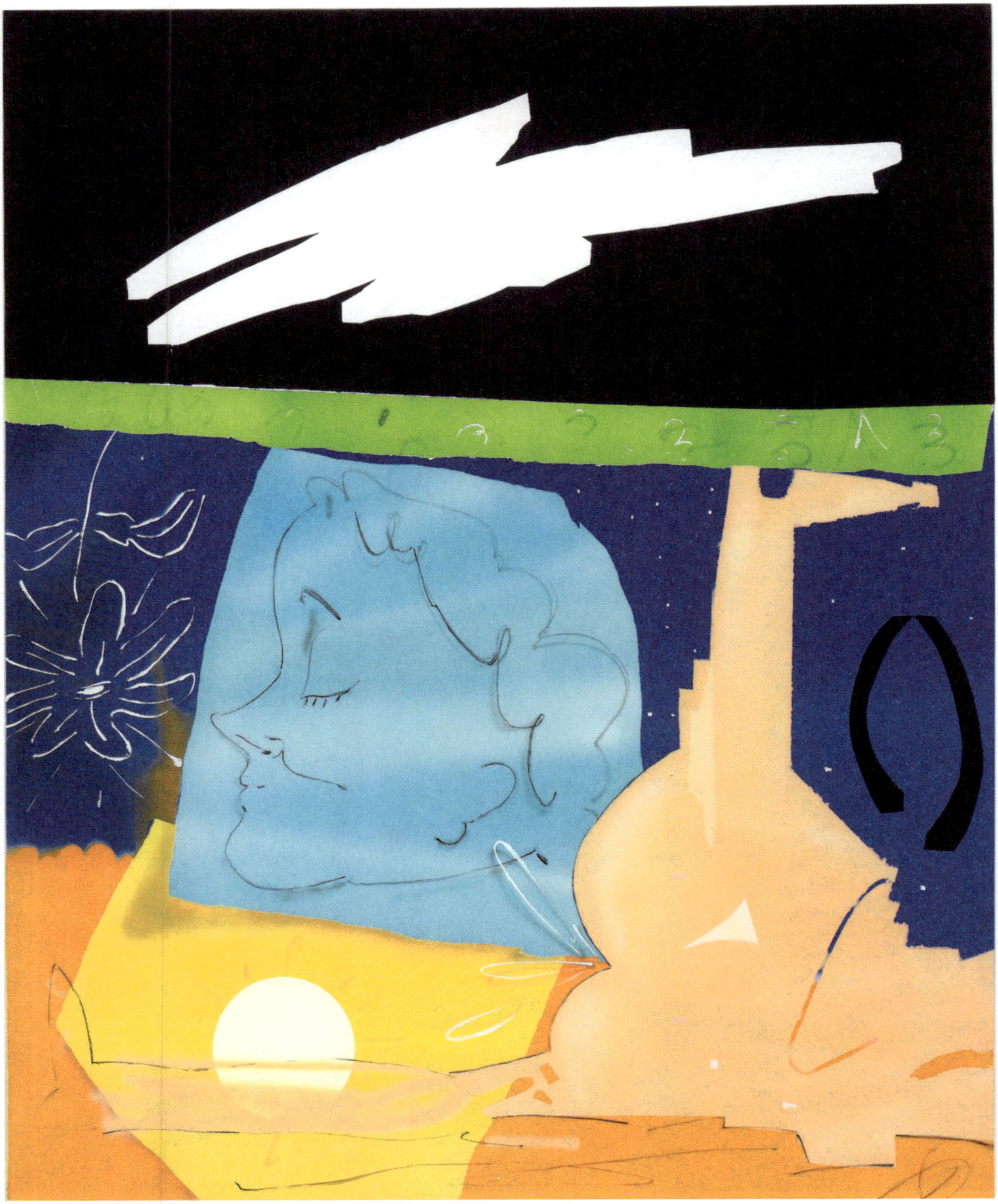

*How to Choose a Right Perfume in a Suspended World?*, 2019. Acrylic on canvas, 120 × 100 cm

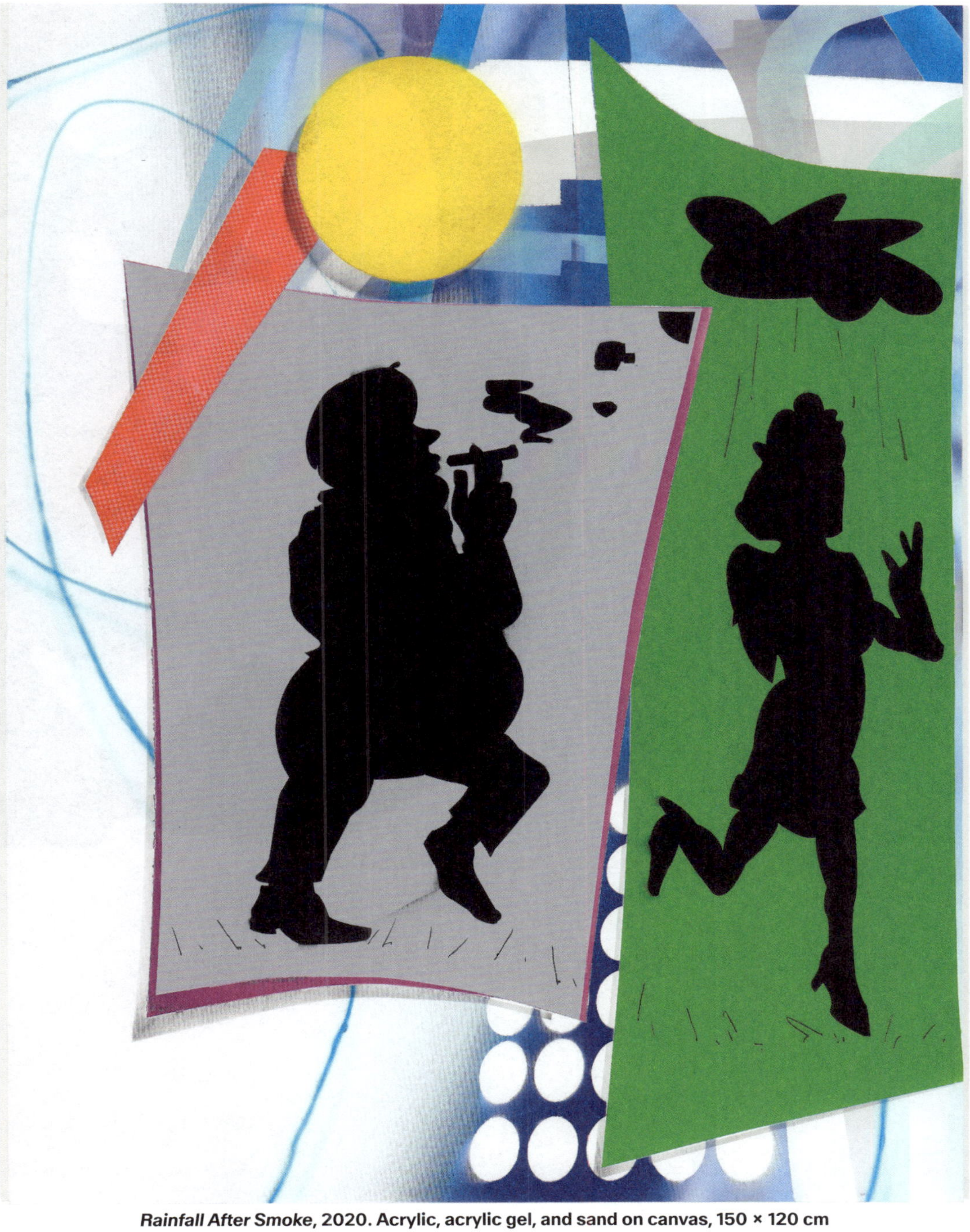

*Rainfall After Smoke*, 2020. Acrylic, acrylic gel, and sand on canvas, 150 × 120 cm

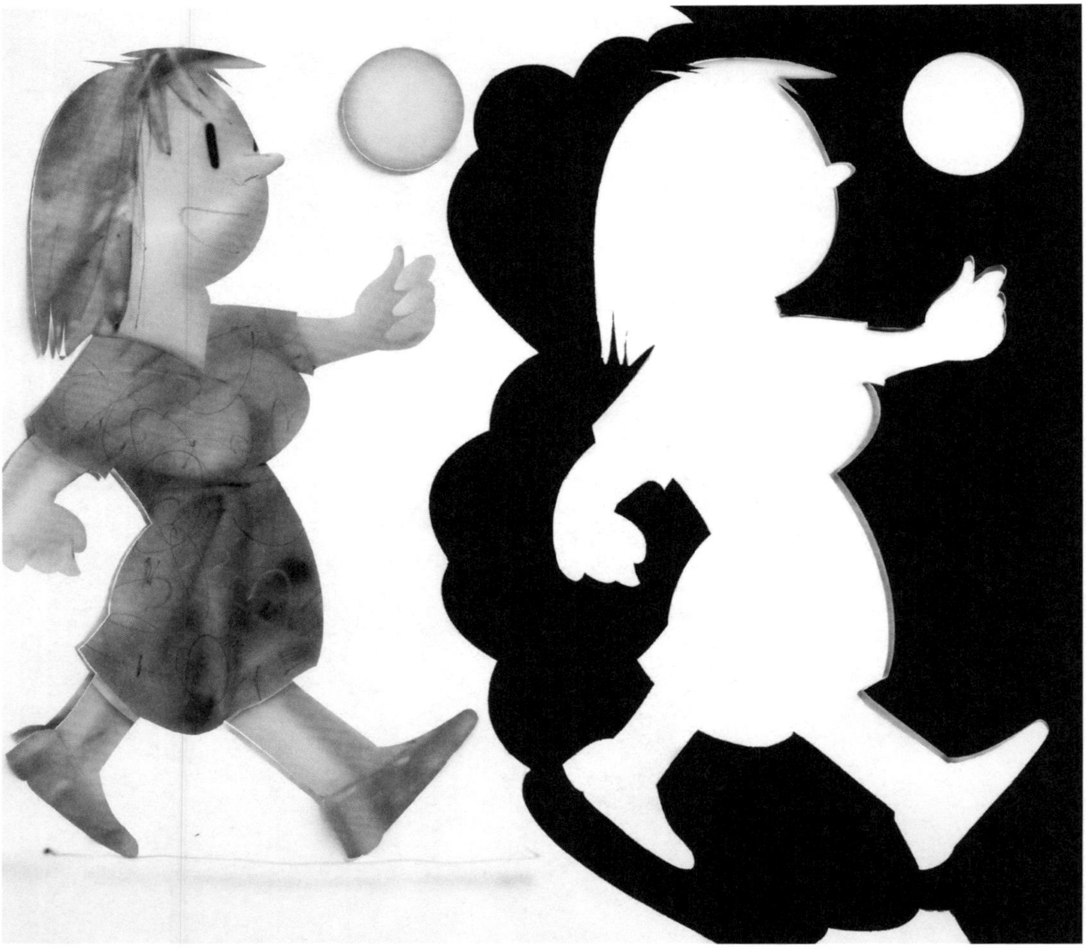

*Full Cycle,* 2021. Acrylic on canvas, 130 × 150 cm

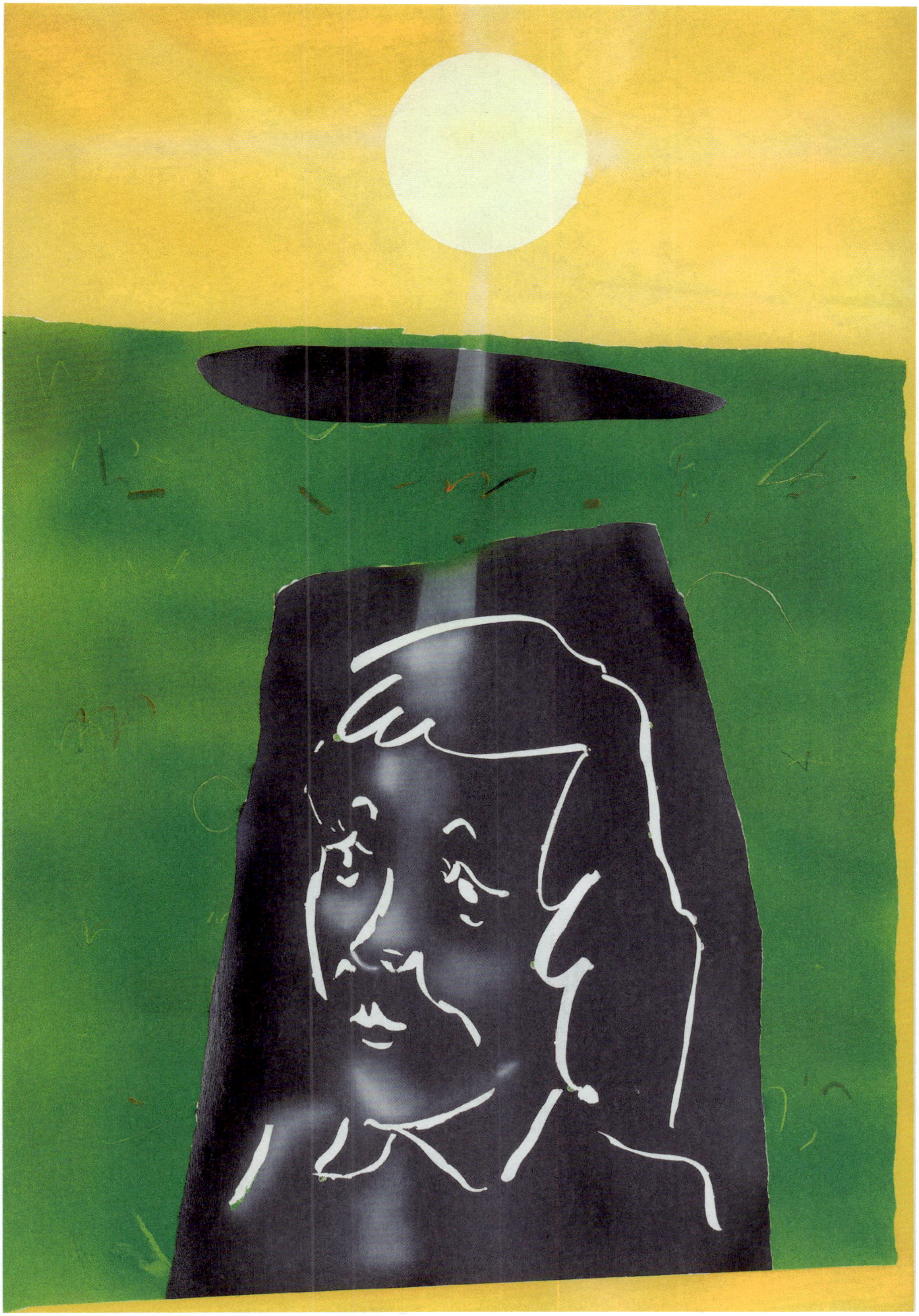

*Untitled, 2019*. Acrylic on canvas, 100 × 70 cm

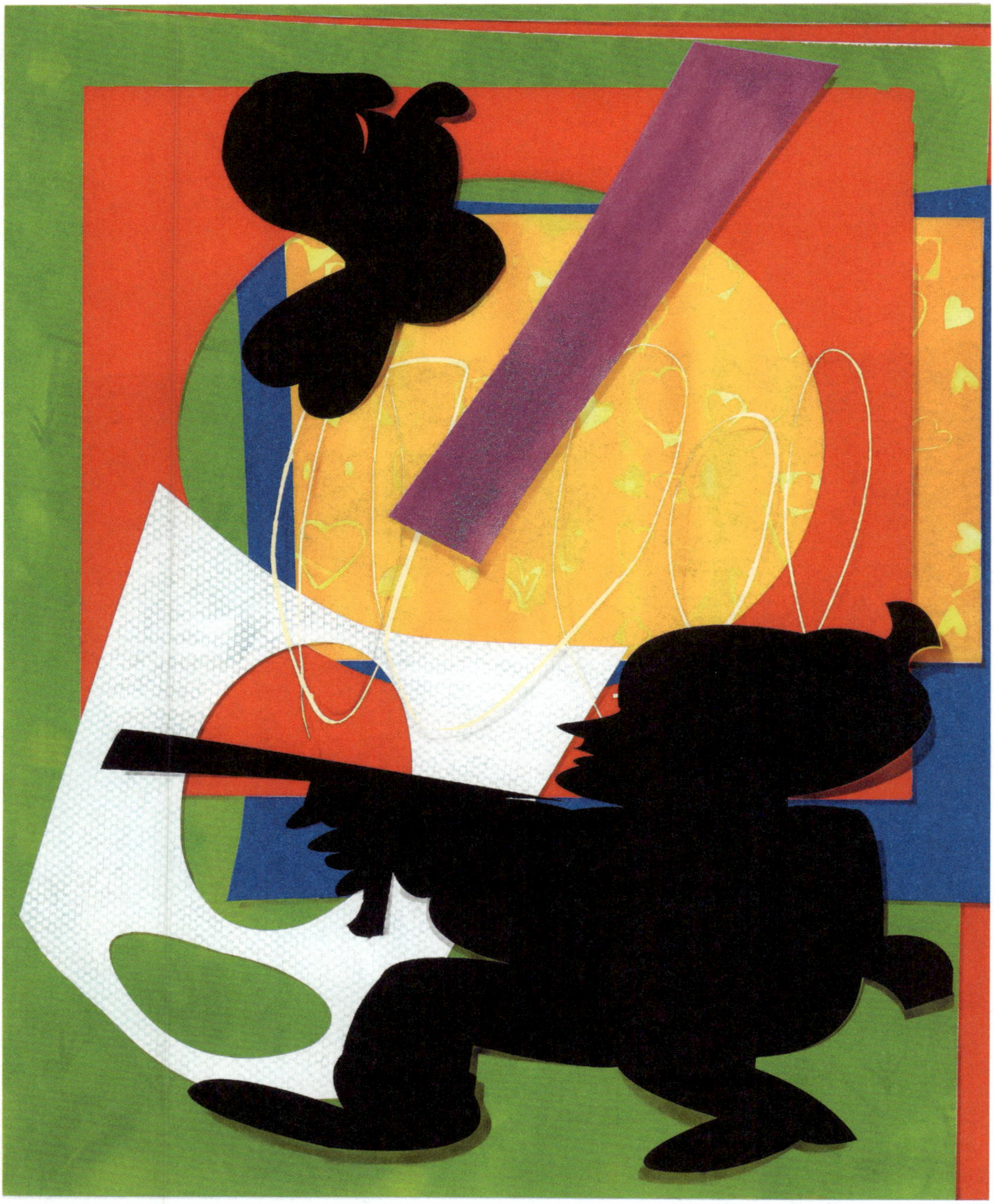

***Rabbiting in the Hunting Ground*, 2020. Acrylic on canvas, 180 × 150 cm**

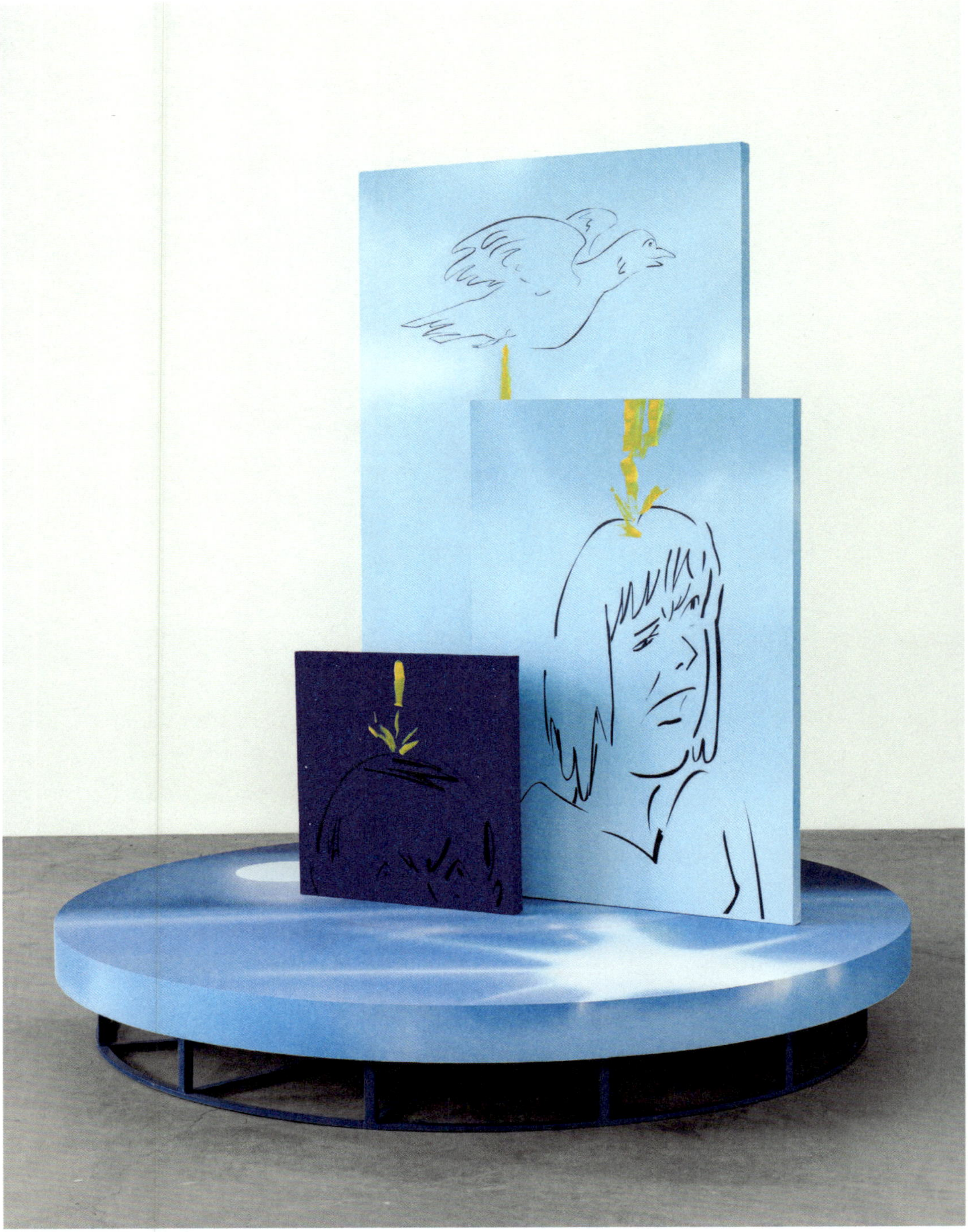

*Everything Started from the Day, Earth Turned and Turned, and One Bird Pooped on My Head*, 2023.
Acrylic on canvas, rotating base, 50 × 50 cm, 100 × 70 cm, 150 × 90 cm Ø 75 cm

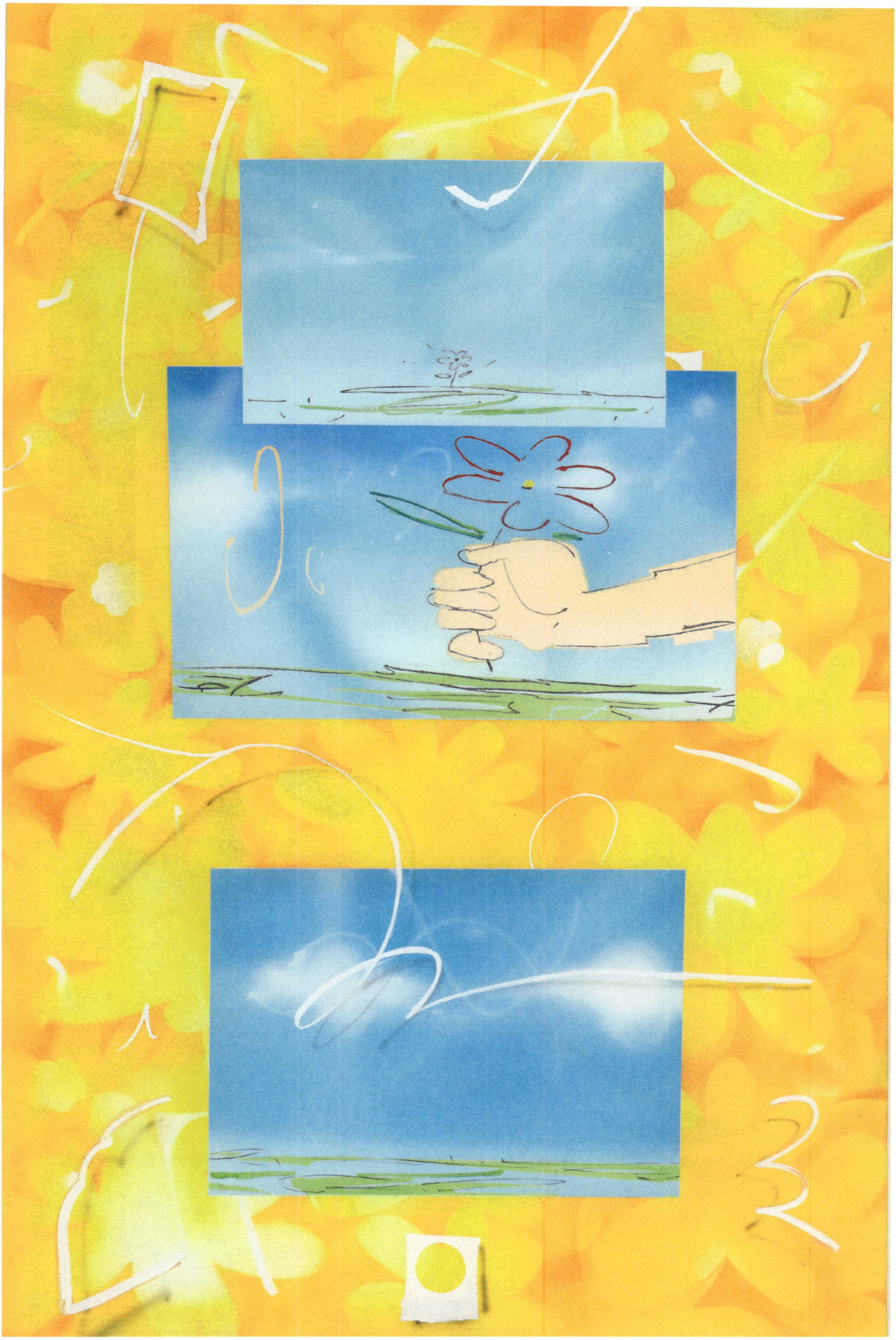

*Where Is the Flower Gone?*, 2019. Acrylic on canvas, 150 × 100 cm

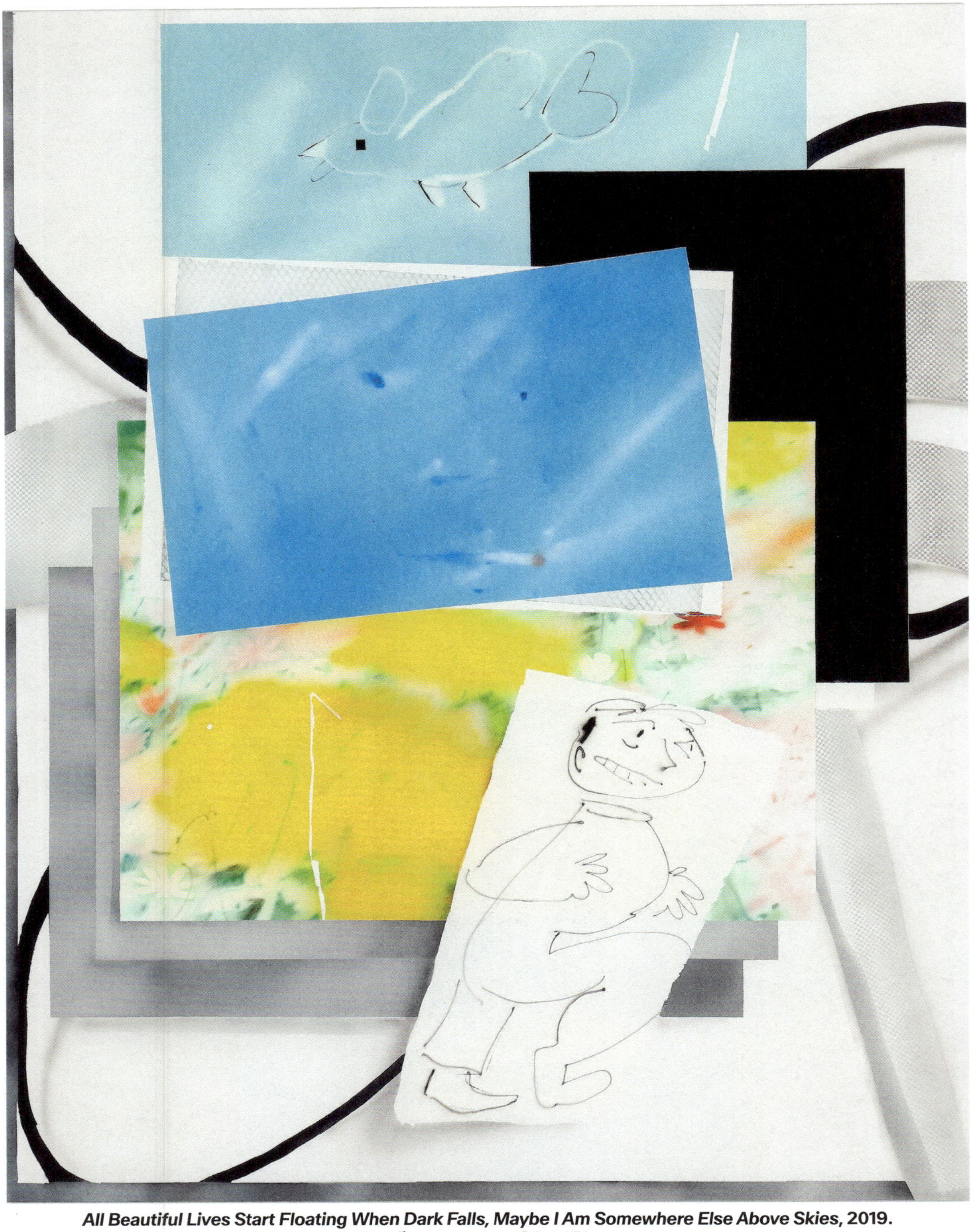

*All Beautiful Lives Start Floating When Dark Falls, Maybe I Am Somewhere Else Above Skies*, 2019.
Acrylic on canvas, 185 × 151 cm

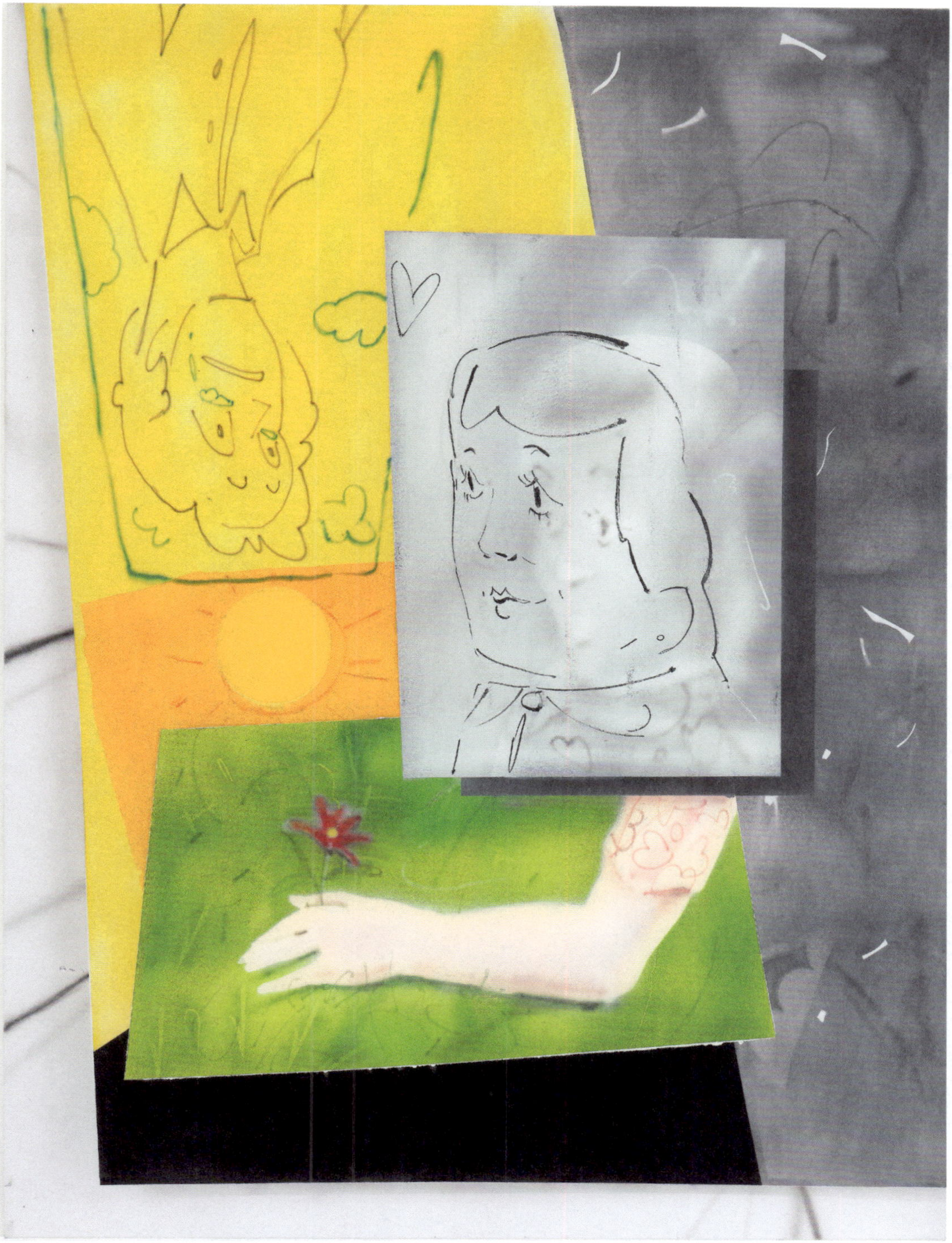

*I Died but I Still Love You*, 2019. Acrylic on canvas, 139 × 107 cm

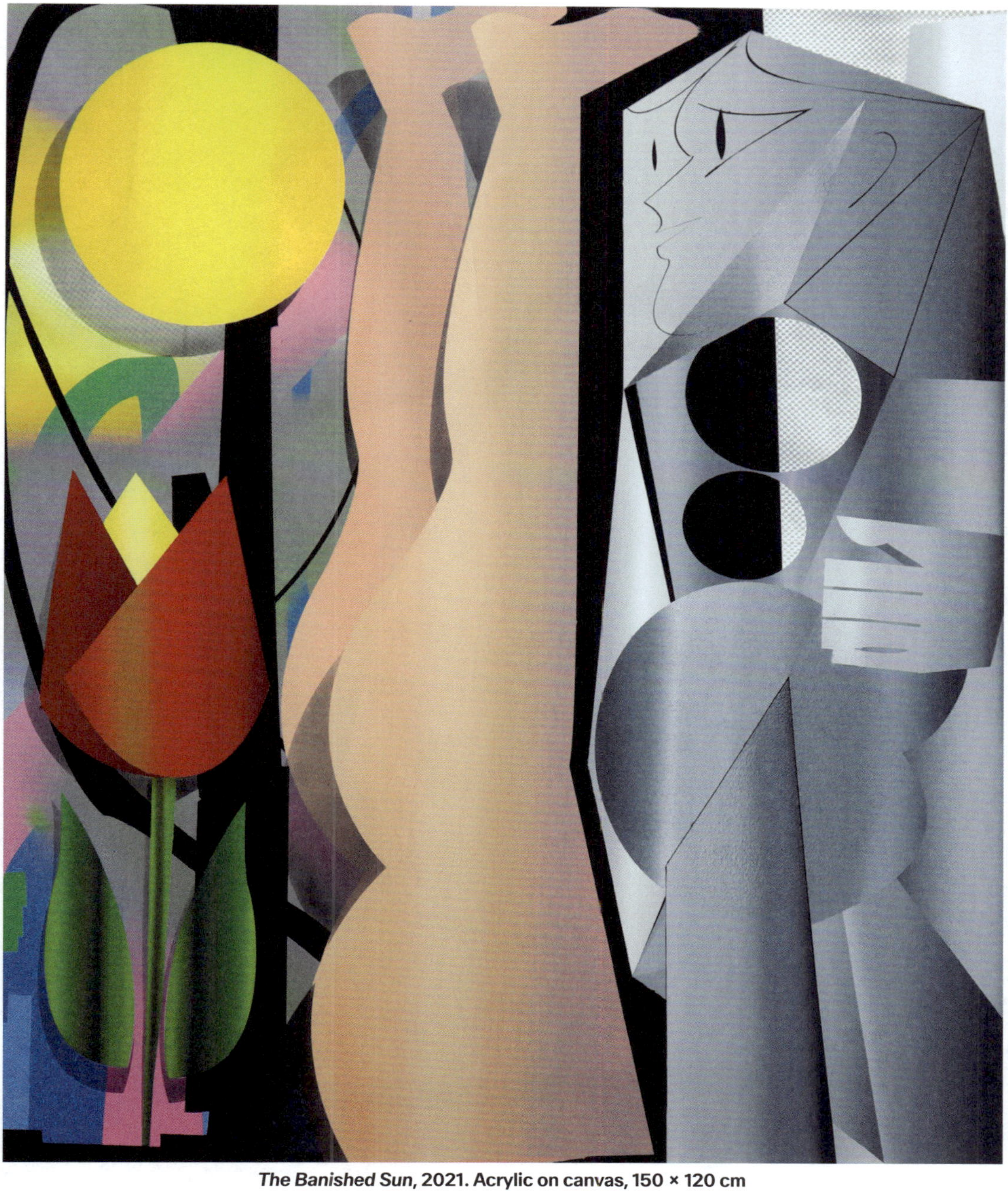

*The Banished Sun*, 2021. Acrylic on canvas, 150 × 120 cm

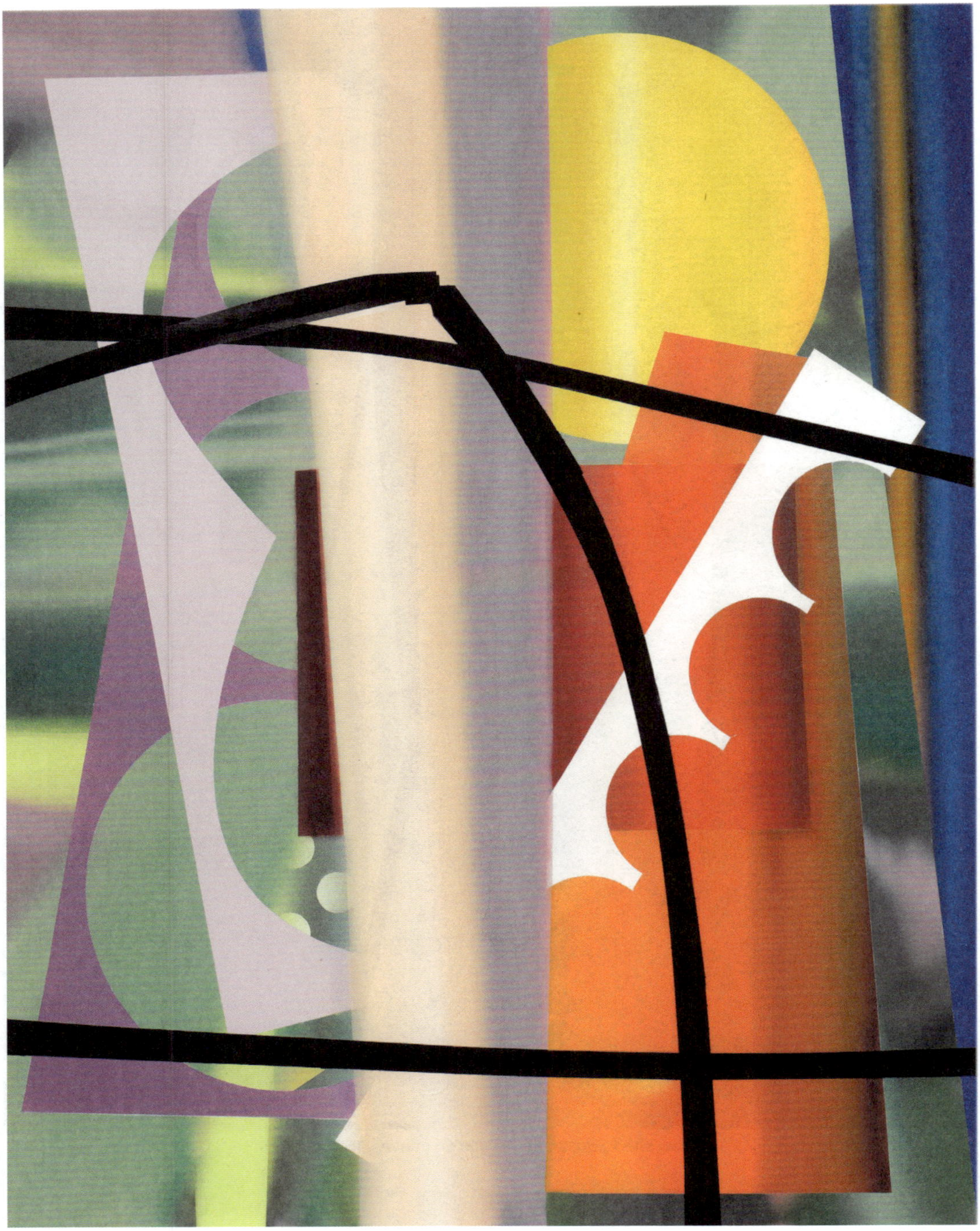

*Return Sun Melts Bodies into One*, 2021. Acrylic on canvas, 150 × 120 cm

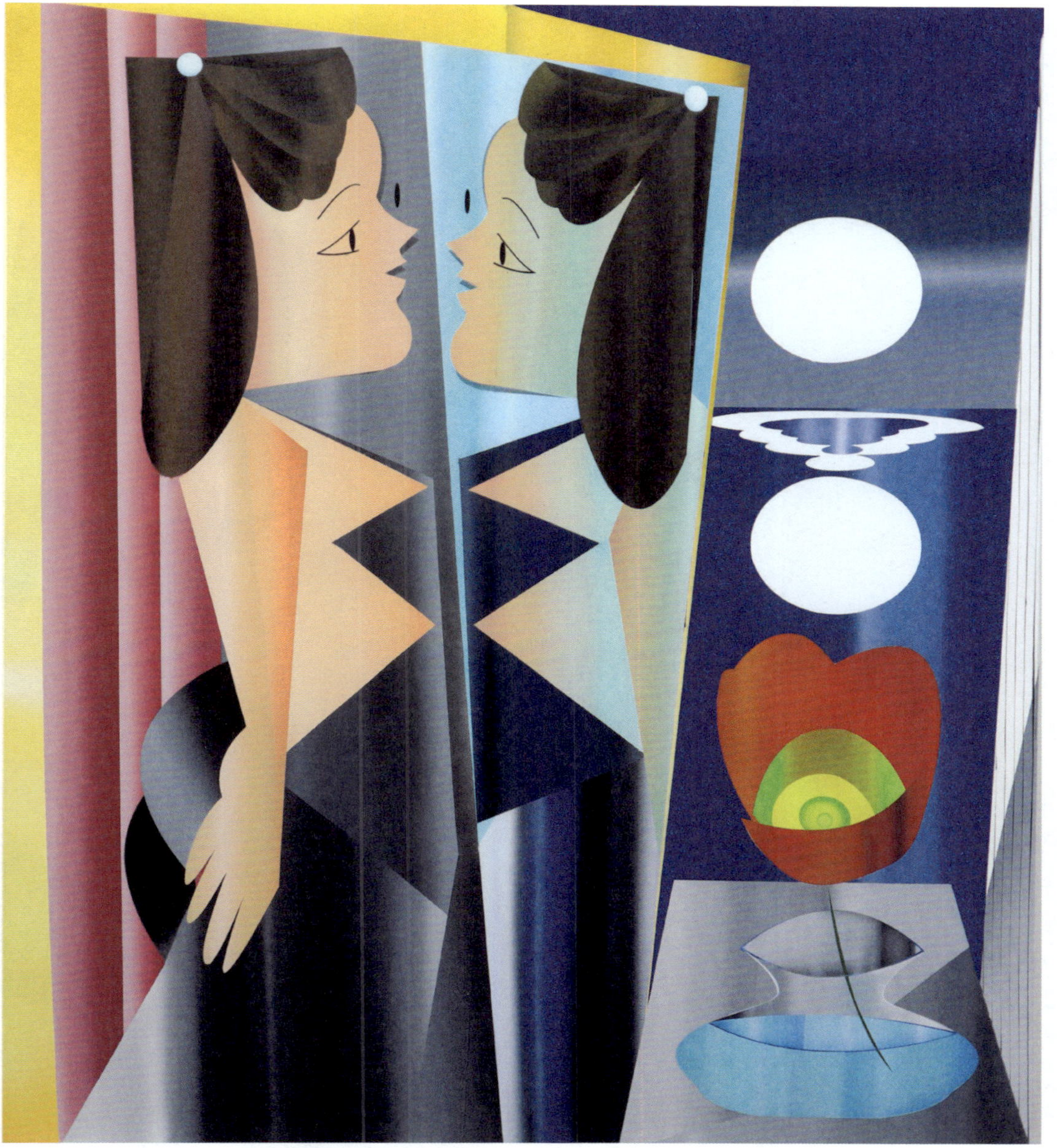

***Look at the Mirror***, 2021. Acrylic on canvas, 150 × 130 cm

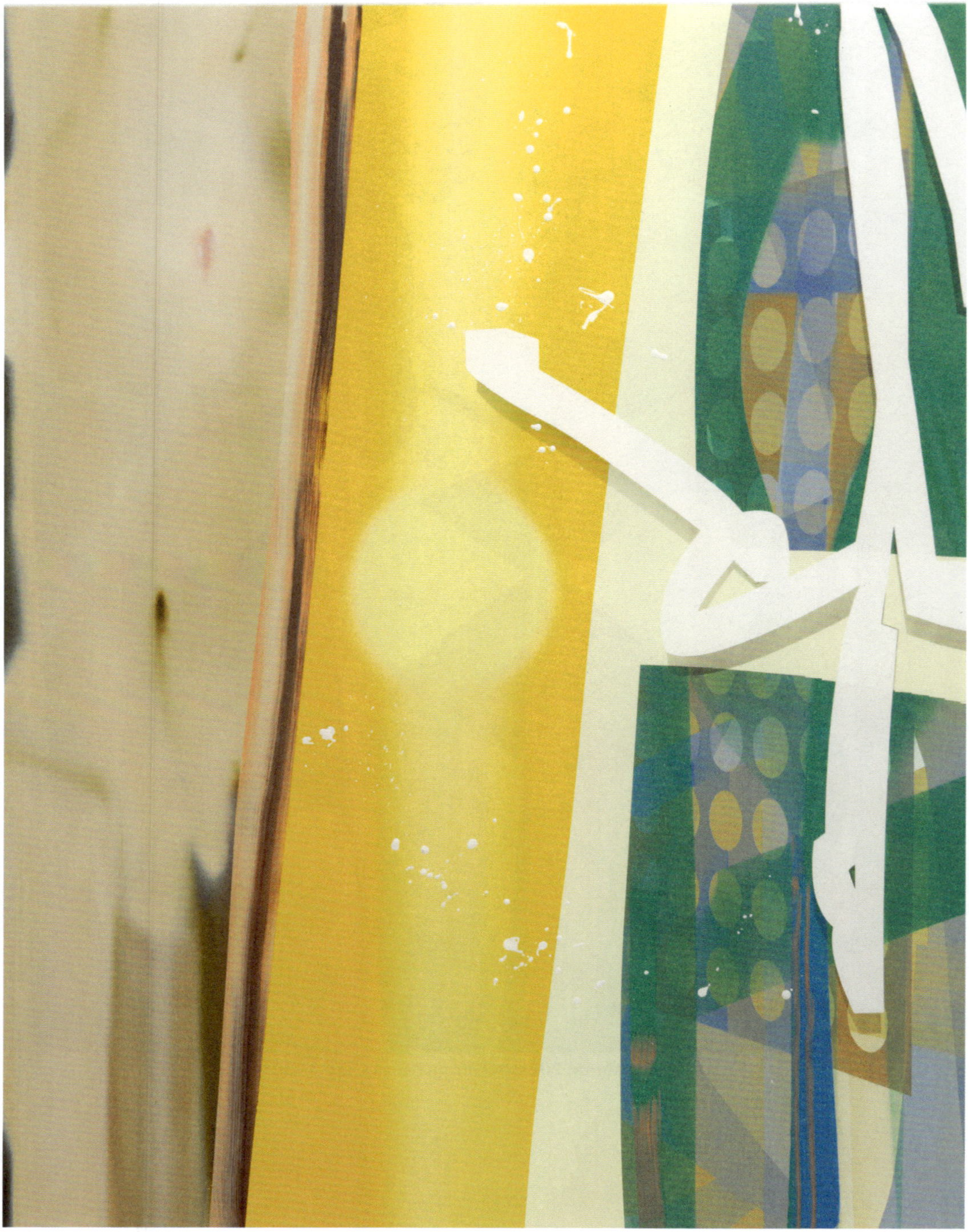

*The Long Days of Summer Melt Thirsty Bodies into Water*, 2022. Acrylic on canvas, 150 × 120 cm

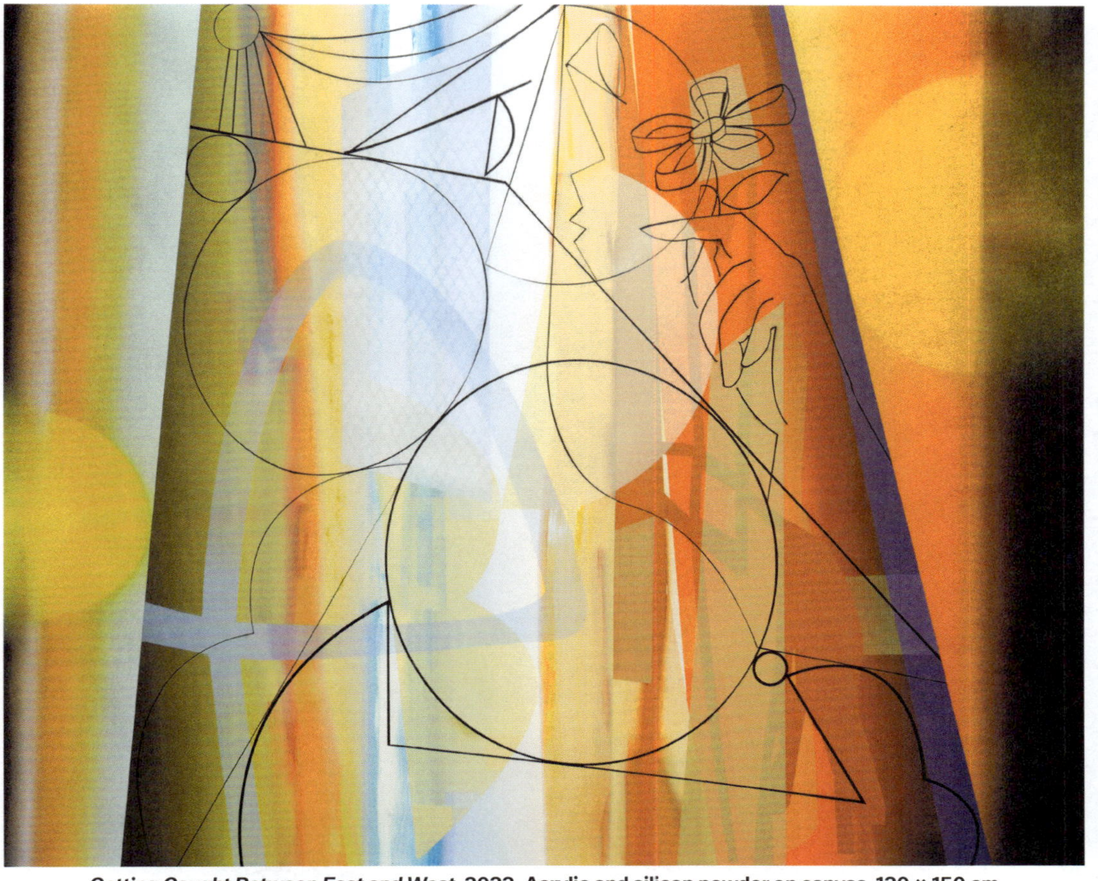

*Getting Caught Between East and West*, 2022. Acrylic and silicon powder on canvas, 120 × 150 cm

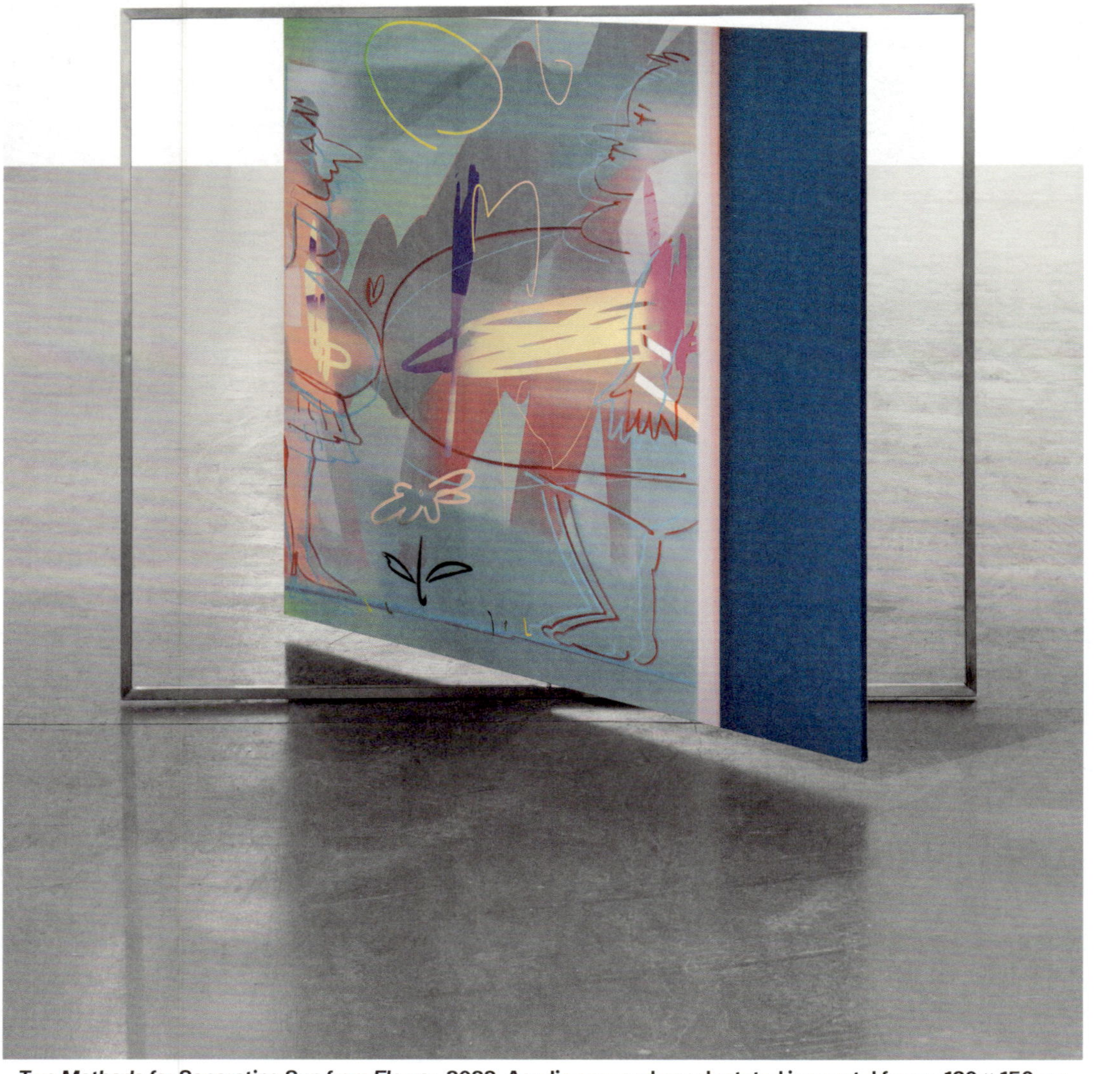

*Two Methods for Separating Sun from Flower*, 2022. Acrylic on wood panel rotated in a metal frame, 120 × 150 cm

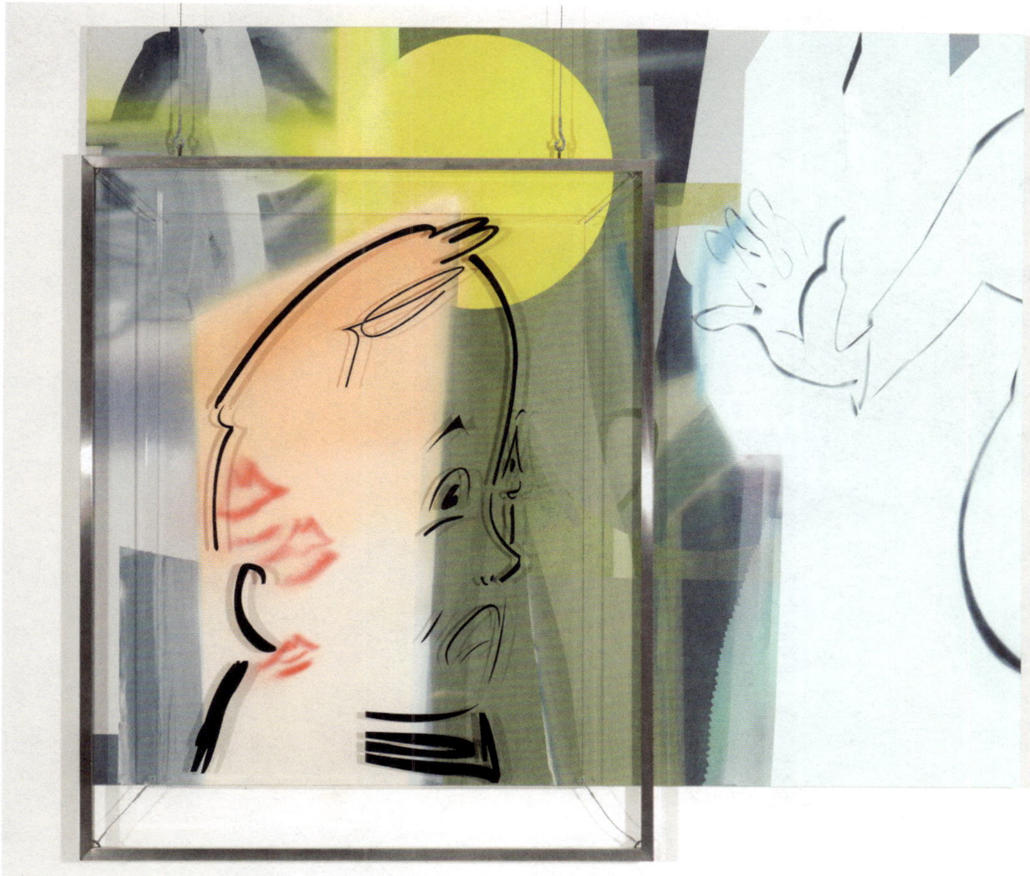

*Everything Vanished Except Lipstick Traces on Skin*, 2022. Acrylic on canvas and Plexiglas inside steel frame, 120 × 150 cm

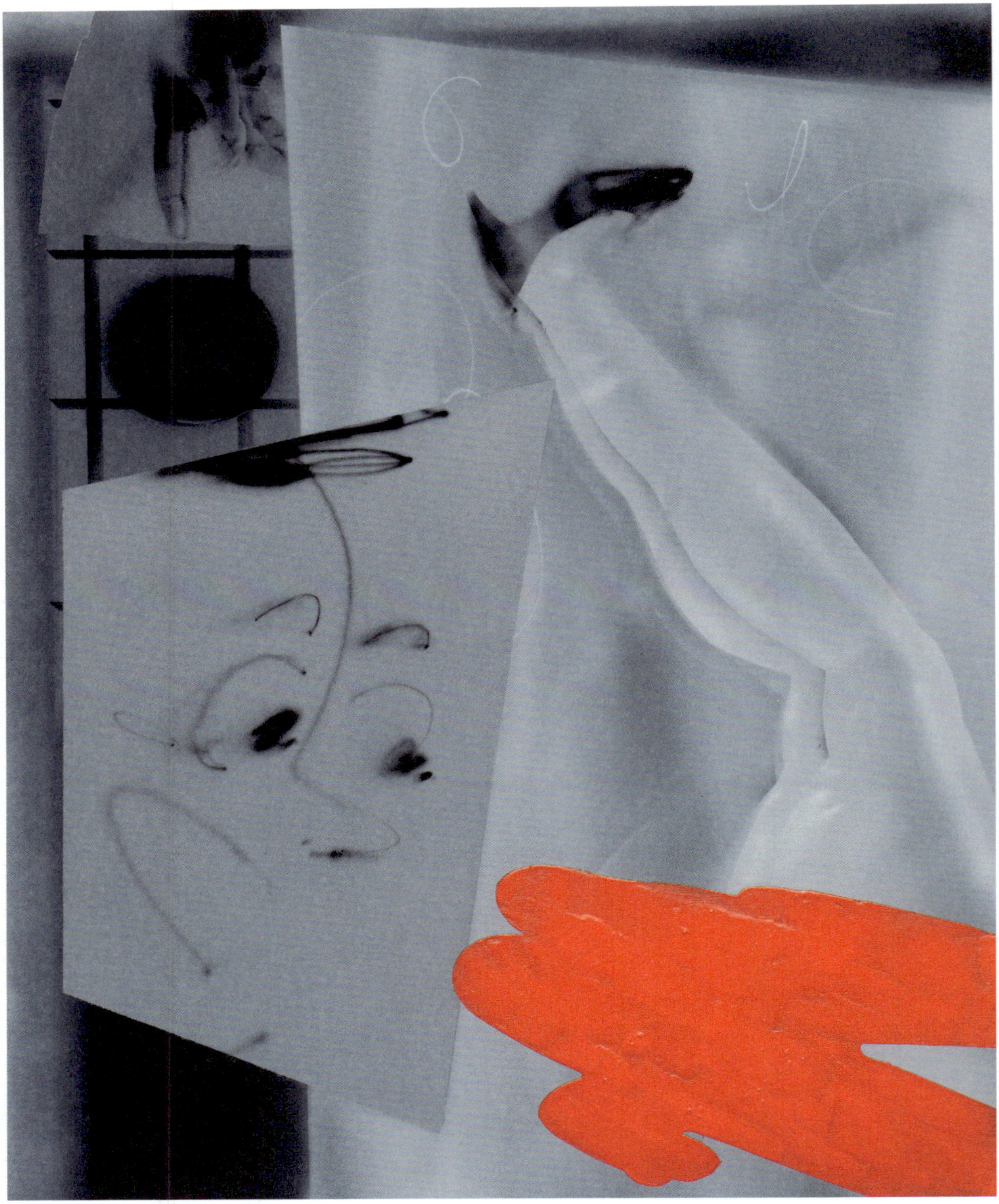

*The Eye, The Eyehole, The Hole*, 2020. Acrylic and wood glue on canvas, 120 × 100 cm

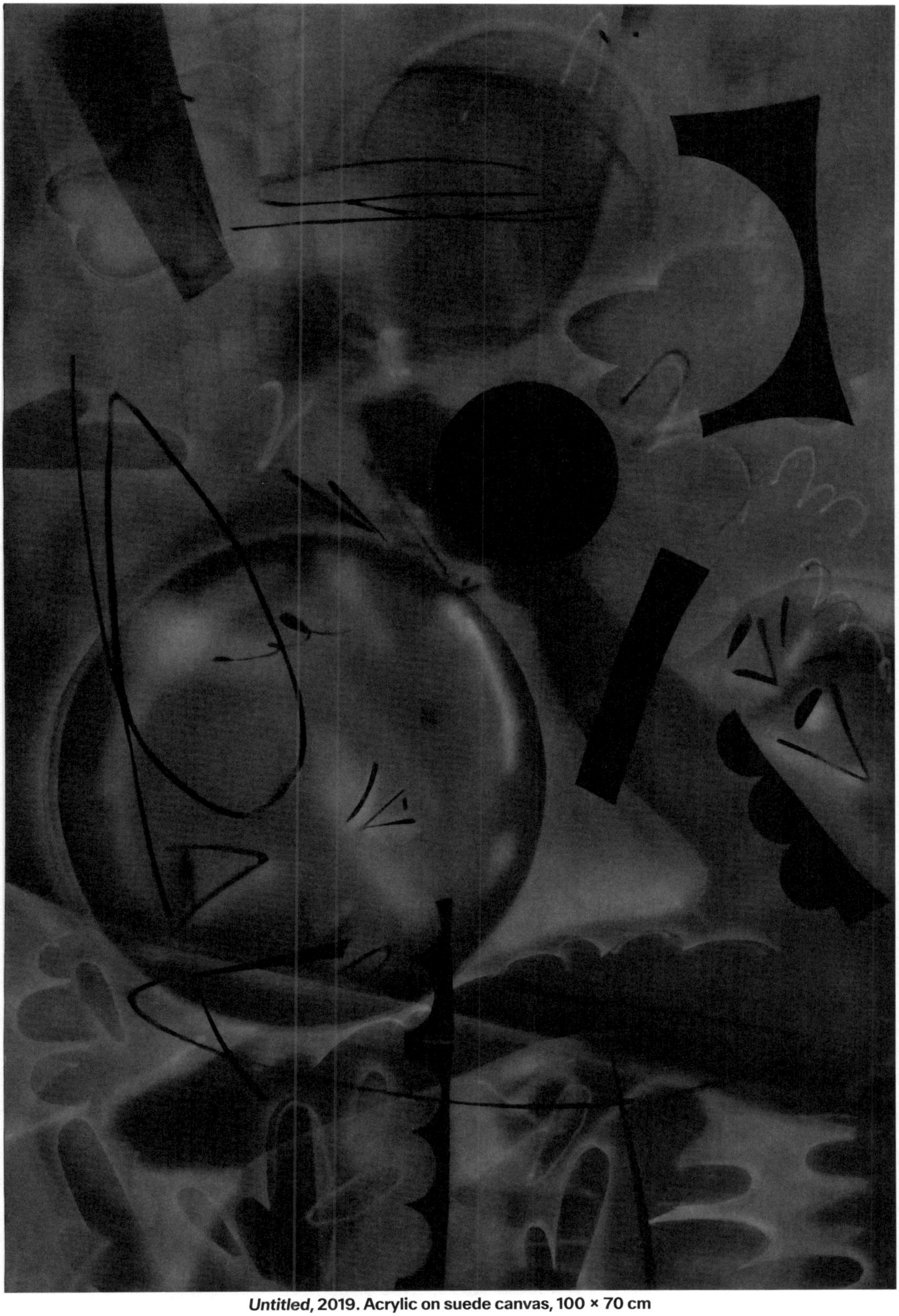

*Untitled*, 2019. Acrylic on suede canvas, 100 × 70 cm

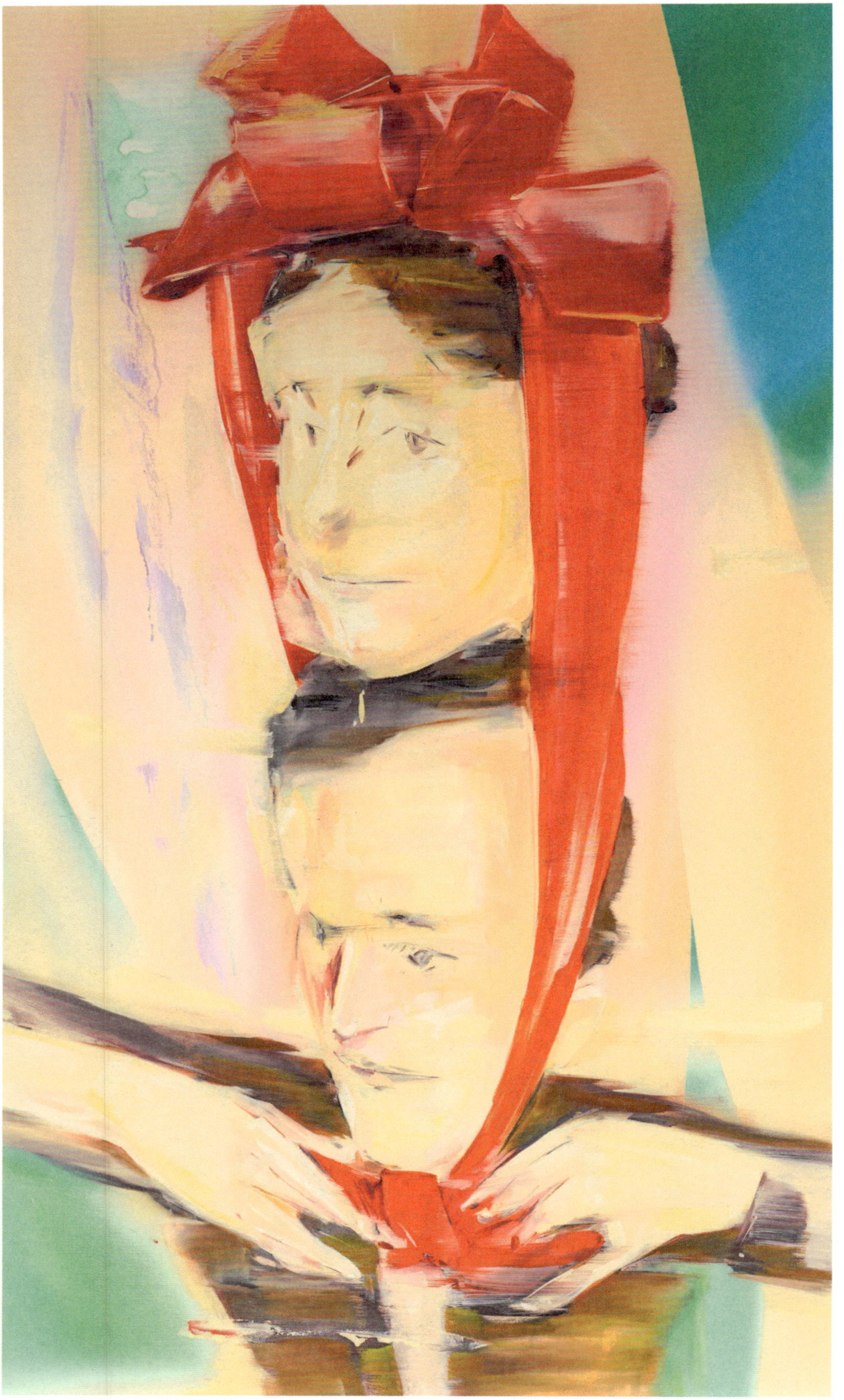

*Red Ribbon*, 2022. Oil on canvas, 150 × 90 cm

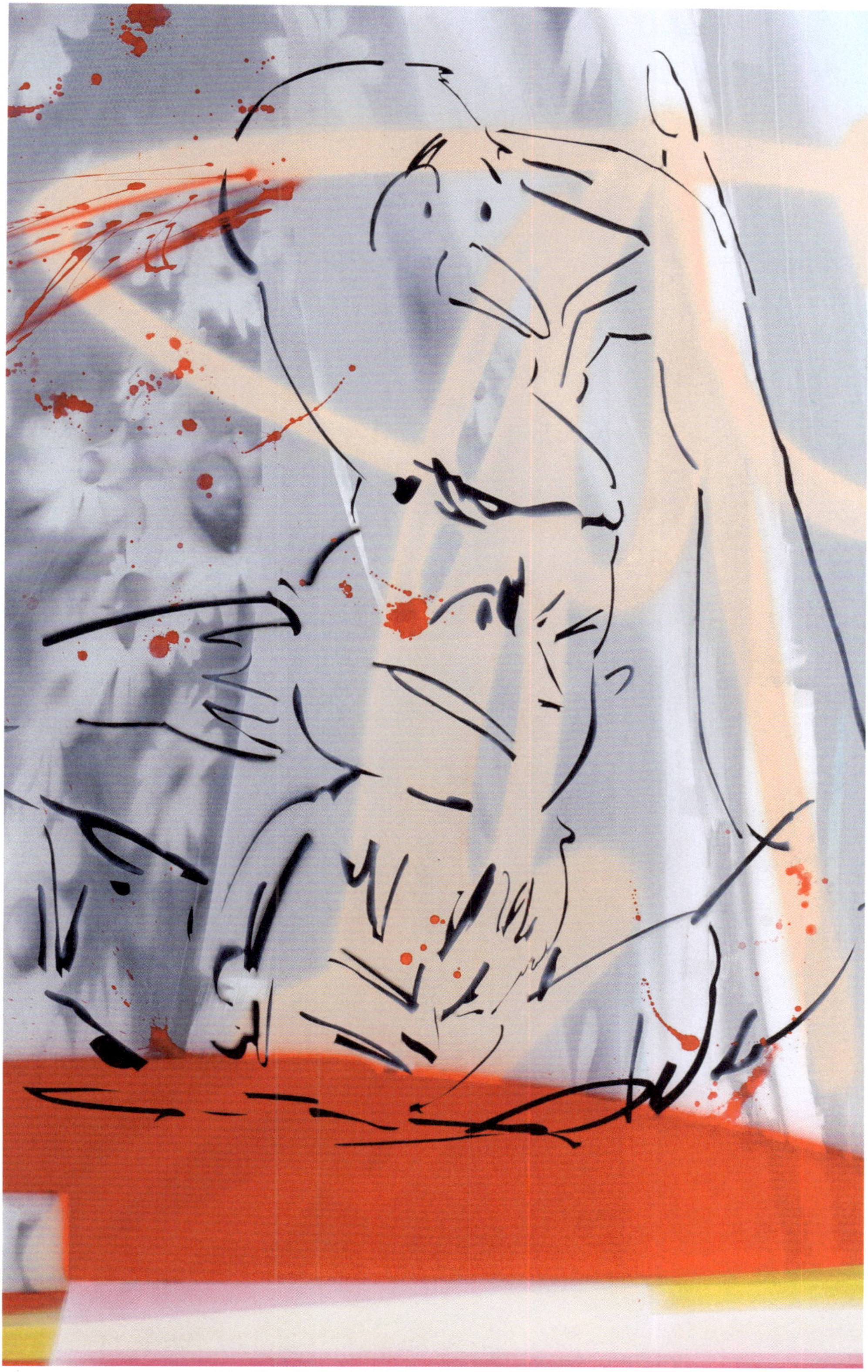

*The Final Point*, 2022. Acrylic on canvas, 150 × 95 cm

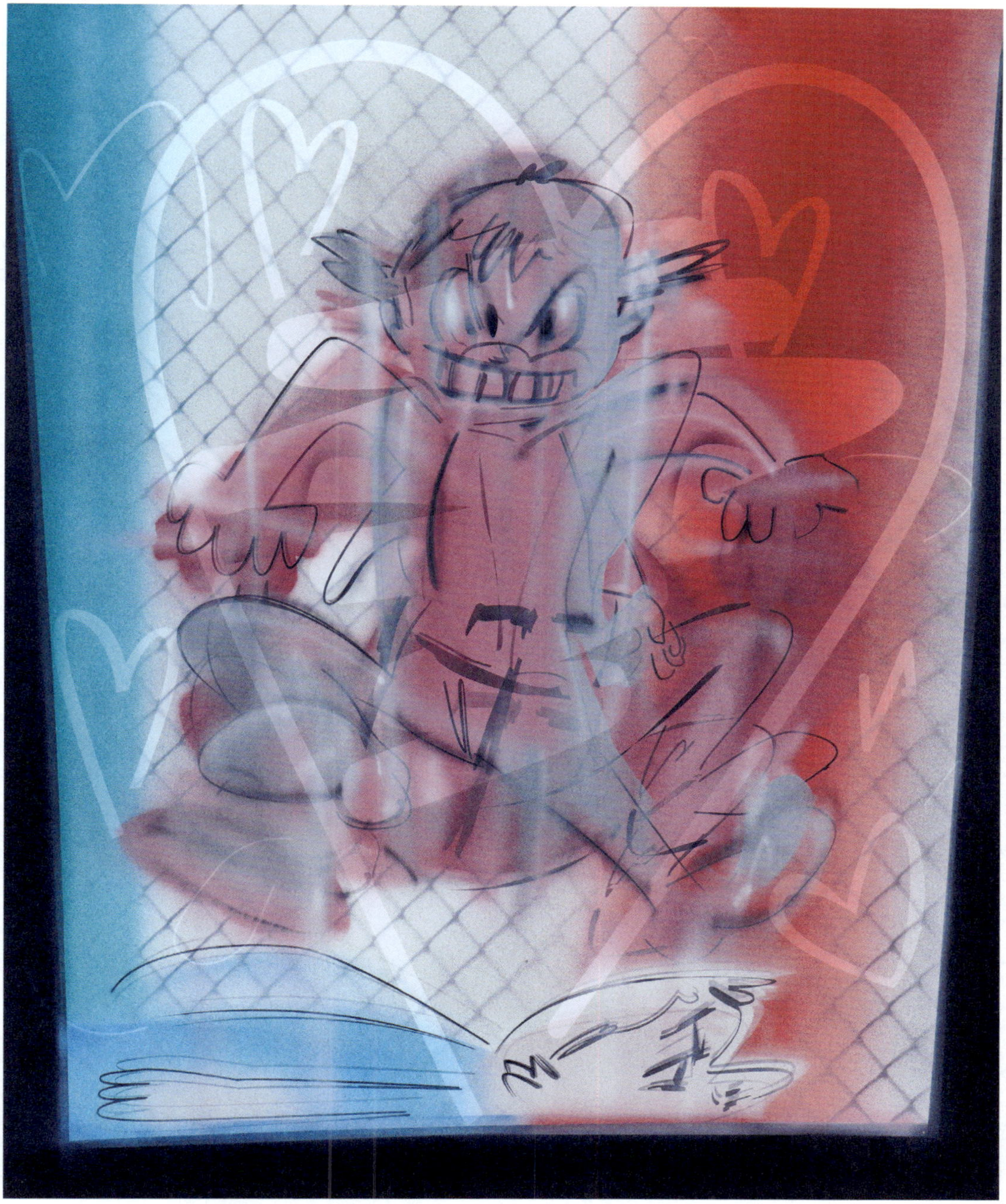

*I Am Angry, but Everything Is Fine*, 2022. Acrylic on canvas, 120 × 100 cm

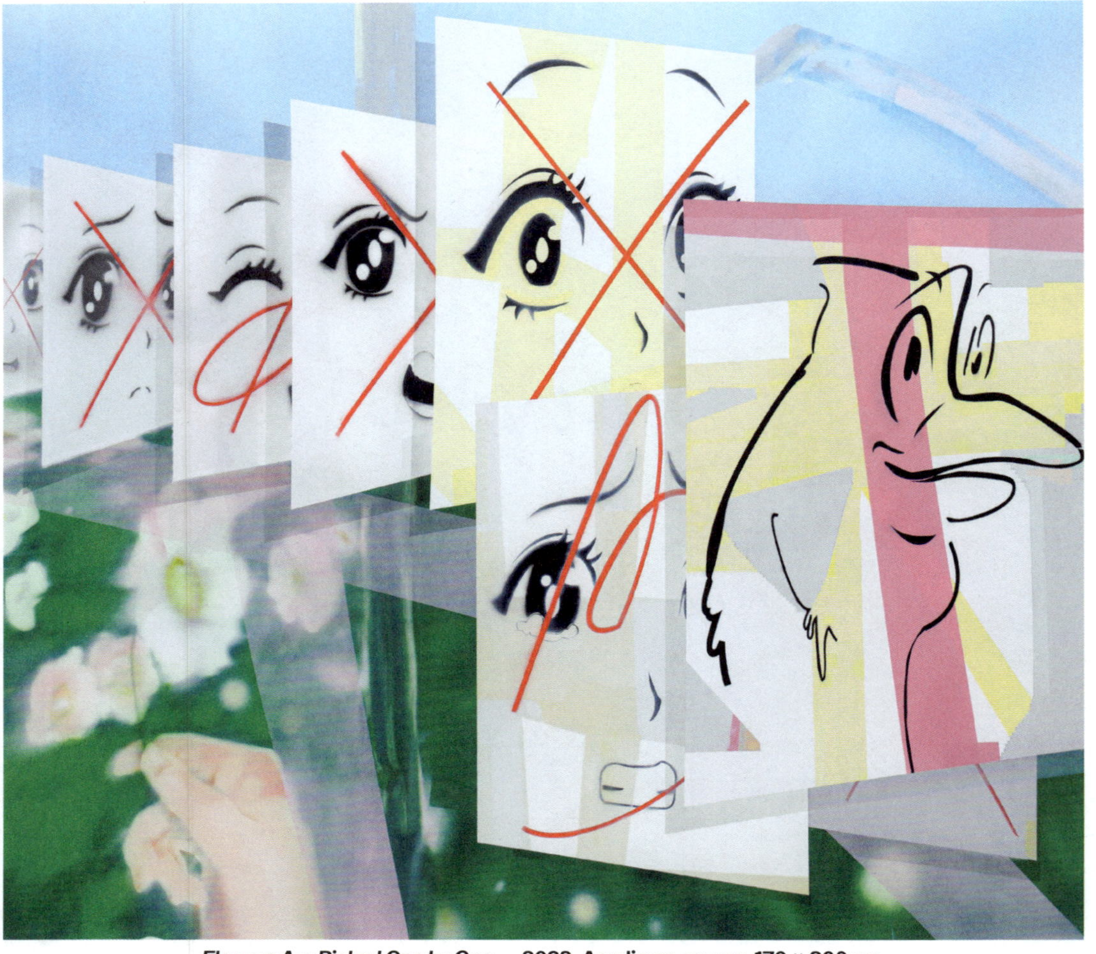

*Flowers Are Picked One by One…*, 2022. Acrylic on canvas, 170 × 200 cm

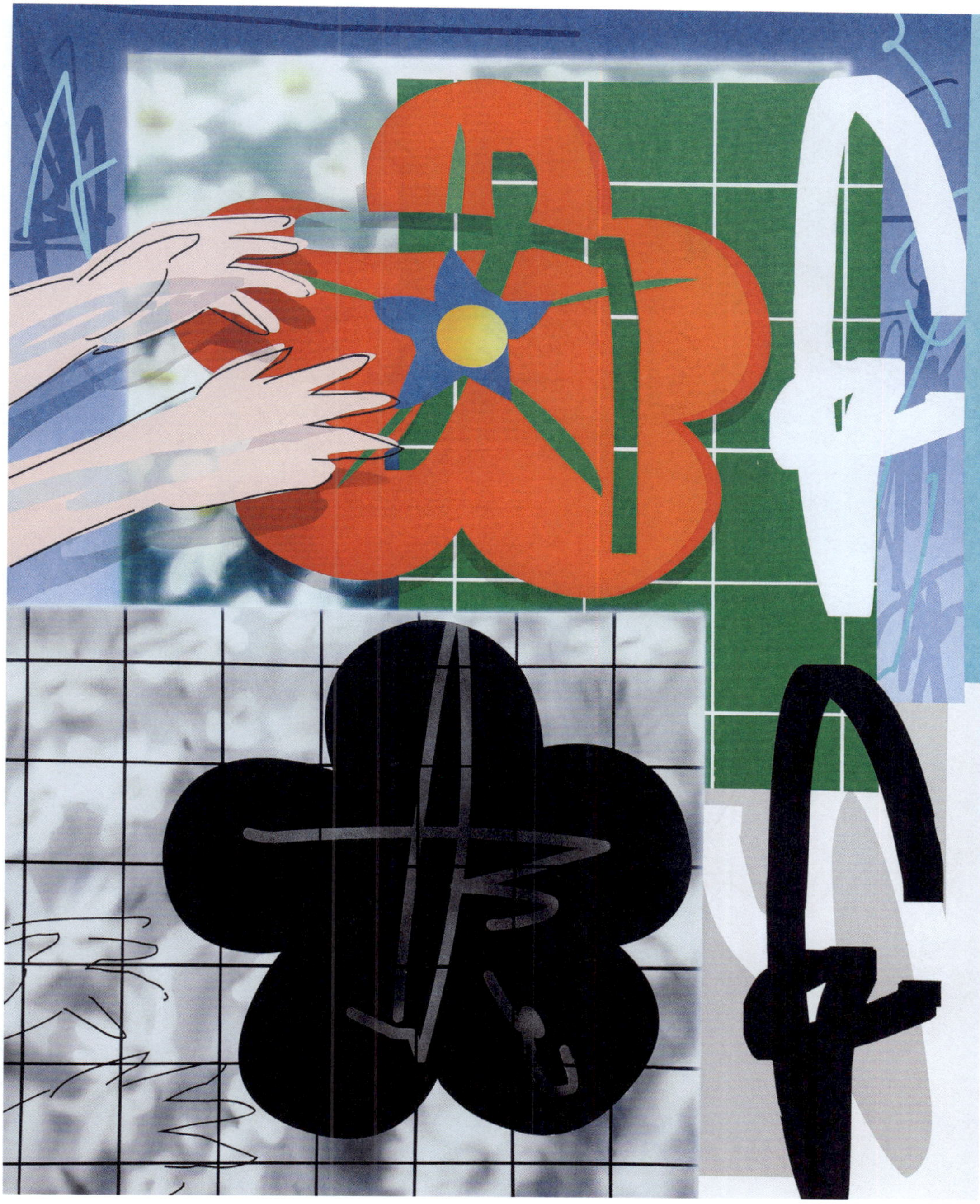

*Even the Last Red One…*, 2022. Acrylic on canvas, 180 × 150 cm

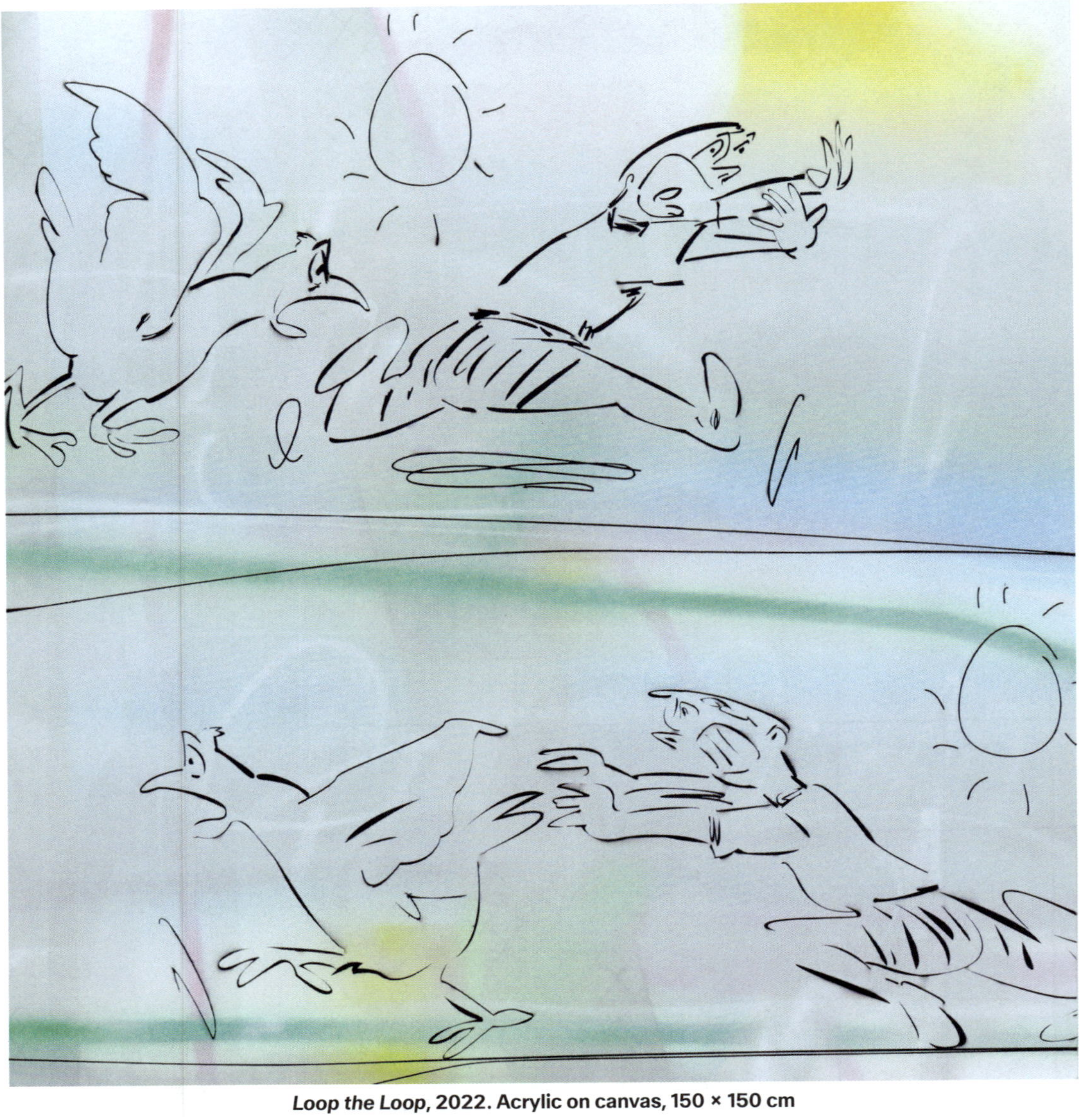

***Loop the Loop*, 2022. Acrylic on canvas, 150 × 150 cm**

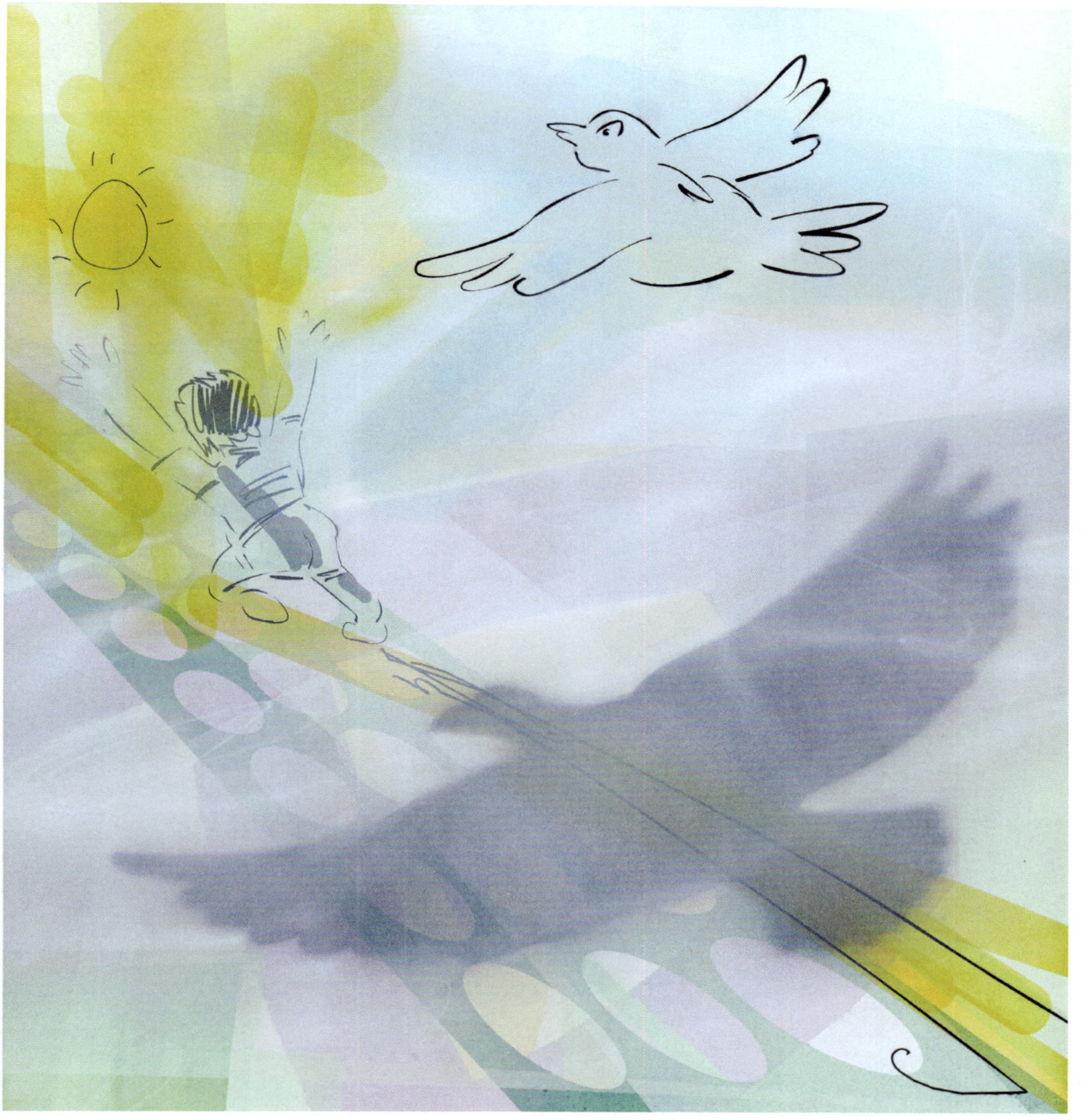

*The Wrong Shadow*, 2022. Acrylic on canvas, 158 × 150 cm

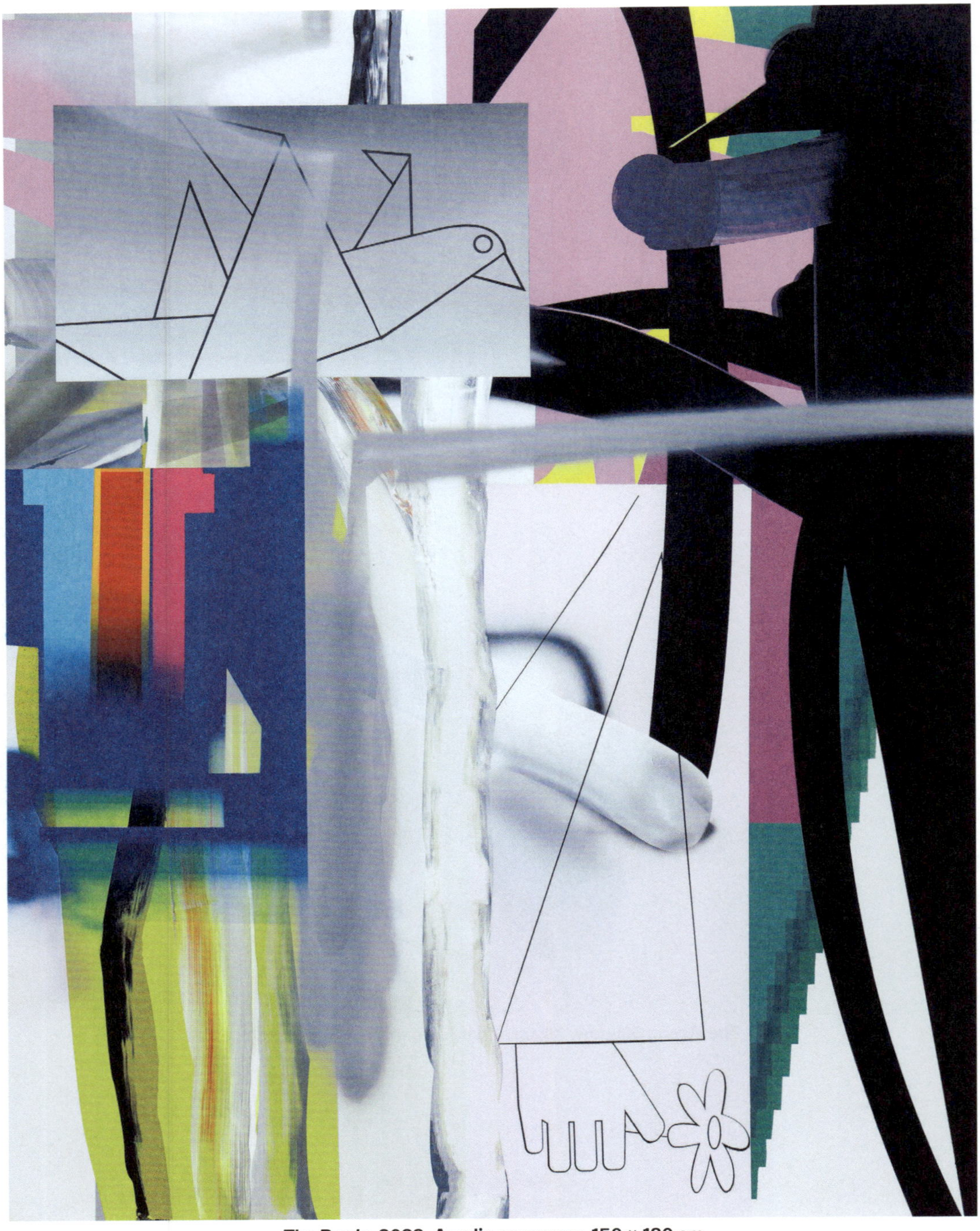

*The Bardo*, 2022. Acrylic on canvas, 150 × 120 cm

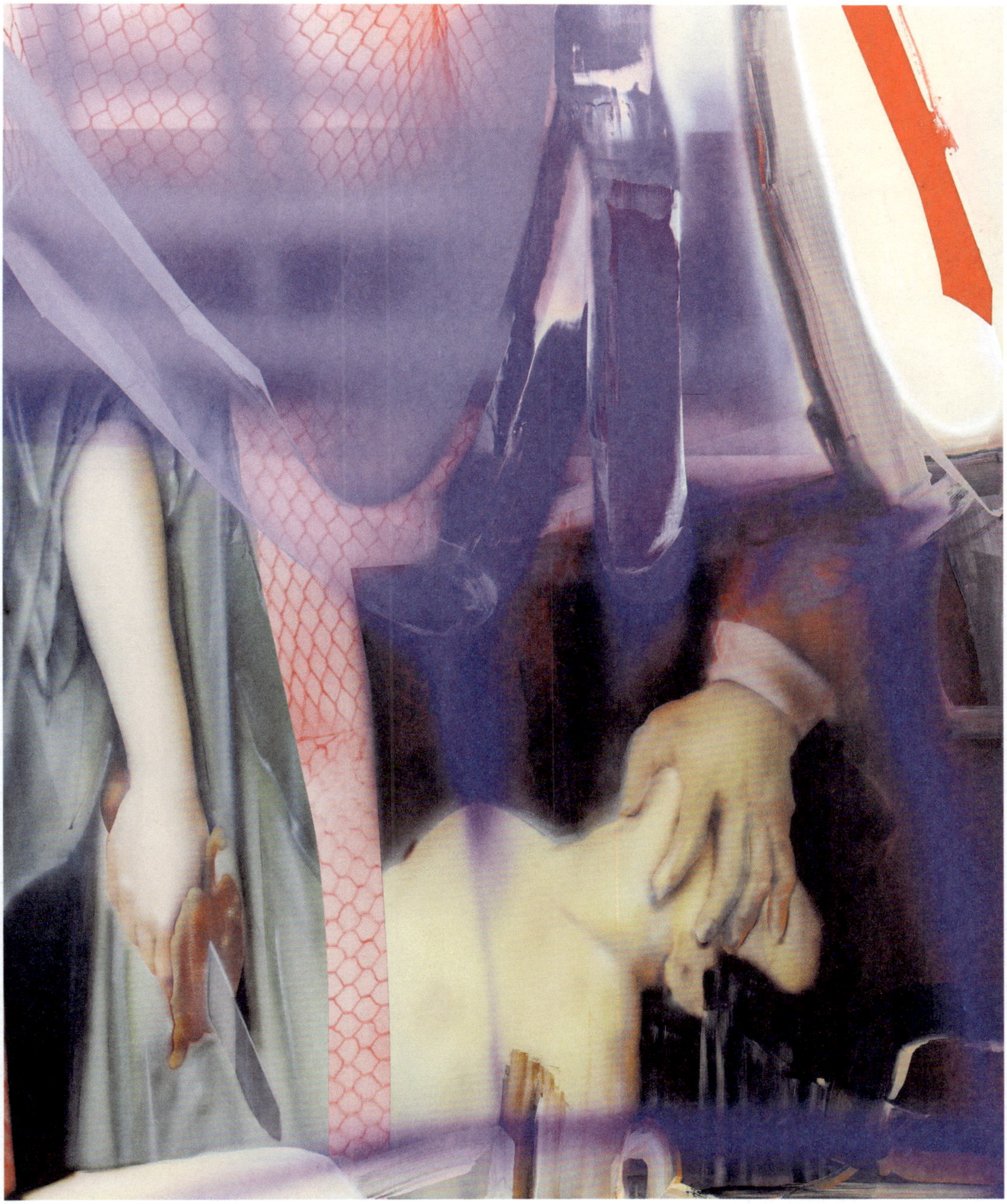

*Purple is Healing the Wound between Sword and Neck*, 2022. Acrylic on canvas, 180 × 150 cm

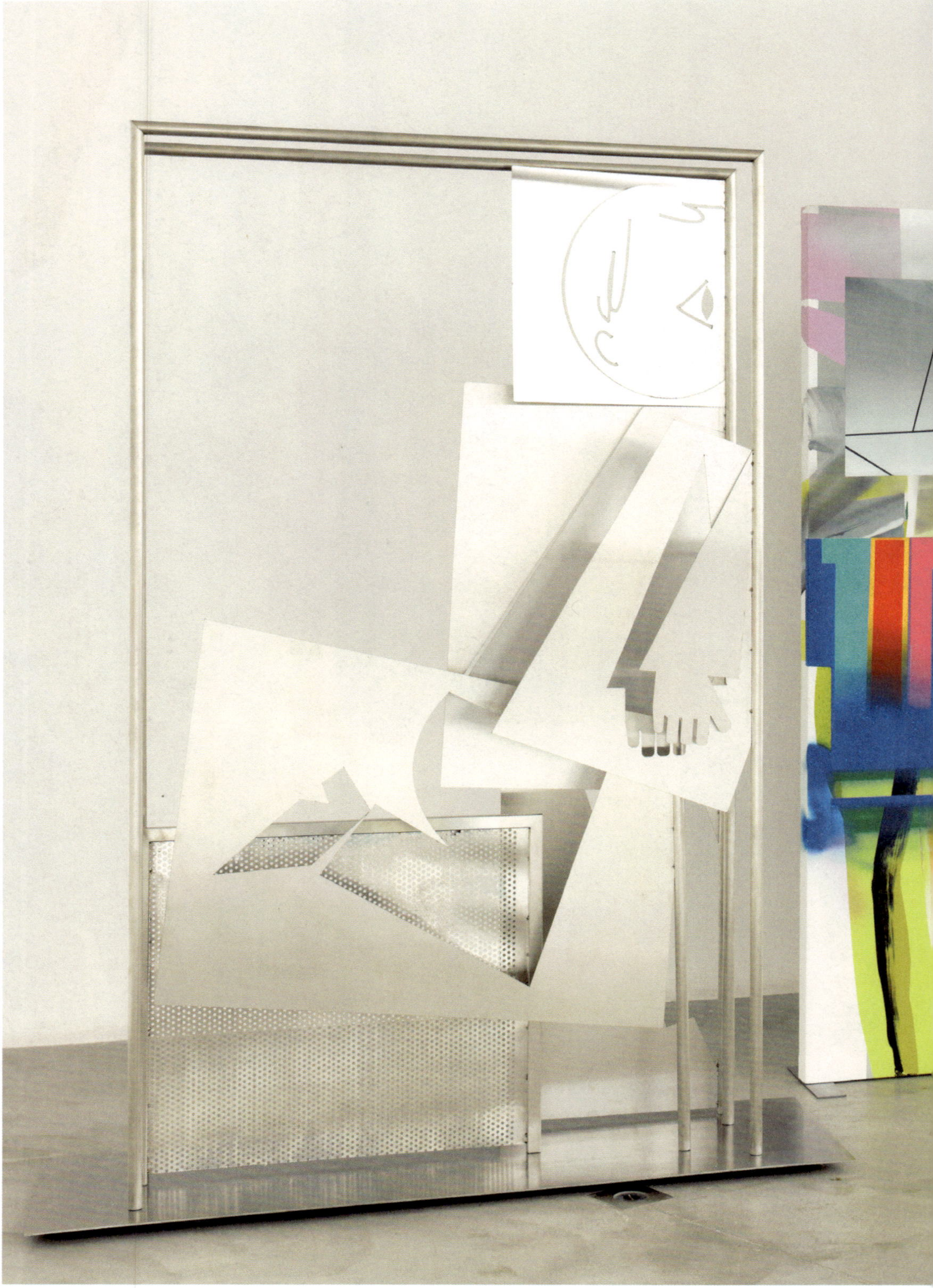

***Another world is waiting for us*** **at Galerie Nathalie Obadia, Brussels, 2023. *Farewell to My Shadow*, 2023. Steel, 150 × 120 cm*;* *The Bardo*, 2022. Acrylic on canvas, 150 × 120 cm*;***

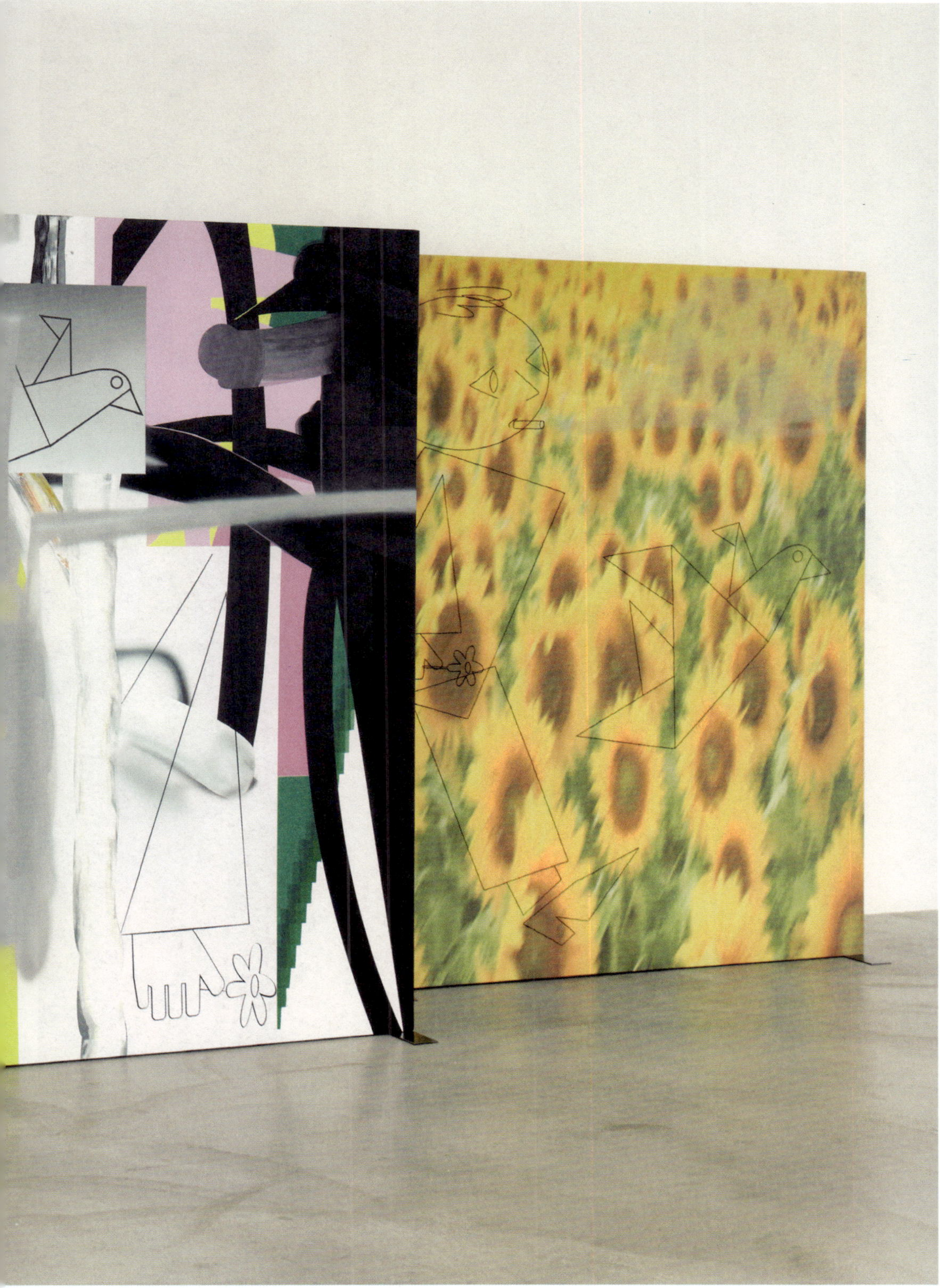

*Just for a Second / Heaven Unveiled Itself / The Sun Returned to Flowers / And the Bright Guilty Word Was Invented: Sunflower*, 2022. Embroidery on printed velvet, 150 × 120 cm

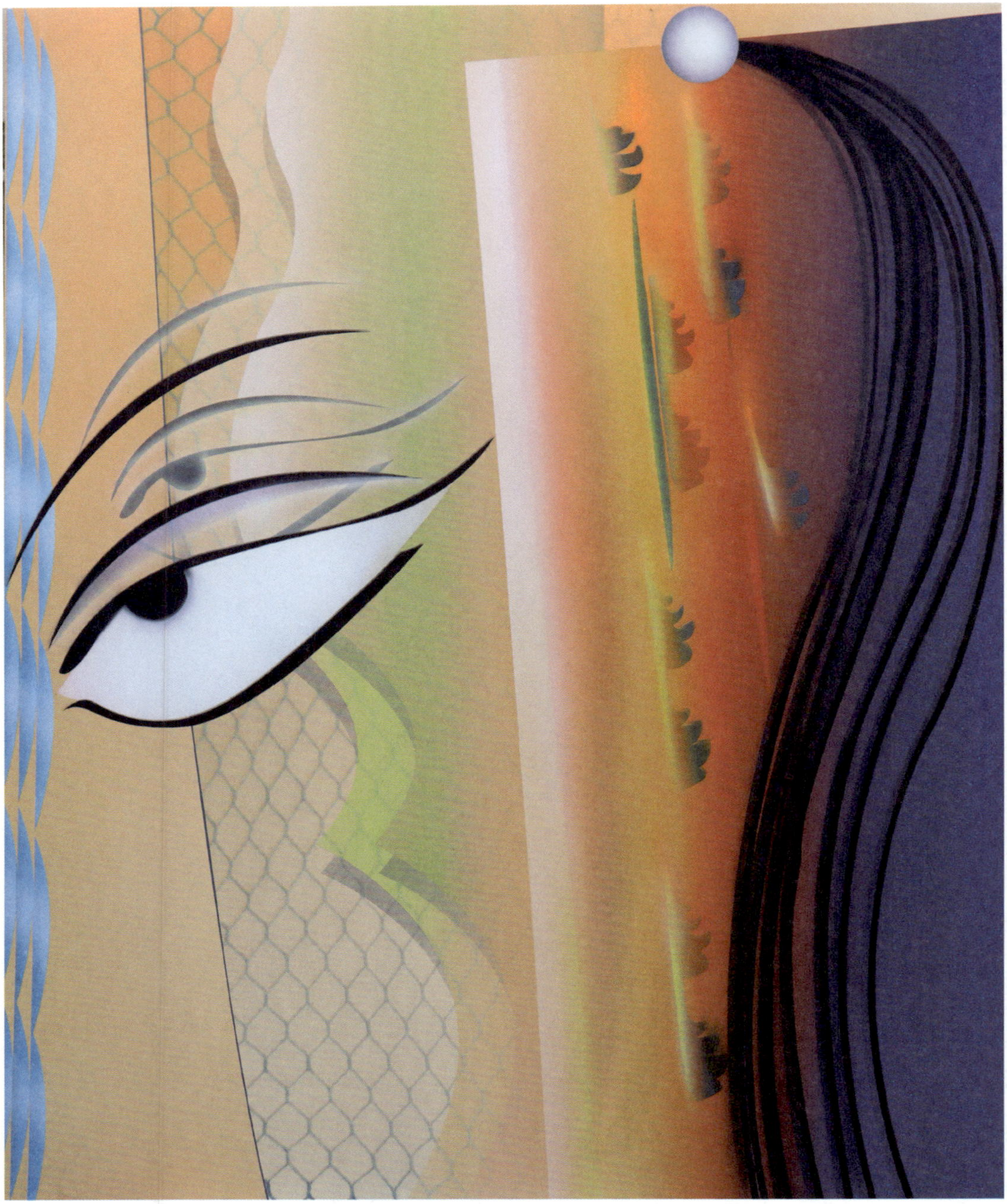

*Water Like Mirror / Hugged My Profile Face in the Red Hot Sky and Now/ My Full Portrait Is Unveiled / in the Soaked Chilled Sky*, 2023. Acrylic on canvas, 120 × 100 cm

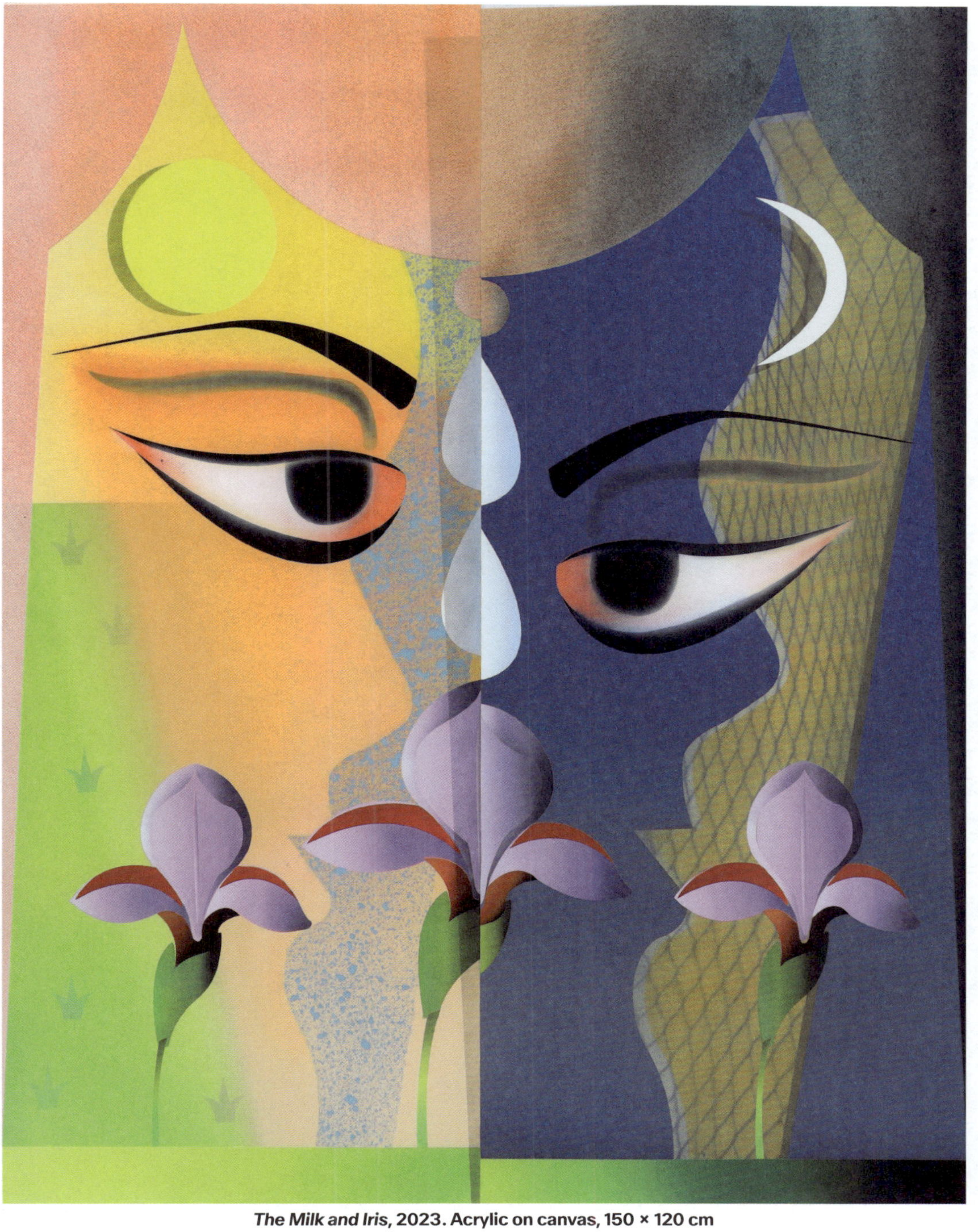

***The Milk and Iris*, 2023. Acrylic on canvas, 150 × 120 cm**

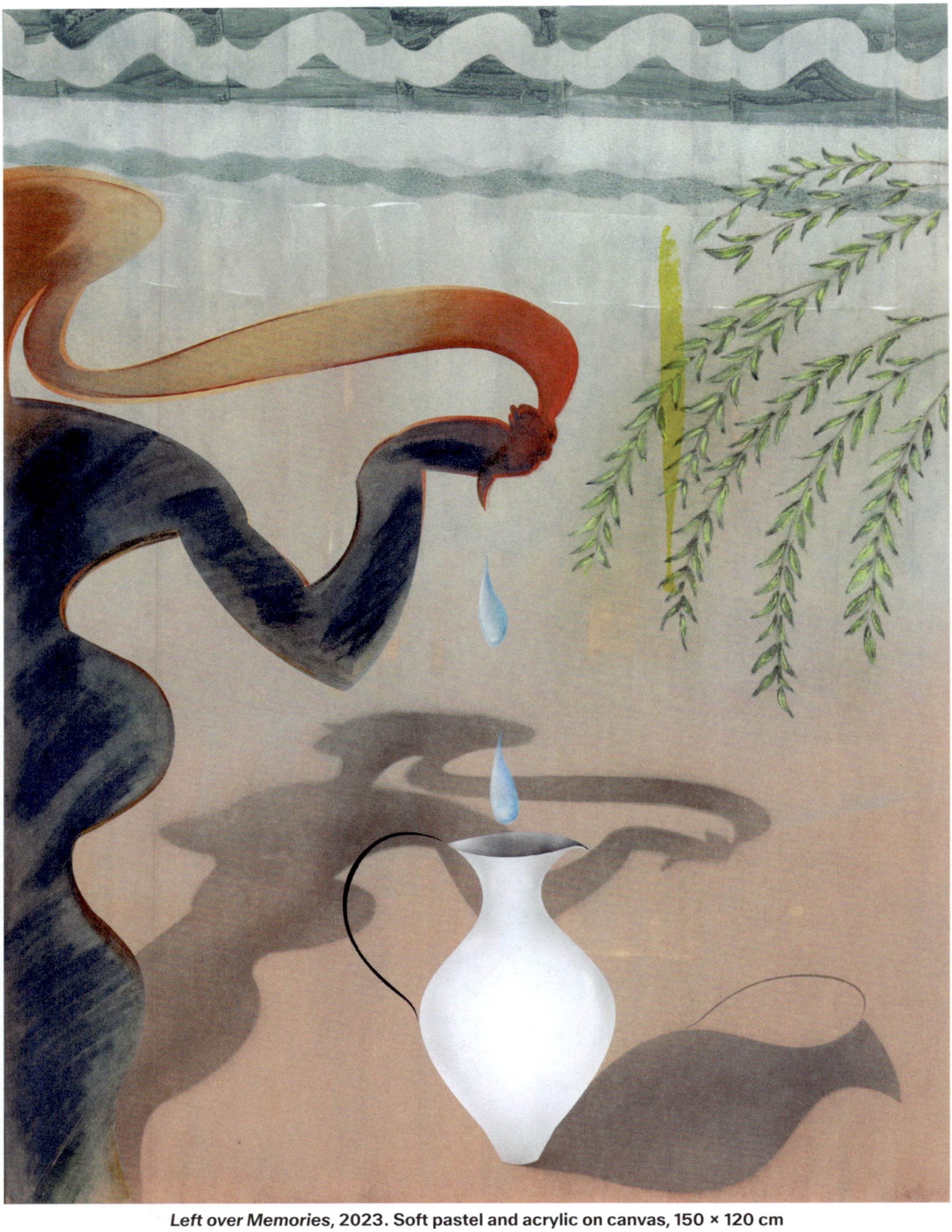

*Left over Memories*, 2023. Soft pastel and acrylic on canvas, 150 × 120 cm

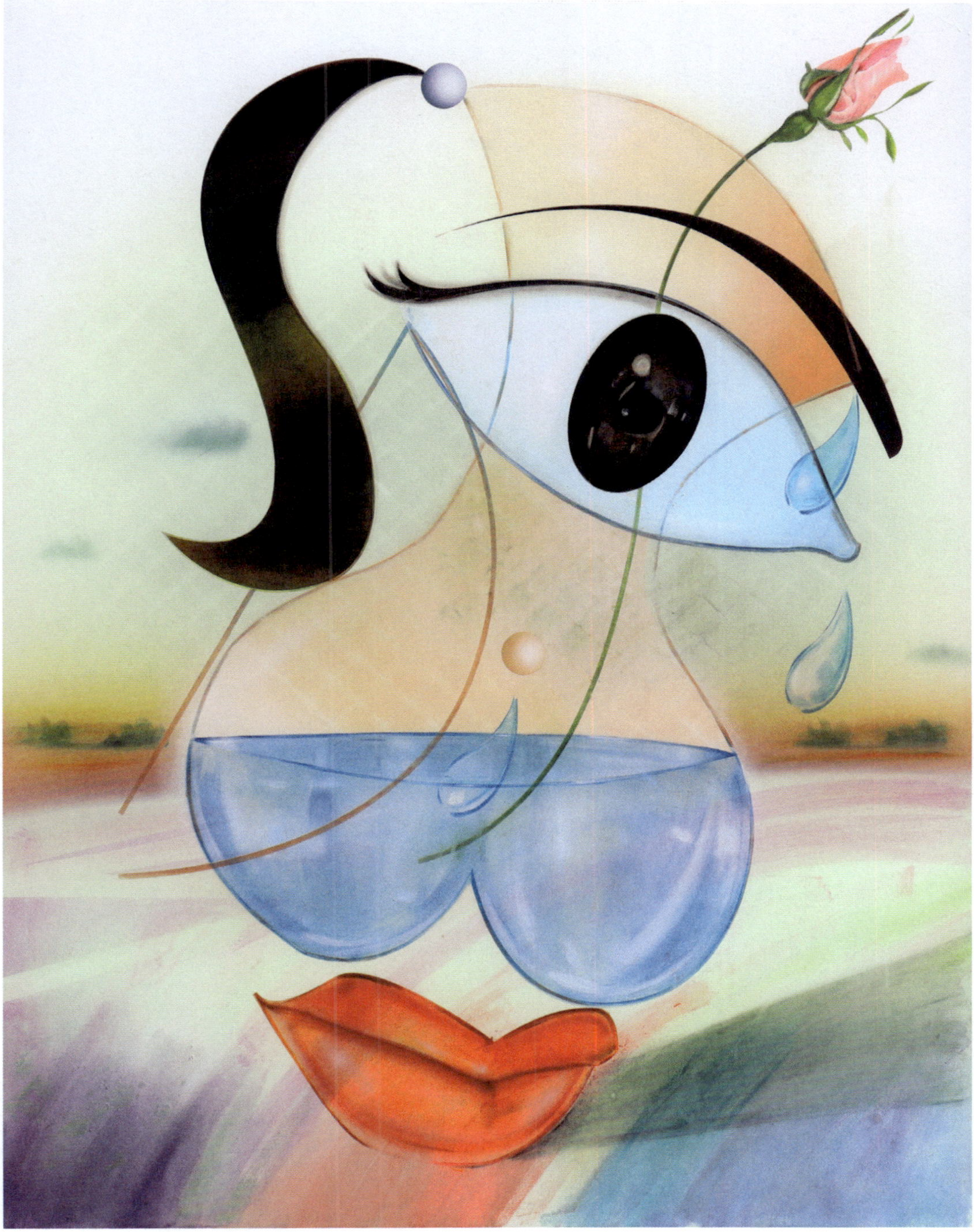

*Woman holding the vase / The Vase Holding the Flower / The Lips / The Eyes / The Vase Fit Water and Light in Herself*, 2023. Soft pastel and acrylic on canvas, 150 × 120 cm

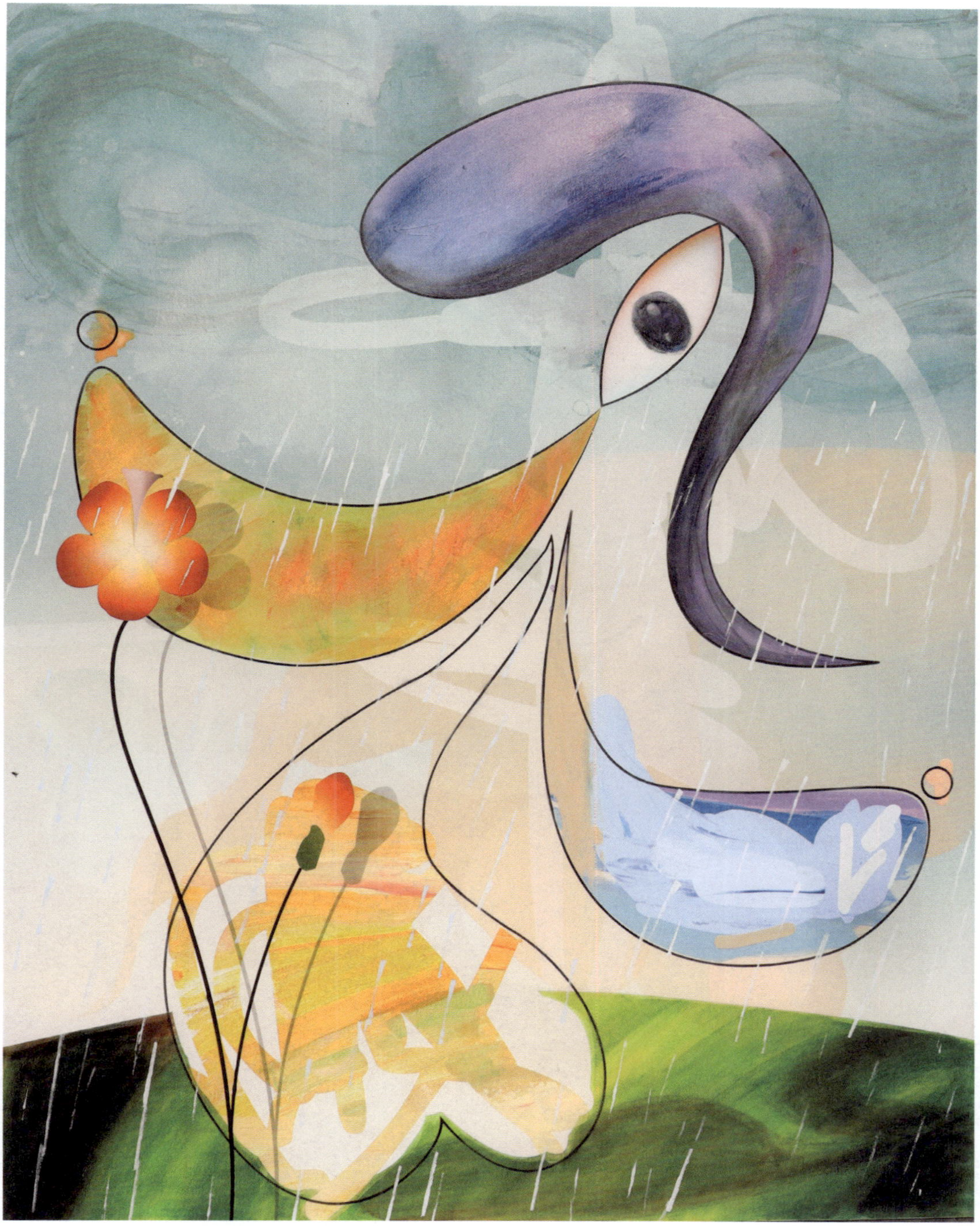

*Rainy Day*, 2023. Soft pastel and acrylic on canvas, 150 × 120 cm

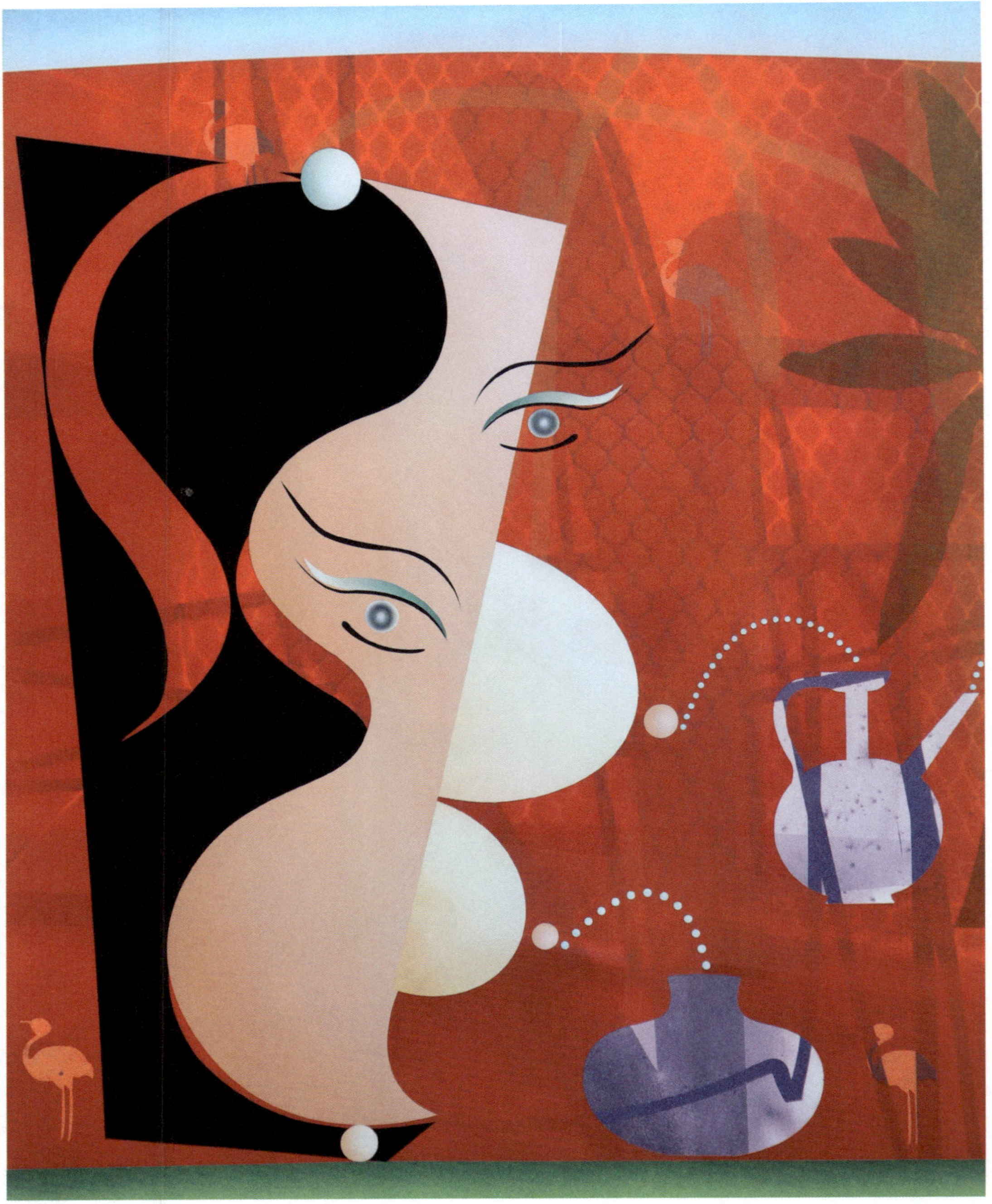

*Spread Your Soul on The Vermilion Soil,* 2023. Acrylic and silicon powder on canvas, 150 × 120 cm

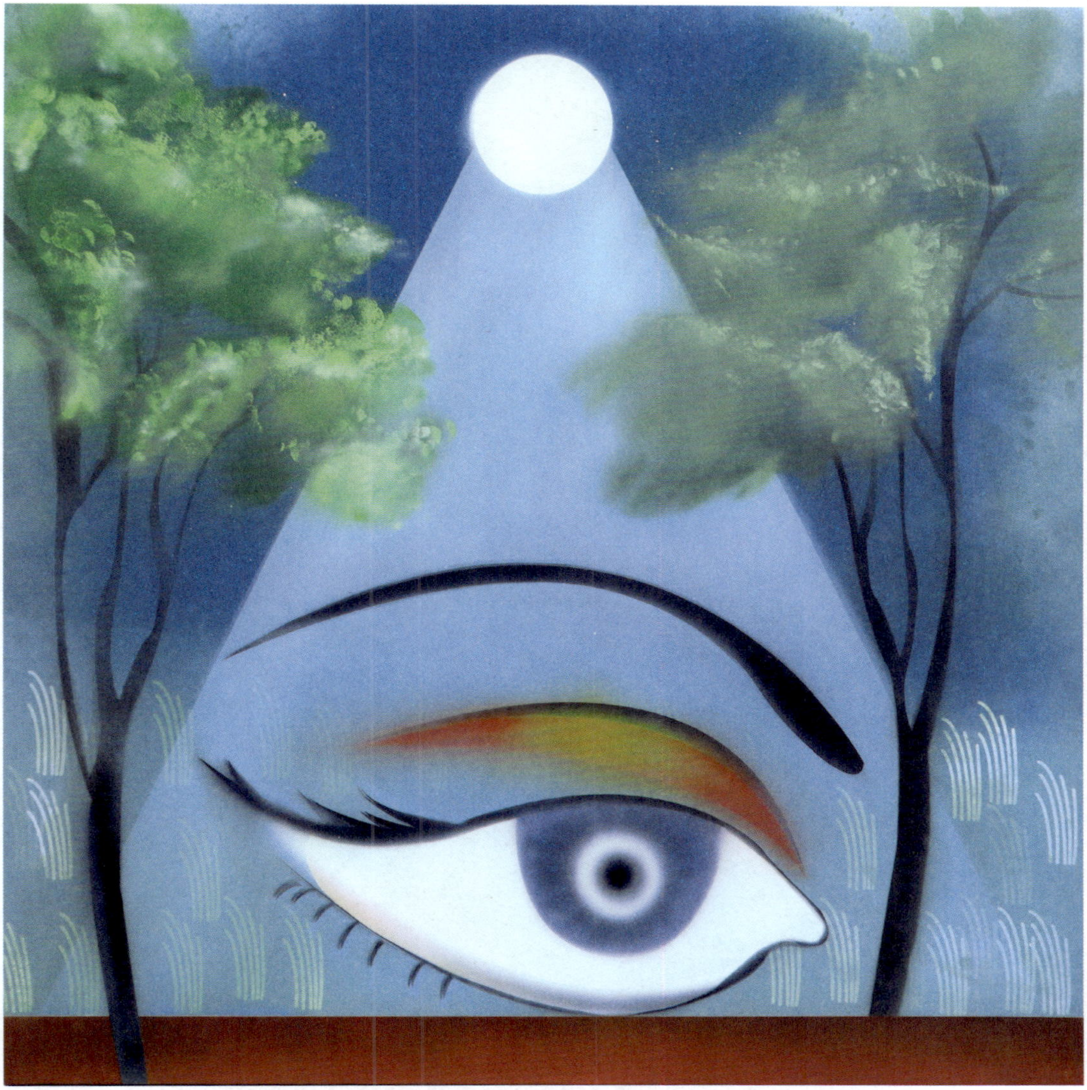

*Moonlight*, 2023. Acrylic and silicon powder on canvas 150 × 150 cm

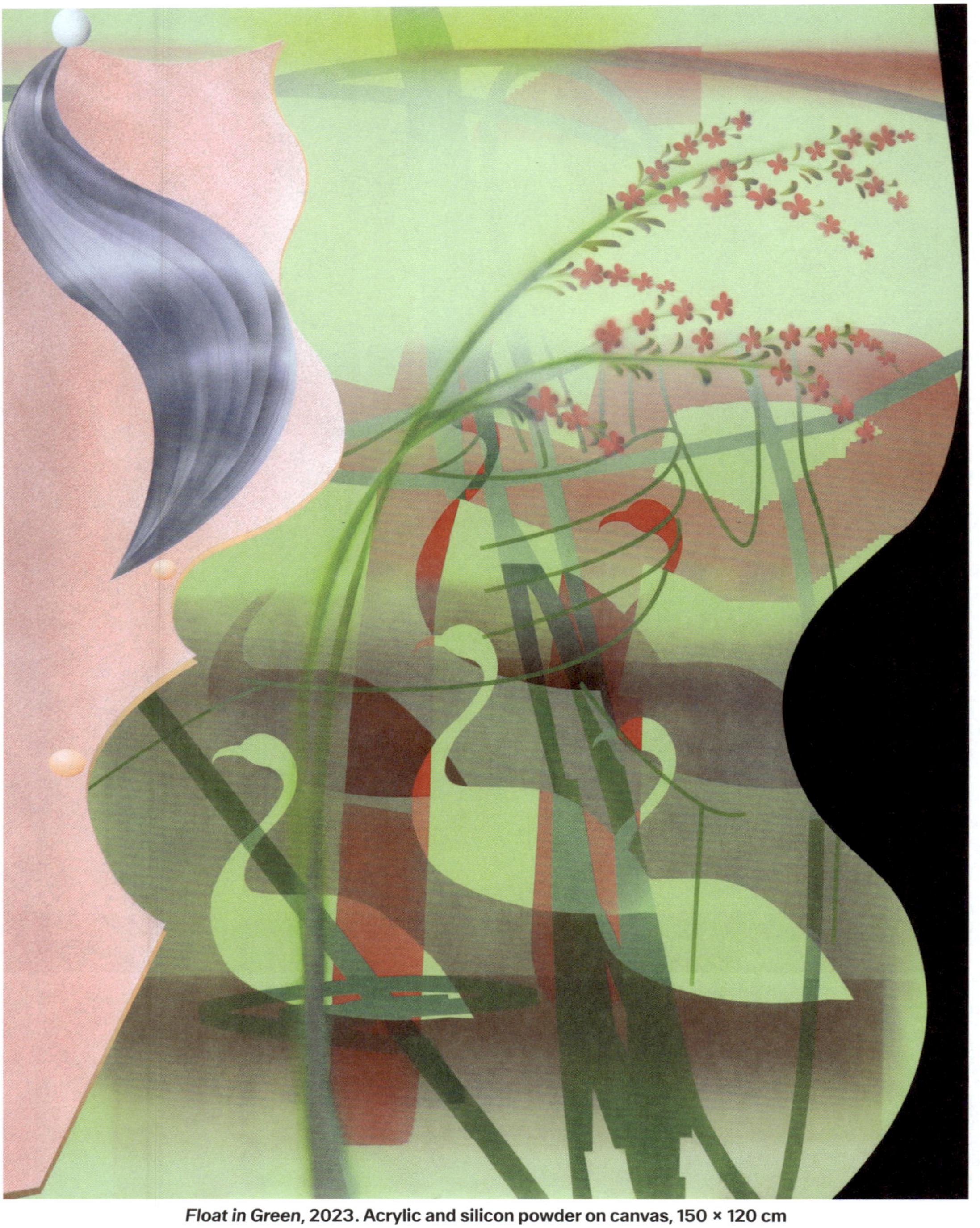

*Float in Green*, 2023. Acrylic and silicon powder on canvas, 150 × 120 cm

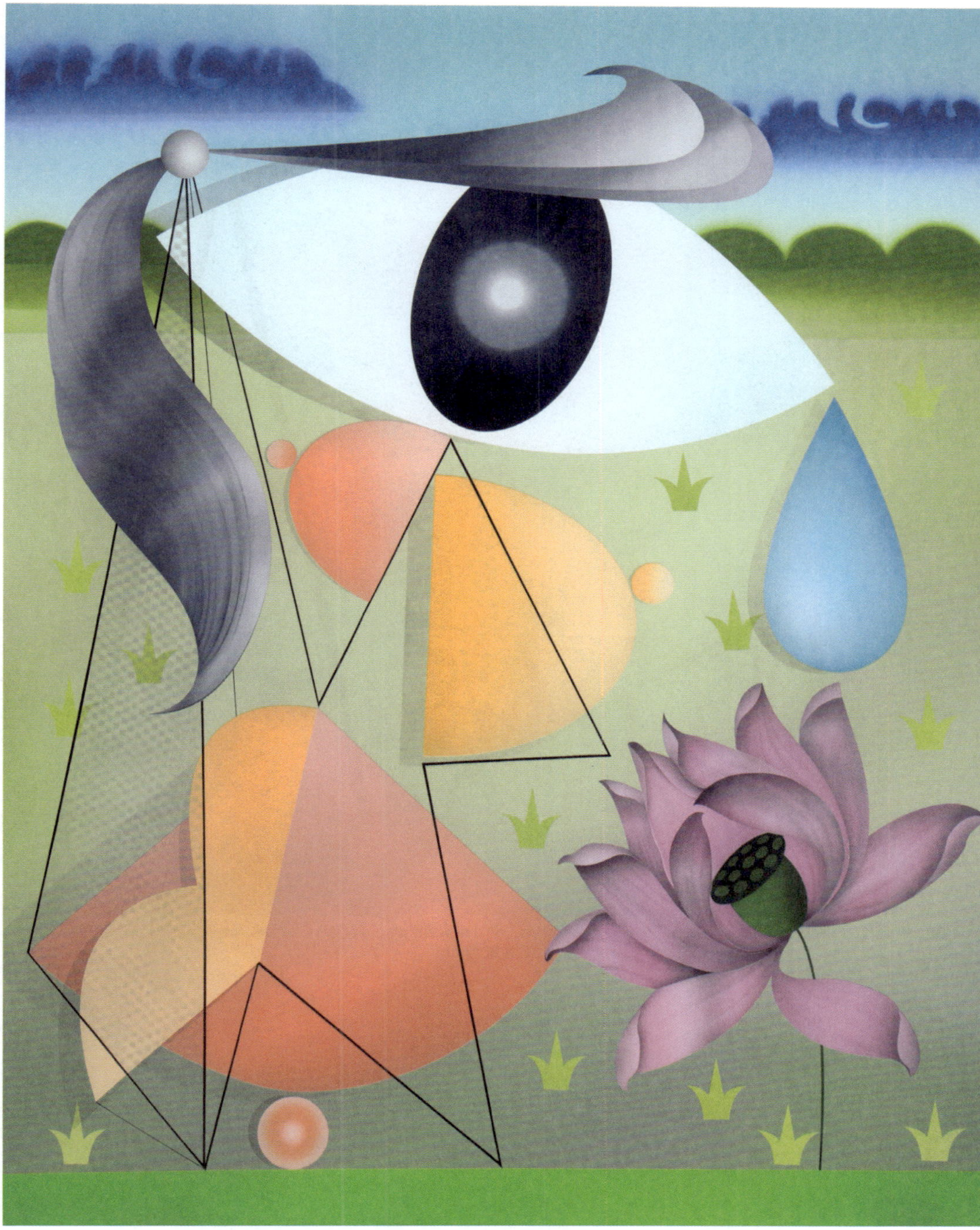

*Shahrivar Like a Tear Drop Decided to Fall This is Liberation Time for All*, 2023.
Acrylic on canvas, 150 × 120 cm

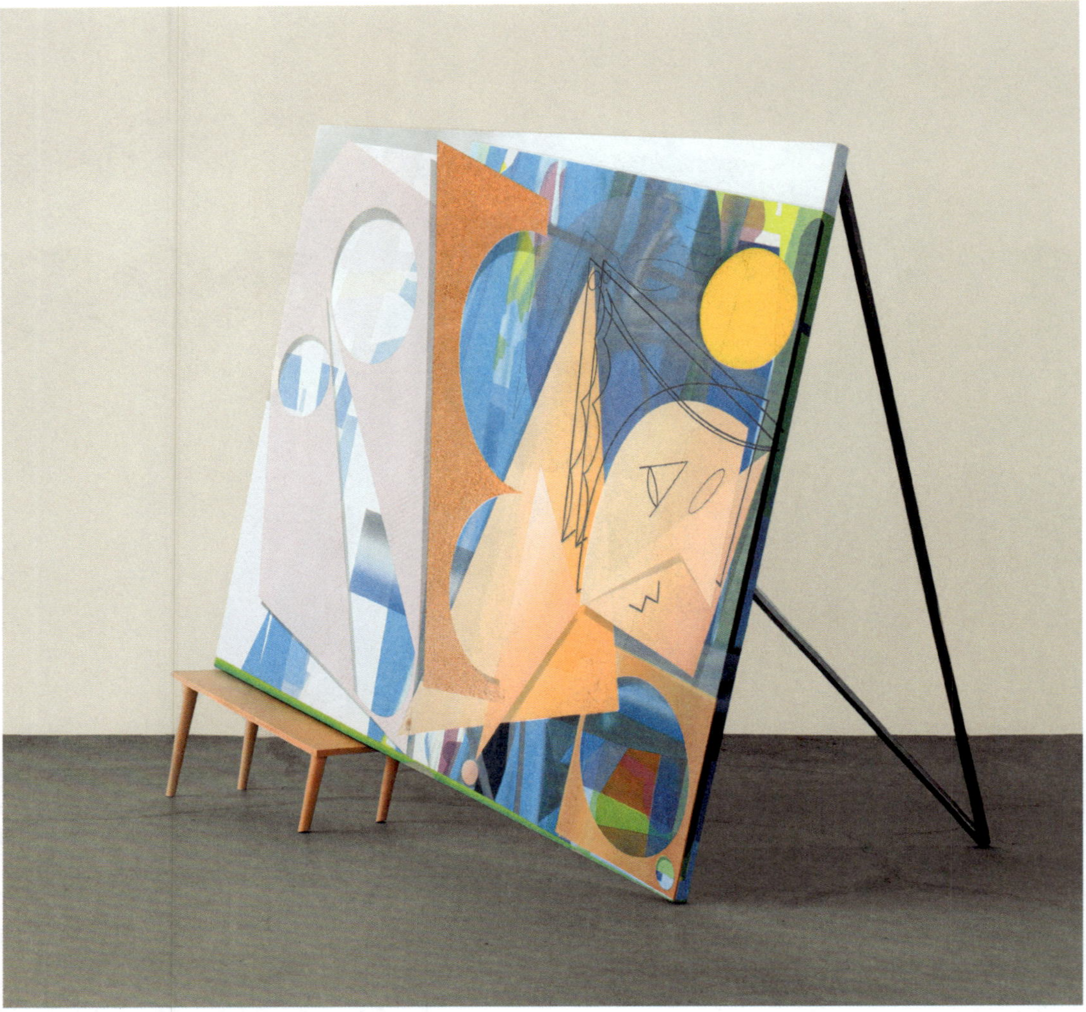

*Don't Push to the Left! Keep Move On*, 2022. Acrylic and silicon powder on canvas, wooden table, and metal, 150 × 180 cm

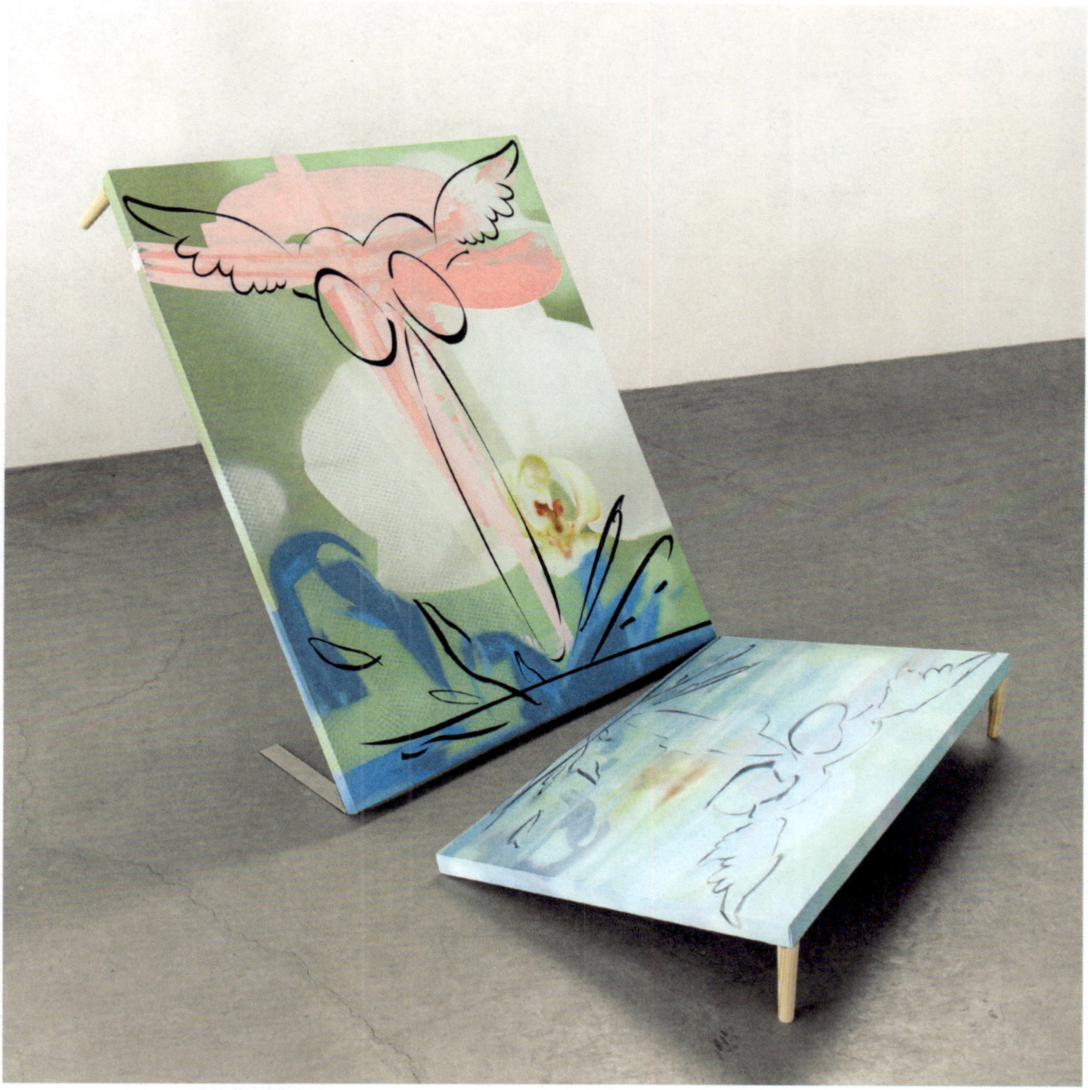

***The Narcissist Awoke and He Faced Broken Bed*, 2023. Acrylic on two canvas and wooden legs, 150 × 120 cm, 75 × 120 cm**

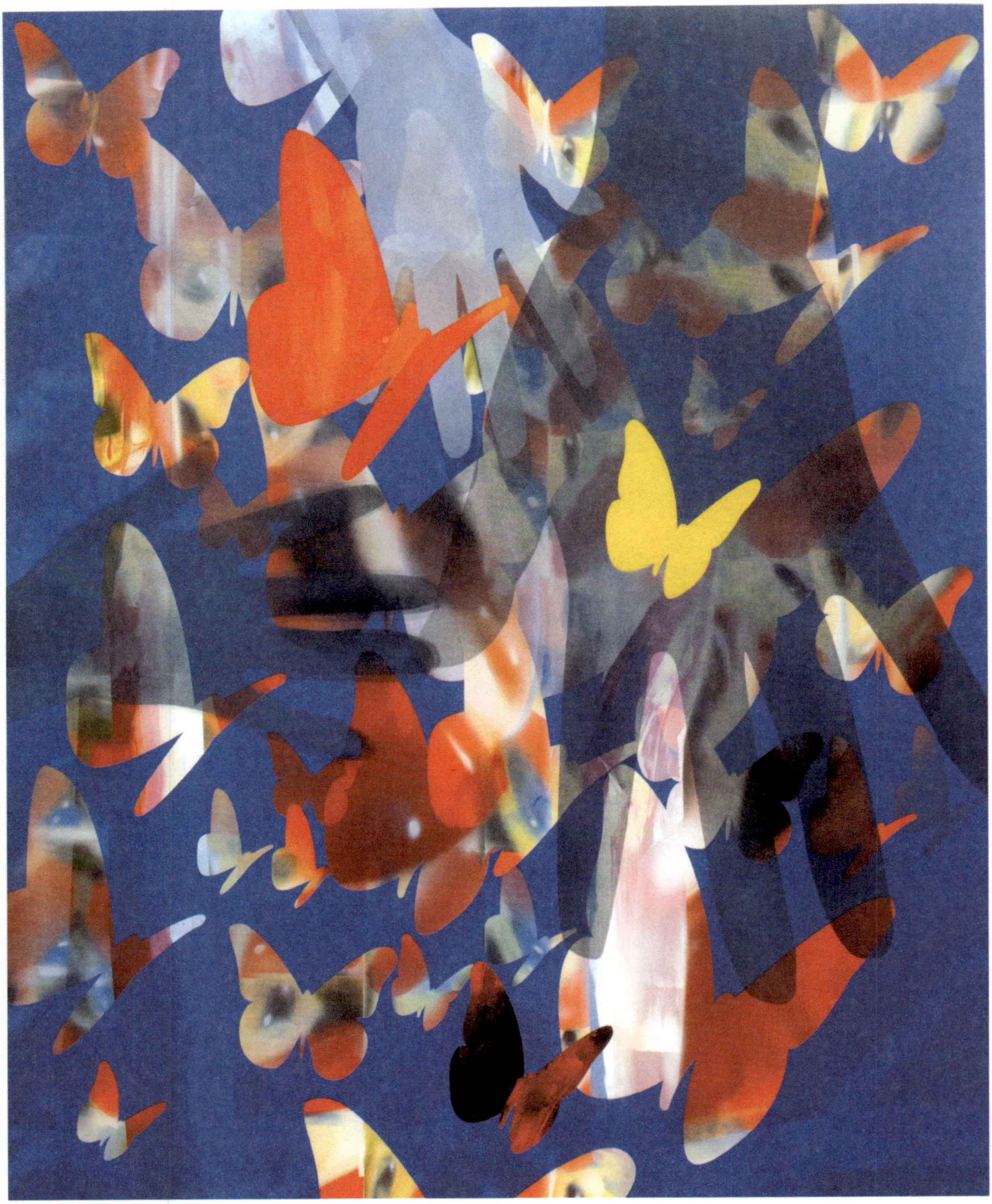

*Oh! Butterflies*, 2023. Acrylic on canvas, 210 × 175 cm

Selected Works 1

Shadows They Cast 99
Lillian Davies

Happiness in the Signifier: 107
A Discussion Between Hoda Kashiha and Loïc Le Gall

Les ombres qu'ils projettent 141
Lillian Davies

Images et bonheur: 147
conversation entre Hoda Kashiha et Loïc Le Gall

آن سایه هایی که می افکنند 173
لیلیان دیویس

شعف در نشانه: گفت‌وگوی هدی کاشی‌ها و لوییک لو گال 181

# Shadows They Cast

Lillian Davies

"I like to hide my nationality at first," Hoda Kashiha told me recently. Kashiha was born in Tehran in the final years of the Iran-Iraq War, a conflict that began with Iraq's invasion of Iran and ended with more than half a million Iranians dead. France and the United States officially supported Iraq, despite suspicions that its military was using chemical weapons. In the summer of 1987, a year after Kashiha was born, I remember seeing a man with a buzz cut and olive dress fatigues on televisions across the American South. It was Lieutenant Colonel Oliver North of the US National Security Council, under investigation for masterminding, despite the US embargo, arms sales to Iran in order to fund Nicaragua's counterrevolutionary Contras. As children on opposite sides of a growing political and ideological divide, Kashiha and I both witnessed flashes of the same dangerously fragmented narrative. Kashiha has dedicated her work as an artist to a study of these fragments, as well as the shadows they cast.

Kashiha grew up in Iran's capital, where she participated in after-school programs at the Institute for the Intellectual Development of Children and Young Adults. Referred to as Kanoon, an abbreviation of the name in Farsi, these programs began in the 1960s, when Farah Diba helped her friend Lily Amir-Arjomand establish a children's library. Shelves were filled with children's books from abroad, translated into Farsi, and Kanoon soon began publishing Iranian stories and hosting youth workshops for creative writing, theater, and cinema. "Kanoon would become a sort of incubator for some of the country's most celebrated artists," and still operates, in a decreased capacity, today.[1]

As a child, Kashiha often visited the Tehran Museum of Contemporary Art, designed by Kamran Diba and inaugurated in 1977. Iran's first open-air art fair, spread across the museum's gardens the following summer. State sponsorship of the arts had begun in the 1950s, and the first Tehran Biennial drew international crowds in spring 1958. The Office of Fine Arts (later the Ministry of Culture) provided access to jobs in the cultural sector, artistic commissions, and connections to a rising collector class.[2] With public and private support for the arts in place, a first generation of modern

1 "Institute for the Intellectual Development of Children and Young Adults," *Bidoun*, winter 2009, https://www.bidoun.org/articles/institute-for-the-intellectual-development-of-children-young-adults.

2 See Media Farzin, "A Short History of Art Exhibitions in Iran, 1946–78," in *Iran Modern*, ed. Fereshteh Daftari and Layla S. Diba (New York: Asia Society Museum, 2013), 67–71.

artists emerged, of whom Bahman Mohasses (1931–2010), maker of "surrealist, iconoclastic" paintings and sculptures, is perhaps best known.[3] Bedjat Sadr (1924–2009), a contemporary of Mohasses, is a vital reference for Kashiha. About her photo collages, Sadr was clear: "We must use and take everything that can express the feelings of our time, tear off pages from magazines, glue them, and find again new tools."[4] Photographer Shadi Ghadirian (b. 1974), mentored by Bahman Jalali, is one of the best known of Iran's second generation, which developed after the Islamic Republic overthrew the shah and cut many international ties.

Like painters Sam Samiee (b. 1988) and Ala Dehghan (b. 1982), Kashiha, belongs to a third generation of artists that emerged post-9/11 and following the arrival of auction houses in the region (Christie's inaugurated its Dubai auction in 2006). This was a time when it became common again for Iranian artists to study and exhibit internationally. If there is one historical event that defines the country's currently emerging fourth generation, Kashiha tells me, it's Instagram.

Kashiha attended Narjes, a private girls' school in central Tehran, before studying fine arts at the University of Tehran, where she earned her BA. At the university's central library, nudity in books of European painting is systematically redacted. This act of censorship transforms the reproduced images—imagine Alessandro Botticelli's *The Birth of Venus* (1485–86) as wide black marks emerging from a watery landscape—and insinuates a general prohibition on European-style painting. When Kashiha arrived at Boston University a few years later, she was making drawings—not surprisingly, perhaps, given the artist's background, as well as her skill for dark humor. (US painter Amy Sillman has observed that all great comic painters are drawers at heart.)[5] In Boston, Kashiha's professor Dana Frankfort pushed her to move to canvas.[6] The young artist's confidence grew in this new medium and expanded scale. As Kashiha worked toward her MFA in painting, she opened her first solo exhibition at Etemad Gallery in Tehran.[7]

After her studies in the United States, Kashiha returned to Tehran in 2016, a moment of mounting sanctions and rising political unrest. As respite, and a method

3
Morad Montazami, "Moderne et contemporain: usages et enjeux en historiographiques compares," lecture at ARVIMM (l'Unité d'arabe de l'Université de Genève, de l'Institut d'étude de l'Islam et des sociétés du monde musulman et l'École normale supérieure), Centre Pompidou and EHESS, Paris, 2018.

4
Behdjat Sadr on her photo collages, 1995, quoted in Behjat Sadr Press Release by Cyrus Goberville and Daniele Balice (April 5–June 1, 2019), Balice Hertling Galerie, Paris.

5
Amy Sillman, *Faux Pas: Selected Writings and Drawings* (Paris: After 8 Books, 2020), 207.

6
Frankfort "was so sharp," Kashiha recalled with admiration in a conversation with the author on June 14, 2024.

7
Historically a dealer in Islamic art, Etemad was the first Iranian gallery to open a branch in Dubai, the city a veritable motor (particularly since the first Art Dubai in 2007) in the international development of the Gulf art world.

*Melt in the Ocean*, 2017. Oil and spray paint on canvas, 140 × 120 cm. Photo: Artist Studio 

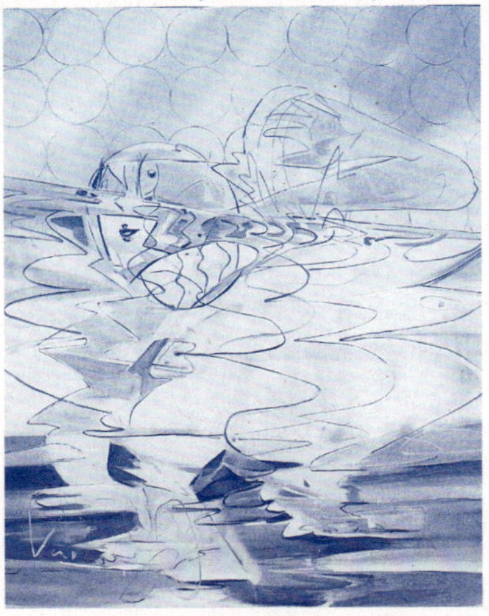

to attain the balance and flow she seeks in her studio work, she began daily yoga and regular swimming. In her canvas *((Swimming and Melting))* (2017), Kashiha plays with the immersion and erasure of a fragmented figure, mobilizing Dada techniques to disrupt a screen-like digital landscape infused with readymade cartoon imagery. The following year, Kashiha exhibited her canvas *Dream Makes Cloud* (2018)—a juxtaposition of how doll-like faces across swatches of blue spray that resemble shard of glass—in Paris. The work was included in the exhibition *Oil of Paradis*—a subtle reference to the

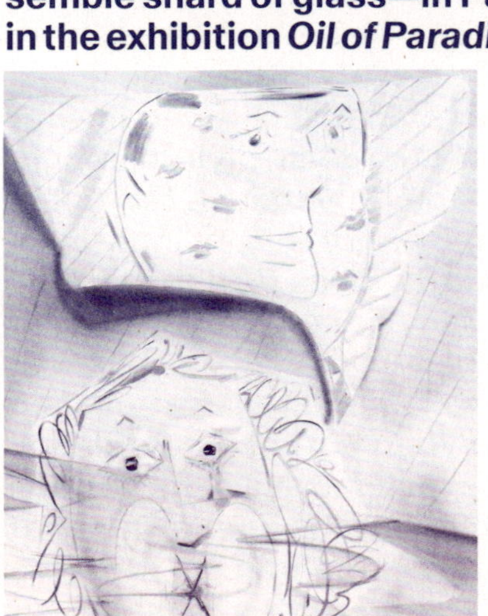

*Dreams Make Cloud*, 2018. Acrylic and oil on canvas, 120 × 100 cm. Photo: Artist Studio

Persian Gulf's petroleum industry—curated by Harmoz Hematin, founder of Dastan's Basement, and hosted at Galerie Balice Hertling. Kasha's painting hung alongside works by Mohasses, Parvaneh Etamadi (b. 1948), and Samiee. On a visit to Iran hosted by the Pejman Foundation the previous year, Parisian gallerist Daniele Balice had met Kashiha in her Tehran studio as well as Hematian.

At the start of the pandemic, Kashiha left Tehran for a property about an hour outside the city center, and she's been based there ever since. In a converted former warehouse large enough to accommodate a tennis court, Kashiha made her studio. The space, with its evocations of sport and discipline, suits her well: "I consider painting a way to think. I try to create a playground for myself."[8]

8
Email to the author, April 2022.

Opening in summer 2020 at Galerie Nathalie Obadia in Brussels, during a short lapse in Belgium's pandemic restrictions, Kashiha named her first solo show in Europe *Dear St. Agatha I Am Witness of Your Tears In the Land of Tulips*, for the patron saint of martyrs and rape victims. In the titular work, a tortured female figure, seemingly watched by a giant pair of anime eyes, collides with an expanse of vermilion tulips. Native to Iran, tulips are the country's national flower. Legend has it that a red tulip grows in each place a patriotic soldier dies.

Soon after, the artist accelerated her desired "destruction of linear narrative," affixing each of the eight

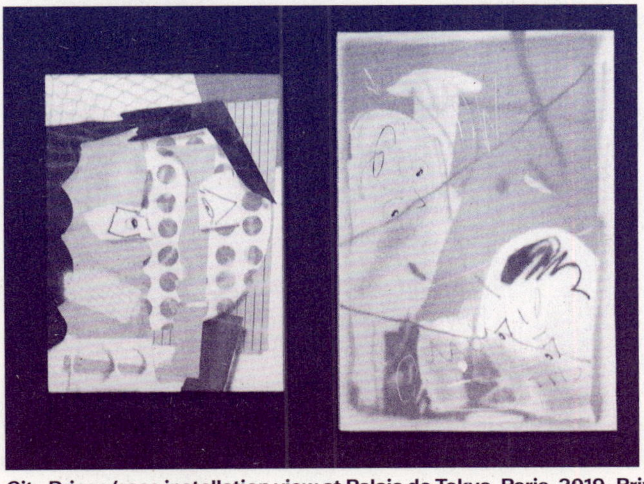

*City Prince/sses* installation view at Palais de Tokyo, Paris, 2019. Private collection

9
Email to the author, April 2022.



*I'm Here, I'm not Here* installation view at Passerelle Centre d'art contemporain, Brest, 2022. Photo: Aurélien Mole

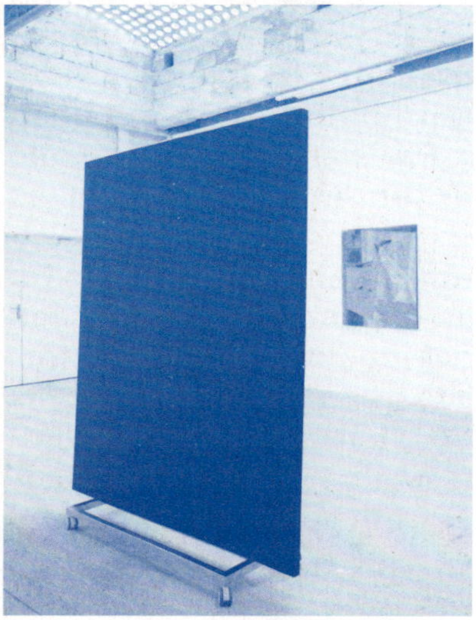

large-scale paintings that constitute *In Appreciation of Blinking* (2020–21) to its own wheeled metal stand.[9] For this work, Kashiha appropriates Caravaggio's *The Incredulity of Saint Thomas* (1601–02) and crafts a jump-cut progression of collaged imagery covered in washes of black acrylic that extend progressively lower on each canvas. By the last painting, *Back as Black*, the entire source composition is submerged in darkness. Her midnight monochrome recalls Kazimir Malevich's *Black Square* (1915) as well as Sadr's extensive use of black oil paint, a medium curator Fabrice Hergott reads

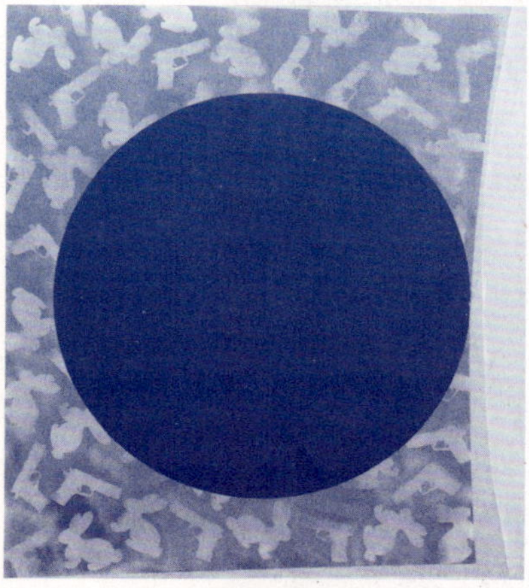

*My Sincere Love to Kazimir Malevich, Black on Black*, 2020. Acrylic on canvas, 150 × 130 cm. Photo: Matin Jameie

as a symbol for "the immense stain . . . that this oil represents in the history of Iran."[10] The black square also echoes the social media response to Iran's political uprisings in late 2017 as well as Blackout Tuesday, organized following police killings of Breonna Taylor and George Floyd in the United States.

During Kashiha's winter 2022 residency in Brest, France, CAC Passerelle curator Loïc Le Gall suggested she consider metal, as Sadr had, not just as a support, but as a medium. The artist's incorporation of this industrial material makes sense. The geometries Kashiha crafts in found metal repeat the stencil-cut shapes that structure many of her compositions. Most importantly, perhaps, Kashiha's sculptures cast shadows. And the shadow, like Gabriel García Lorca's *duende*, embodies a richly nuanced creative space. As Clarice Lispector writes in *Água Viva* (1973), "To remake myself and

10 "The immense stain, the indelible oil slick like a gob that this oil represents in the history of Iran, through which this country was restored to the rank of producer, eliciting covetousness and the darkest passions of the human soul." Fabrice Hergott, "Spirals," in *Behdjat Sadr: Traces* (Paris: Zamân Books, 2014), 8.

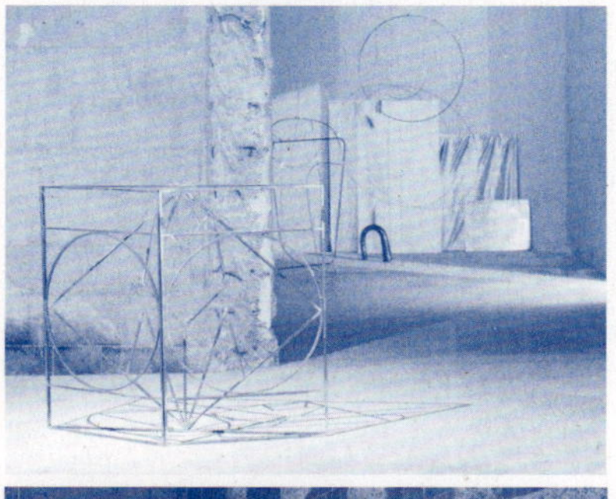

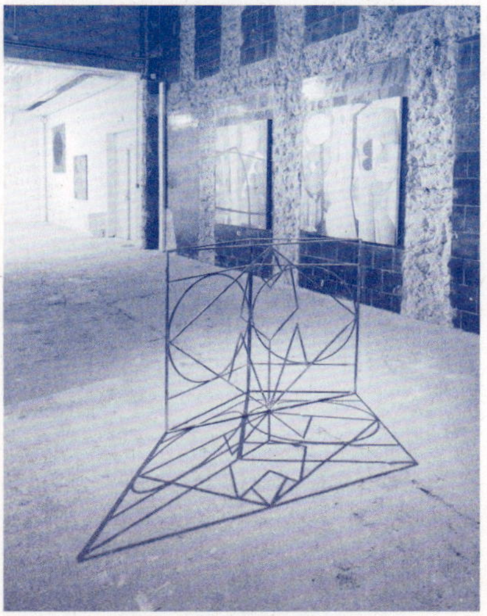

*I'm Here, I'm not Here* installation view at Passerelle Centre d'art contemporain, Brest, 2022. Photo: Aurélien Mole

remake you I return to my state of garden and shadow, cool reality."[11]

Kashiha also exhibited her video work for the first time in Brest, revealing her process of testing compositions on screen before placing them on canvas. The animated film she made during the pandemic lockdown, *The Eyes Fill with Brightness Slip Over to the Black Shades* (2021), is another crucial source for the descending darkness of *In Appreciation of Blinking*.

Recently, Kashiha planted sunflowers outside her studio. She loves this flower, and loves Vincent van Gogh's renderings of its radiant blooms in the large-scale canvases he painted at the Yellow House in the south of France. In *Another world is waiting for us* (2023) at Galerie Natalie Obadia, Kashiha's most recent exhibition in Europe, the artist continued her use of the flower motif, pointing to the violence of love, the covetous picking of a precious blossom. Part of this group of works, Kashiha's split canvas *Don't Push to the Left! Keep a Move On* (2023) engages the dynamics of sculpture and pictures a falling, abstracted female form in dangerous disequilibrium. Lately, Kashiha has begun covering her canvases in a pattern of pale shadows. Created with spotlights obscured with vinyl cutouts in the shape of a hand, these severed, outstretched silhouettes grasp at the violence of beauty.

11
Clarice Lispector, *Água Viva*, trans. Benjamin Moser (New York: New Directions, 1973), 11. Here I could just as easily quote Junichiro Tanizaki, *In Praise of Shadows* (1933), given how both writers craft an ode to the creative power of shadow and darkness.

# Happiness in the Signifier: A Discussion Between Hoda Kashiha and Loïc Le Gall

LL: You have a dual background: you studied art in Iran in a fairly traditional way, then continued your studies in Boston. How has this combination of two cultures affected your painting practice?

HD: The school in Iran where I got my BFA was conservative and so traditional. I usually like to have cartoons and caricatures in my works, and I love sharp colors. But at this school, our teachers said I could not bring such things in, or else the work would look cartoonish, or like illustration. And so I tried to censor myself; I felt it was necessary. When I came to the States and I saw such a big range of art, I felt that I could bring everything into my works, everything that I like, and it doesn't matter if it's cartoonish or not. I could mix all of it together! In that moment, I felt like I wanted to learn how to paint on canvas all over again. Indeed, even though my art school in Boston was relatively conservative for the US context, the artists that they invited, and my classmates, had a huge effect on my practice and my sense of what was allowable.

LL: I think your work is very progressive, both in concept and in the way it's painted. You are very influenced by cartoons and comics. Could you tell me more about that?

HD: Where that's from actually? I don't know. When I was a kid, I bought a lot of magazines with caricatures in them—I wanted to become a famous caricaturist. I don't know why. And I've always made a lot of portraits of my family and my friends. I've used cartoons for a long time in my work. I thought it was a good but subtle way, a good approach, to evoke what's happening in Iran. Fiction and content on social networks—and I'm making the link with the culture of cartoons and caricatures—allow an enormous amount of freedom, and I like to draw inspiration from them. Online, content is created almost immediately and reposted, so it goes viral. In a place where that's hard to control, they can peddle alternative stories or black humor. But when you refer simply to the dark, the works become like a drama, and I don't want to make drama work.

LL: The situation and the context in Iran affect your work, certainly. They accompany you every day. It was probably different during your experience in the United States?

HD: You know, every day something happens in my country, and you have to think about yourself, about everything you want. The subjects I deal with also reflect this. That's partly why I left the States. Daily life there perhaps requires less constant questioning than in Iran. But I have the impression that all this underlies my work. When I'm in the studio, my personal stories are intertwined with those of the country as a whole, and even more so with what's happening internationally. Here, every day, something happens and I get inspired by it, but I don't like to talk about it directly. In the end, when I look at my work, I don't think it's Iranian, or even political. I think it's lacking political or cultural borders.

LL: That's true—it's quite impossible to reduce your work to the Iranian context. For sure, there are some typical shapes and patterns that could recall the history of the region, but in the end I could not say, purely from looking at the work, if its maker comes from a Chinese, an Iranian, or a Mexican background. Nevertheless, there's something I notice about you and other artists from Iran, like Tala Madani (b. 1981) for example, namely an ability to handle the absurd.

HD: I'm not sure it's so common currently. It's probably more part of our history.

LL: I'd like to mention an important work you first showed in your gallery in Tehran, Dastan Gallery, then in Europe at Passerelle Centre d'art contemporain, at Galerie Nathalie Obadia, and during Art Basel/Unlimited. It's called *In Appreciation of Blinking* (2021). It's a really different work. It's not just a painting, but also an installation, even a sculpture. I'd like to talk to you about new ways of showing paintings, and about how this medium can be renewed again and again. For that installation, you chose to place the paintings on mobile pedestals to be arranged as you wished in the exhibition space. Why did you make such an unusual choice?

HD: Installing works on the wall—it's so . . . solid seeming. Most of the time, I feel it's just inviting

Untitled, 2024. Ink on paper, 30 x 40 cm. Photo: Artist Studio

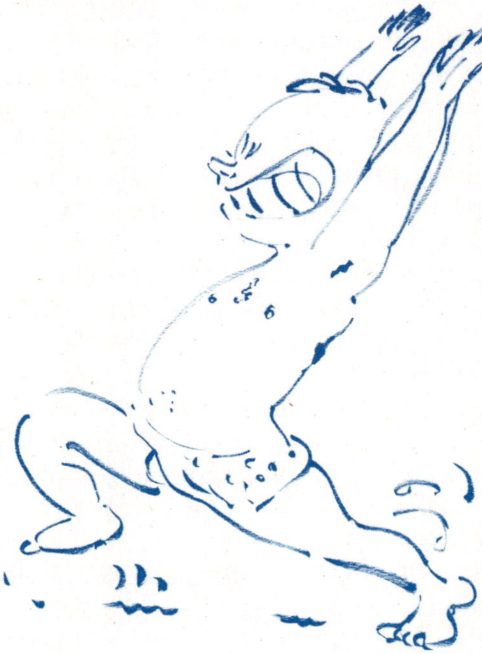

*Can you hear me?!!*, 2024. Ink on paper, 50 x 70 cm. Photo: Artist Studio

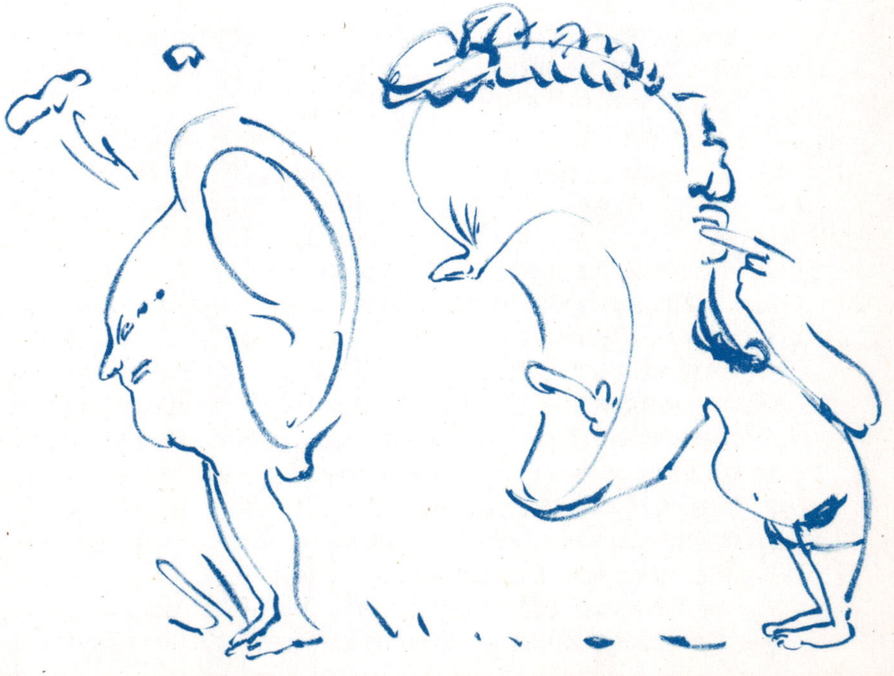

people to look at the work and think, okay, they like it or they don't. The viewer becomes so passive. I wanted to make the scenario more playful by giving visitors this chance to play with the paintings. It's like action and interaction. More and more, I'm thinking about not just the painting that I'm working on, but the space. When I install my canvases in a space, I think about atmosphere, how viewers will be actively involved.

LL: I have the definite impression that your desire to get people involved brings a certain joy to the work. At your 2022 exhibition in Passerelle Centre d'art contemporain in Brest, *I'm Here, I'm not Here*, you again took a particular look at the way visitors view and interact with your work in that you produced new sculptural works and others incorporating light, which I find very playful indeed. How is your work evolving now? Does it increasingly include special displays and installations?

HD: At this moment, I want to play with some fabric and canvas and how to mix them together. Even in my paintings, I'm going in different directions. I'm working on three different, unrelated projects at the moment. One of them is inspired by some Indian miniature painting. One of them is inspired by the Pink Panther cartoons. And the last new body of work is more poetic.

I recently spent some time in New York, and my studio there was small. I had to adapt to the size of the venue. Once again, I produced something very different. I usually try to reject having a signature, recognizable style. When an artist is stuck in a spiral of repetition, I find it so sad, even if the work demonstrates great mastery or technique. Sometimes I'm very satisfied with what I've been able to do in a painting and I'm surprised by it, but I don't want to reproduce it, so I go in the opposite direction for the next work. I hate having certainty in my work, and I think, in this way, the art maintains its playfulness.

LL: I like the way you try to cover your tracks! You mentioned a new series about the Pink Panther—can you tell me more about it? I'm particularly intrigued because at your exhibition in Brest, you showed your short animated films for the first time. These short films are starting points for new paintings, right? 

HD: Sometimes I make sketches on my iPad, which come out like a short video, and then I start a painting along those same lines.

LL: You create moving images, then return to still images. I find this relationship with animated images and cartoons quite magical and beautiful, because it brings with it a pop culture that many people are familiar with and can appreciate. To circle back to *In Appreciation of Blinking*—the first time you exhibited it was in Tehran, and you had to cover up some of the painting. Was it because of censorship?

HD: I was not allowed to show part of the work—a man with a tongue. I had to cover it. In the end, it was interesting because I covered the tongue with a sticker. And at that time, I was developing another series, *I Am Here, I Am Not Here* (2020), which was about the ofcensorship. This series is about how we can be suppressed, ignored, terminated, or disappeared, by power or by death. I repeated here the same subject as in my paintings. A body is covered with a red mark or a black shape, or is deformed. In some countries, censorship comes to cover with black forms the bodies deemed "immodest," or manifesting protest themes. I tried to find what remains of us after death and our disappearance, when our gaze darkens.

LL: It makes me think of books that are redacted in Iran.

HD: When I was at school, a lot of books were censored, with passages blacked out. I used to wonder: Is it hidden by magic? The nudes and certain figures disappeared. It was interesting because it created a new kind of aesthetic. You knew that there was a nude body there; it's just that you couldn't see it. It makes your imagination fly. What is behind all this? Sometimes, a new version of a painting is curated by the government. These things prompt yet more questions, for instance: If you die or are erased by power, do you still exist? So I made the body artworks *I Am Here, I Am Not Here* and then *In Appreciation of Blinking*, and the work was censored. It felt like things were coming full circle with these ideas.

LL: Images of women are at the heart of your work. And what you're explaining is that the power is suppressing bodies in public space, especially women's bodies. Are you looking for solutions to show these in your work? Because in some of your paintings, you use particular styles that mask or modify the forms, like Cubism for example. I'm thinking of *Looking at the Mirror* (2021).

HD: Bodies are very important in my work. They shape it, actually. When I'm doing an abstract painting, it is coming from the body, which is so abstract, and the viewer cannot understand that. I'm still very interested in this. At the moment, it's at the heart of my research into Persian and Indian miniatures. It's a combination of Cubism, Indian paintings, and Iranian miniature paintings. Again, a female body getting involved with its environment. This idea came strongly in my work after "Woman, Life, Freedom."[1] I've become more curious about hair, and then I started looking at Indian paintings, which have a lot of hair and female bodily forms, which are aligned with nature, with flowers. I started working with a pottery wheel. The vases and other ceramics I made intentionally evoked female bodies. So, yes, the body is a continuous theme in my work.

LL: You find evasive and original strategies for showing bodies. You mentioned deliberately changing your style so as not to get bogged down in commercial monotony, but you've also found a way to keep the bodies throughout. There are different levels of understanding the perpetual change in your style as a painter. I know you often look at social networks, which are a window onto a kind of infinity of images. When you look at artistic content, when you read contemporary art magazines, you see that there are thousands of different styles. When you're on social networks, you have access to the whole world, and that's surely the joy of these tools. Your paintings are often linked to social networks. During major demonstrations in Iran, some people posted black squares on Instagram as a sign

1 "Woman, Life, Freedom" is a slogan that originated within the women-led Kurdish movements, then transcended its initial context and garnered global recognition following the 2022 protests in Iran sparked by the death of Mahsa Amini. The Guidance Patrol, the religious morality police of Iran's government, had arrested Amini for allegedly not wearing the hijab in accordance with government standards.

of solidarity in protest. And you've used this symbol in one of your paintings, for example. It was in *My Sincere Love to Kazimir Malevich, Black on Black* (2020). This was just before the Black Lives Matter movement, which also used the black square as a sign on social networks. Do you often include elements of this kind in your painting?

HD: Yes, but not always, you know. I don't push myself that I should do that, but if I randomly see something and make some relation between my works and that idea, it's coming to my worries. I'm welcome to do that—meaning, to feed them into my work. I think my work is like a trash bin. For me, painting is like that. My ideas come from social media, from cartoonish things, from the news, and then I merge them, all of them, together. I paint them, and then I go for another experience. Regarding the painting you just mentioned, I was thinking about the question of black, because of the strikes, when people shared black squares on their Instagram. And then I started again thinking about the idea of black. I was so obsessed with Malevich at that time, and I found a lot of links between all of these ideas.

LL: It's strange that you became obsessed with black at that time, because your work was the complete opposite, all color.

HD: People say that black doesn't appeal or sell. My work was so colorful, and maybe I was scared of doing black painting. So I purposefully tried to challenge myself that way. I was thinking about the concept of black, and wanted to do something that felt challenging for me.

LL: Can we talk about the humor in your work? The jokes and fun things in your paintings?

HD: I really like to create a moment in the gallery or in the space or everywhere that people can come look at my works and laugh or cry with them, and then leave. When works are just funny, people don't take them seriously. I love to talk about life. After the revolution in Iran ten years ago, I was in my twenties, and when I visited galleries or other art shows in Tehran, I saw a lot of paintings inspired by Lucian Freud and Francis Bacon. So many bad paintings about fragmented bodies. It was just—so ugly. I don't think that we should all talk about happiness only, but this wasn't about aesthetics, about form, it was just about inviting people to ugliness. It was like a prestige, intellectual boast—this announcing, "I have bad feelings about life." The reason I like to bring some funny things into my works is because I want to invite people to see specific points, some dark things that at the same time are funny or interesting. I don't want to only show the ugliness of life.

LL: Your work celebrates life and the fact of being alive. And it's beautiful, especially today when the world is ravaged by destructive policies. Your paintings are like breaths of fresh air, but if you want to delve deeper into their meaning, you have to look at what's going on in the world today. There are so many levels to understanding your work. It's serious, but it's not serious at the same time.

HD: You just articulated a purpose that I have in my work—it's serious but it's not serious. Painting is like a puzzle. You are going in different directions, and then you try to find different pieces and fit them together.

LL: The puzzle is a beautiful metaphor.

HD: *In Appreciation of Blinking* was for me a series about life and death. The fragility of life is important, because life is so tragic.

LL: Tragedy in a series! Have you always worked in series?

HD: I have not always been an artist who thinks in series, but I am increasingly so. Maybe because my mind these days is focused on narrations. My mind likes to tell a story. Yes, that's the reason. My work is getting more and more series oriented because it wants to tell stories.

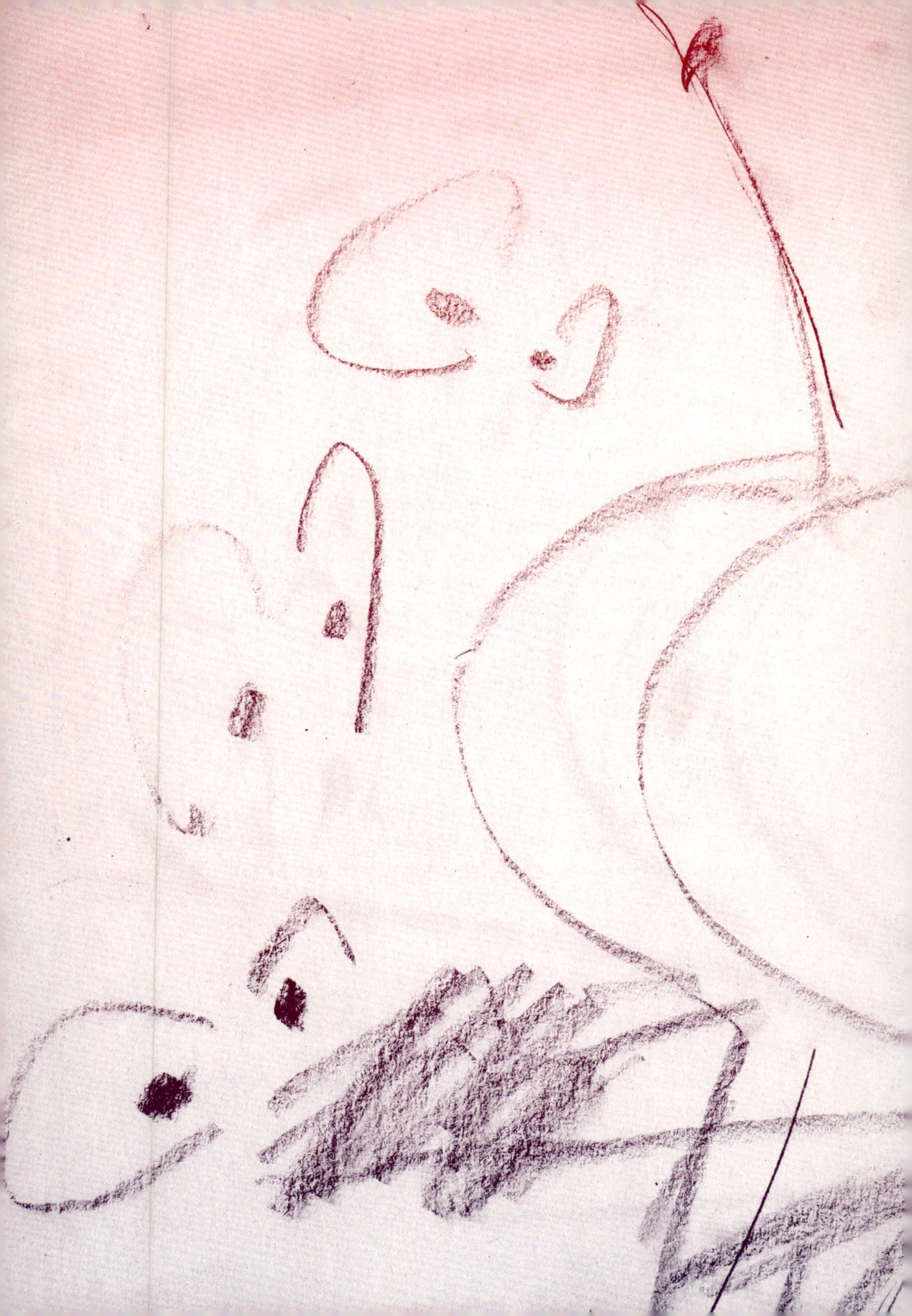

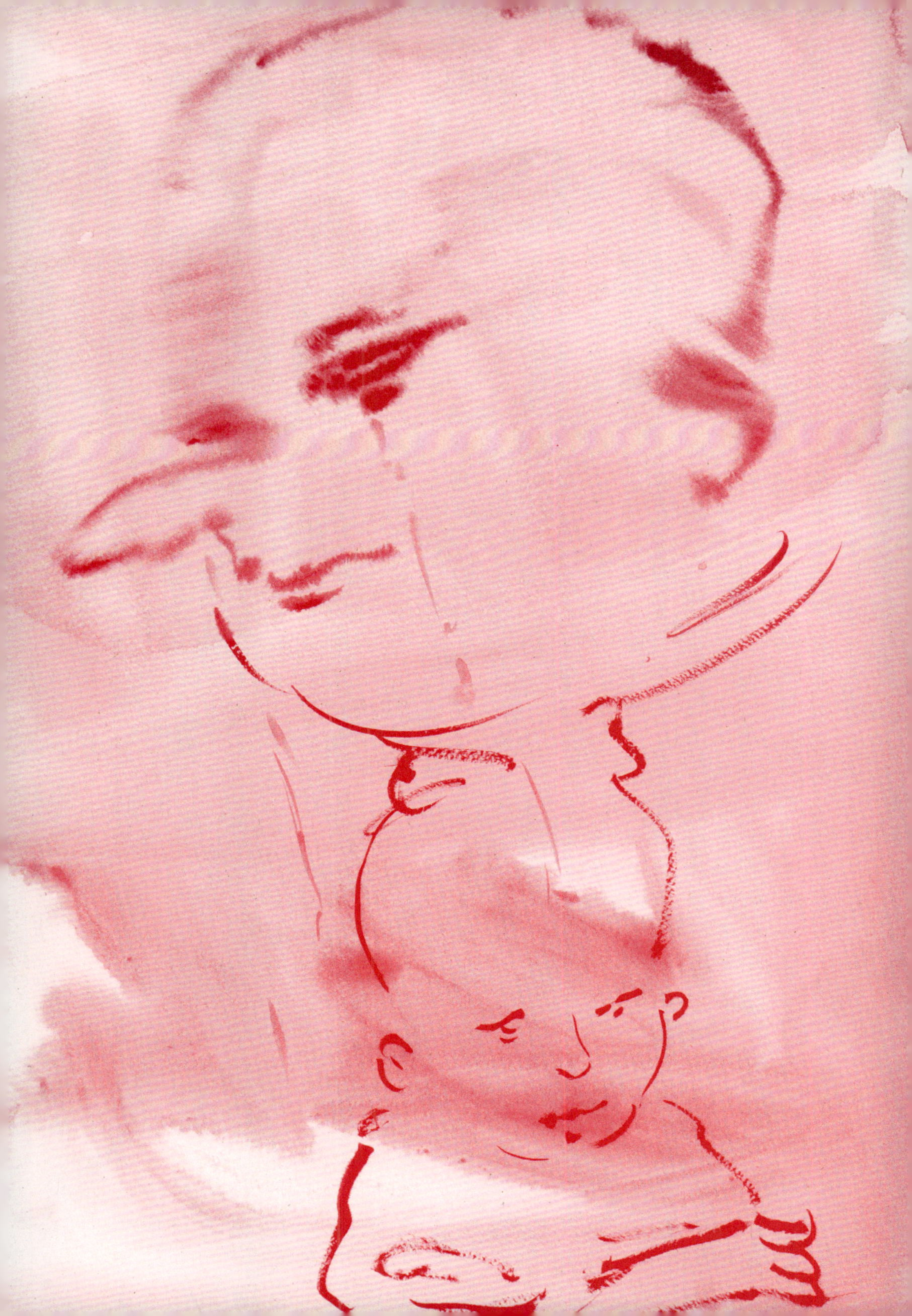

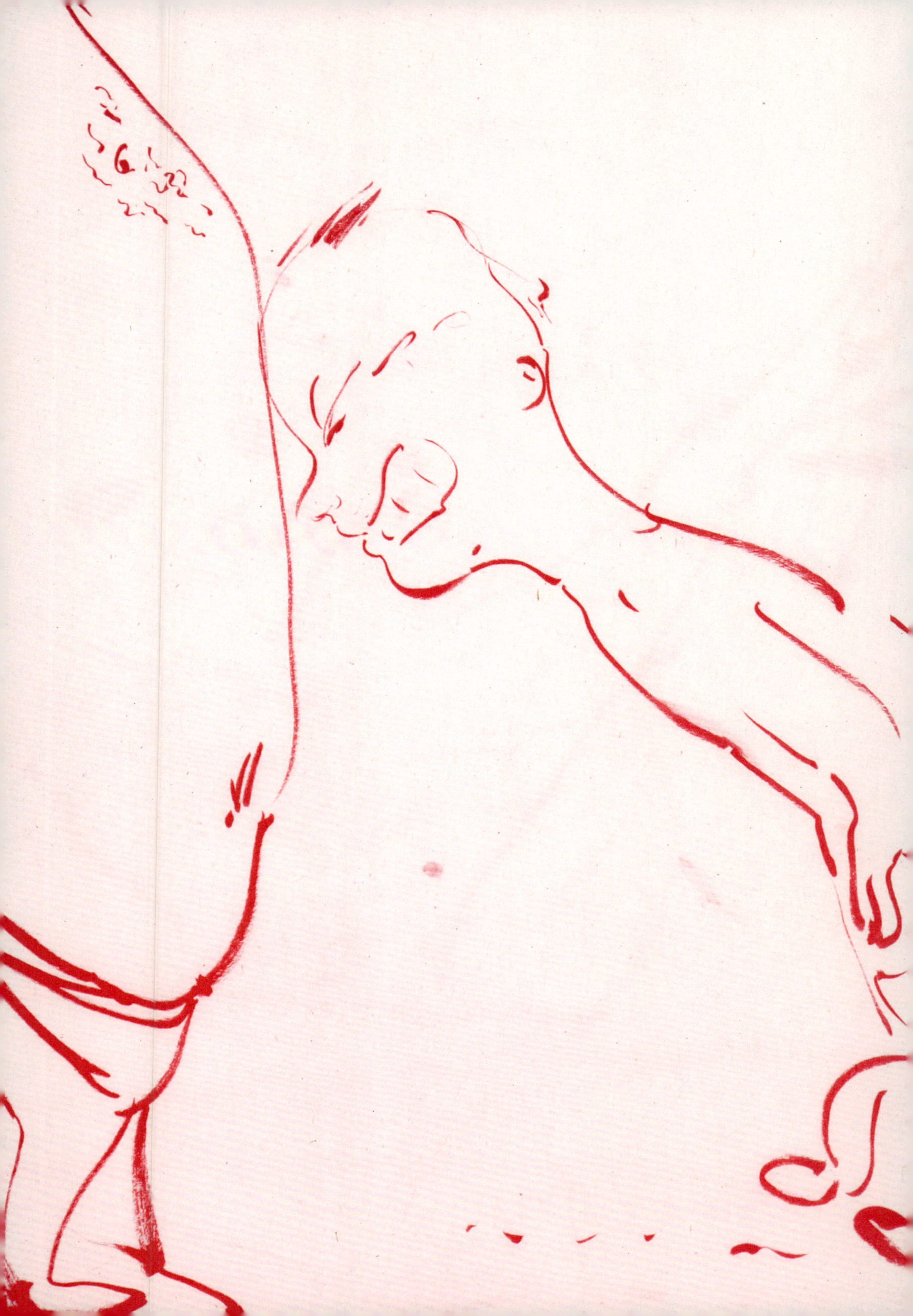

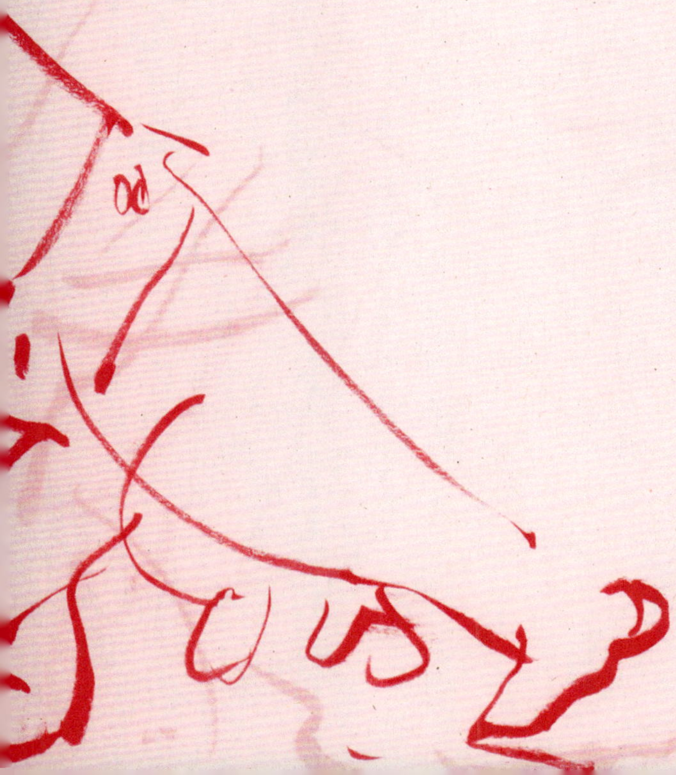

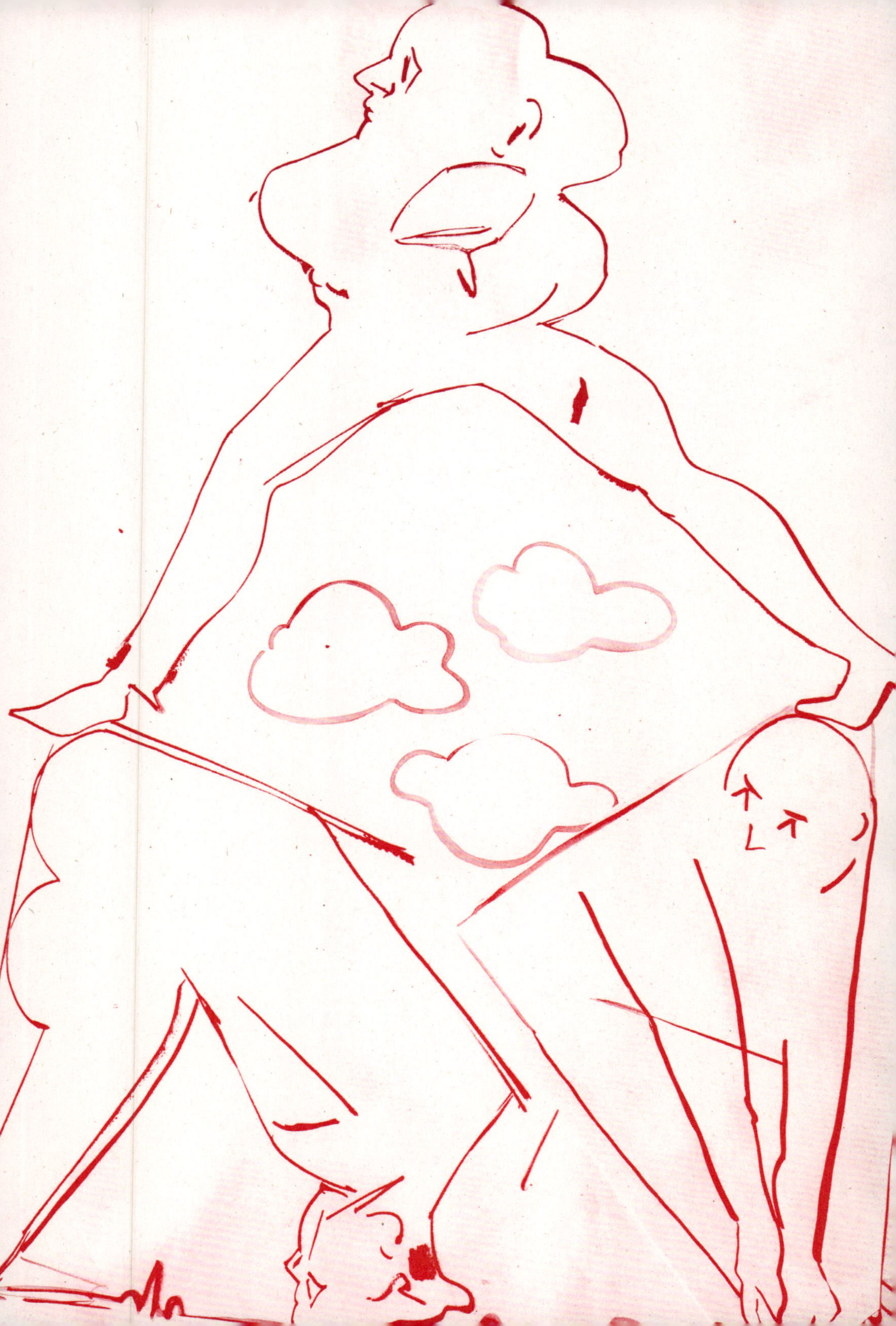

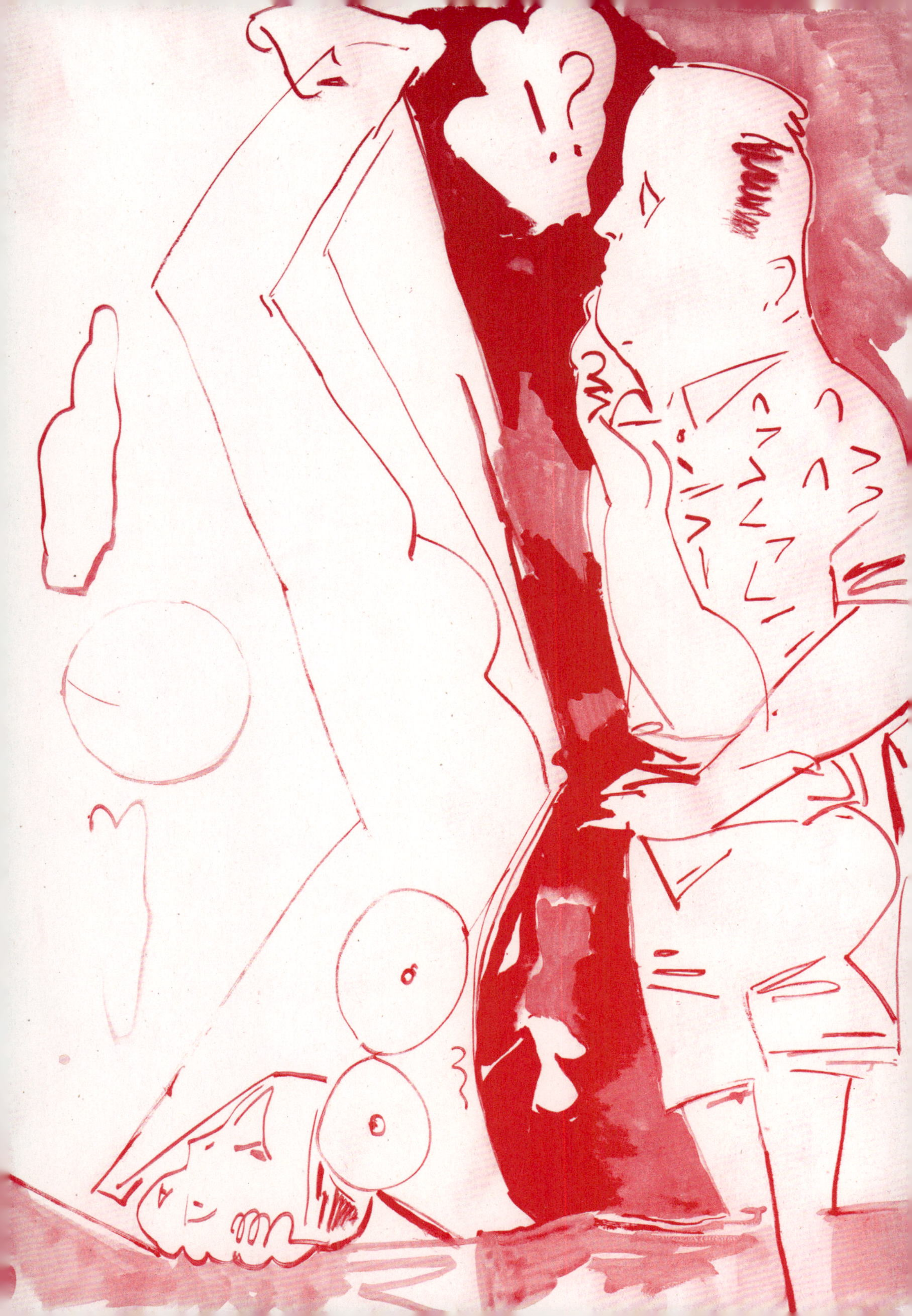

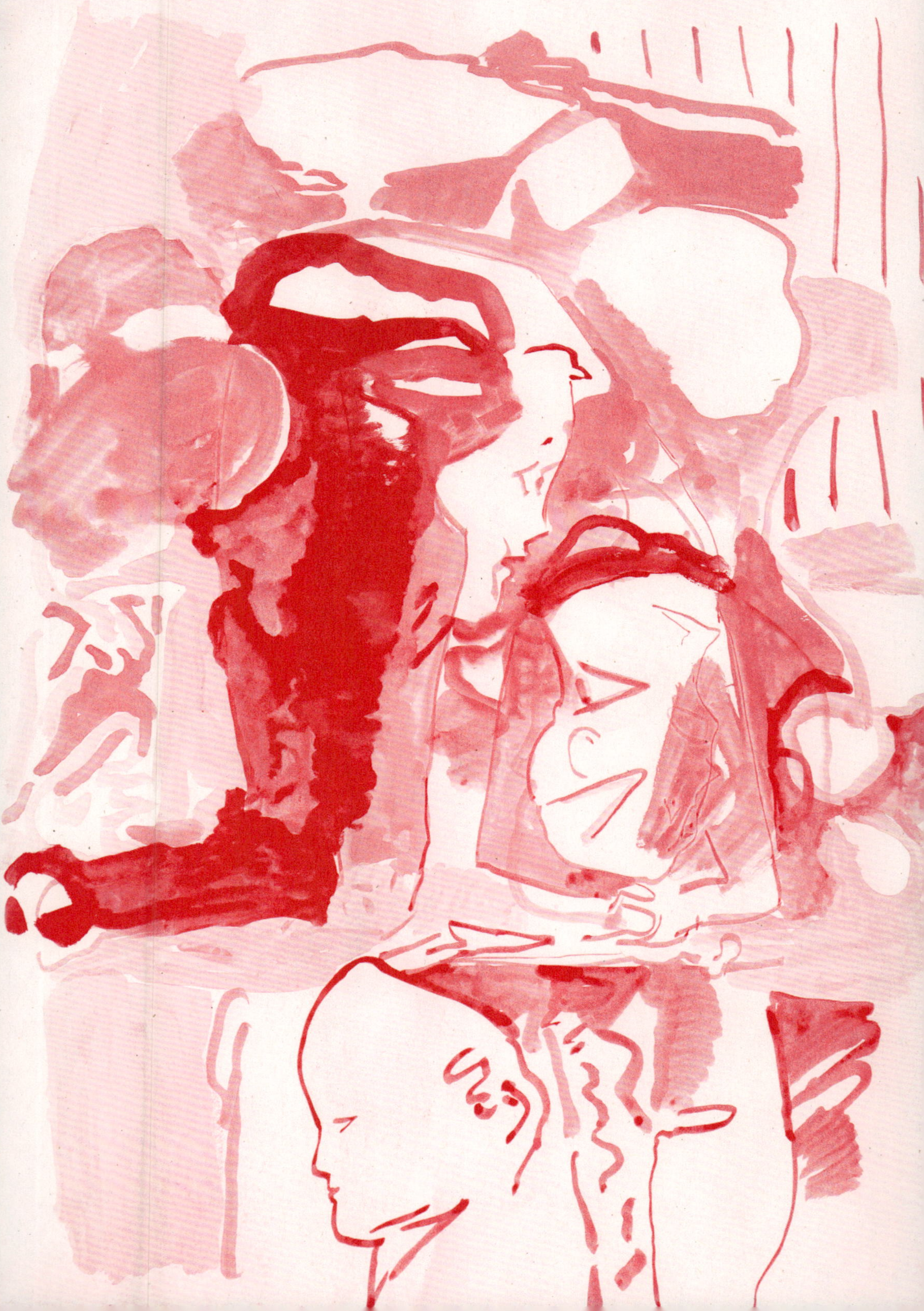

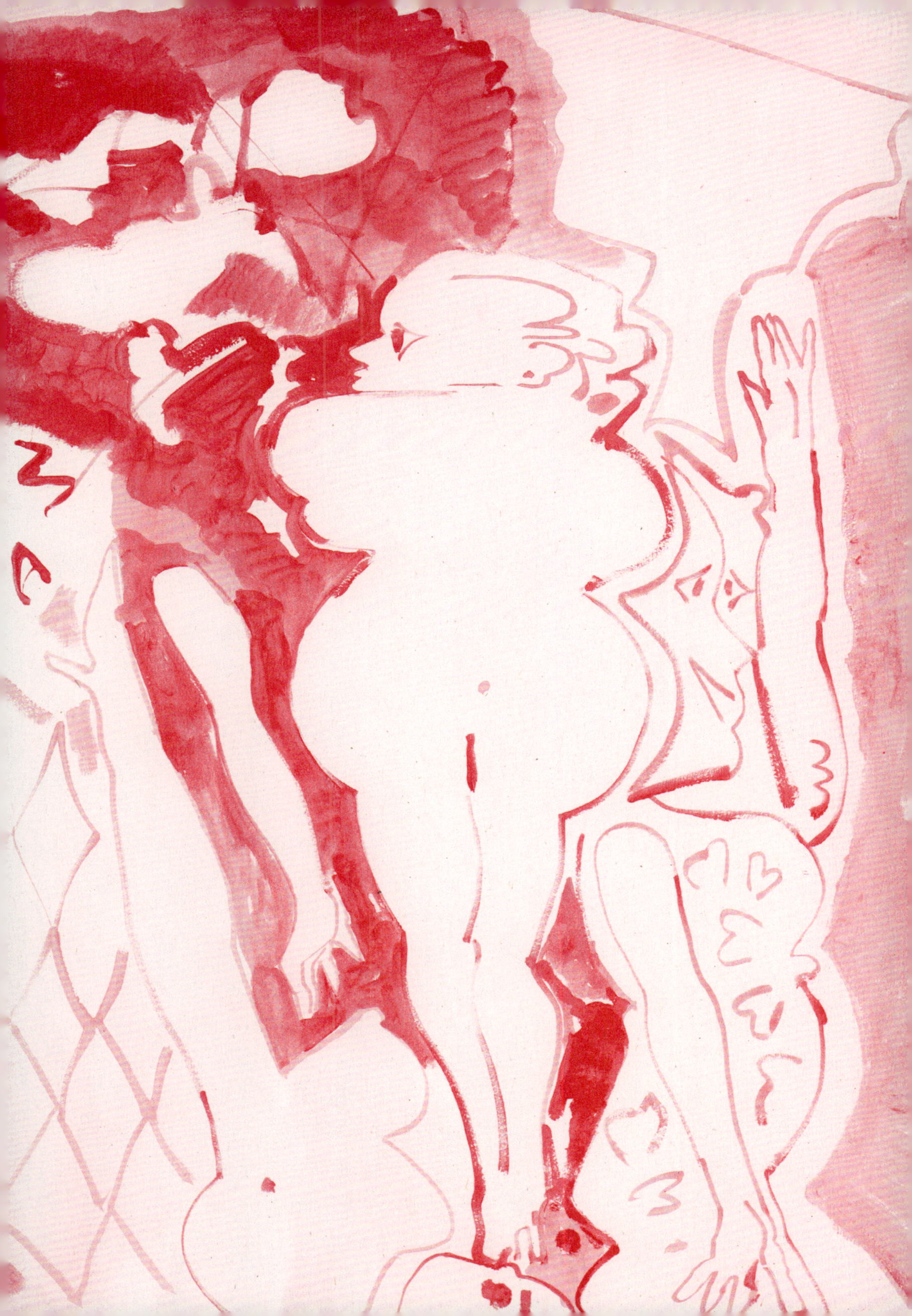

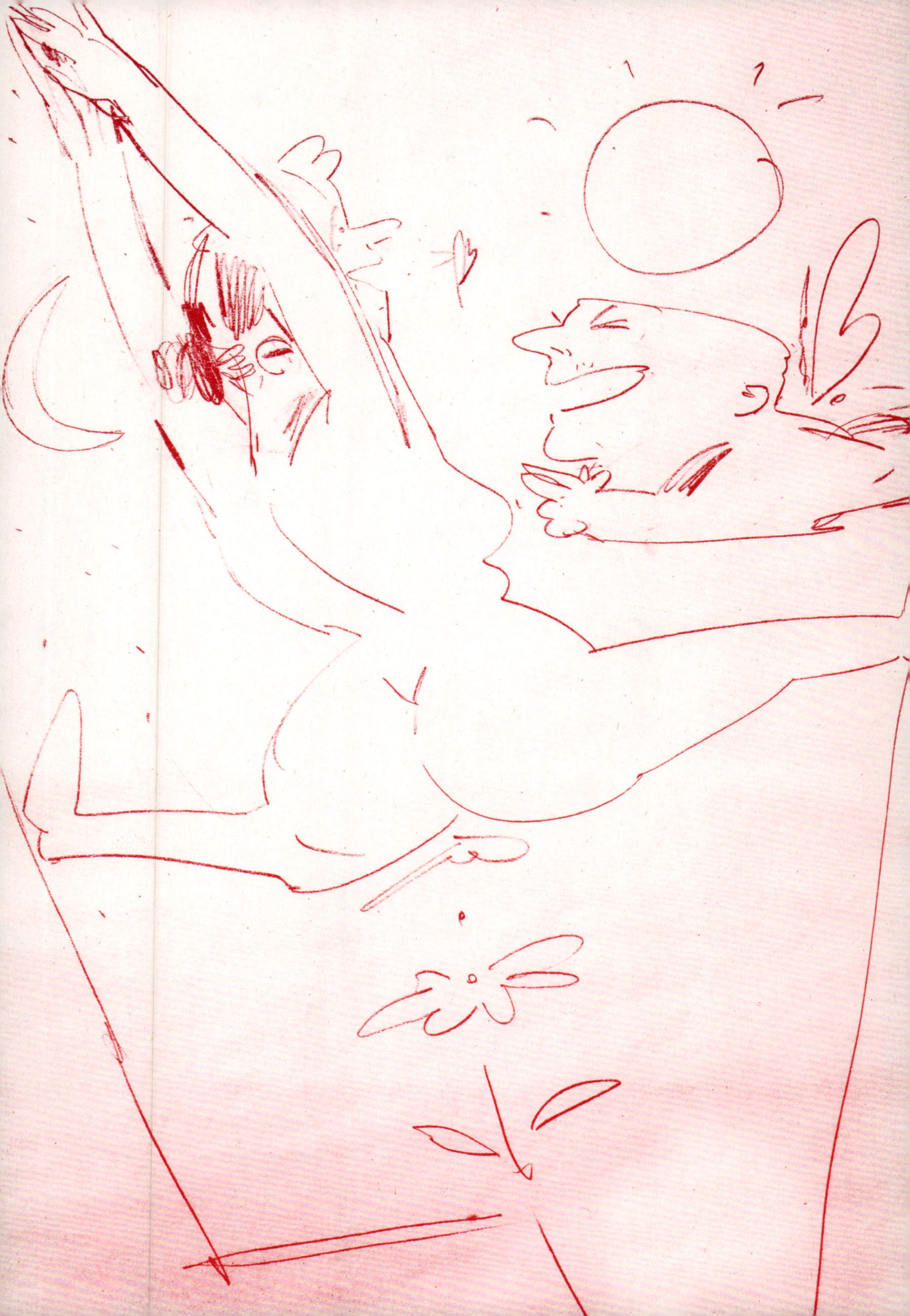

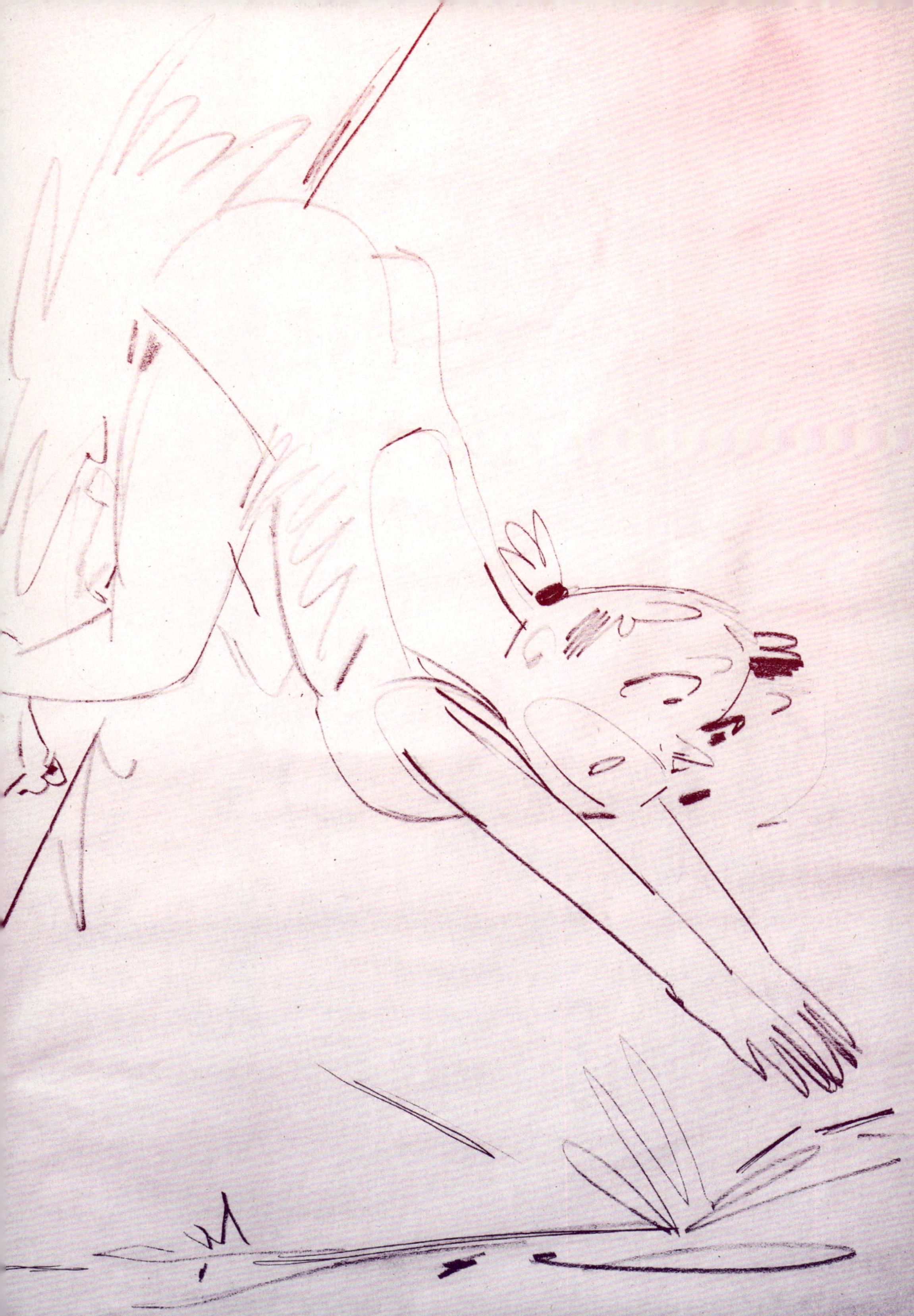

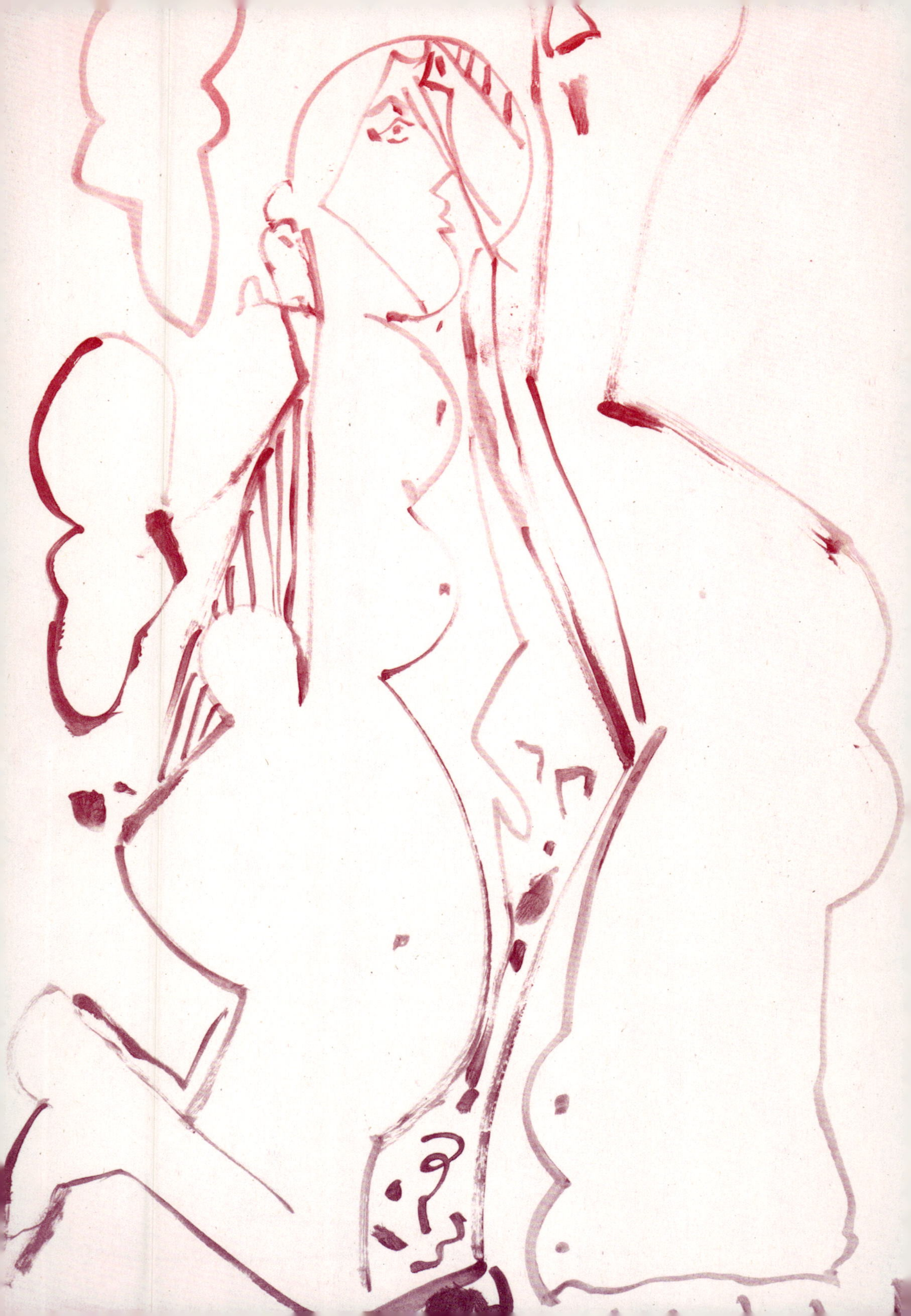

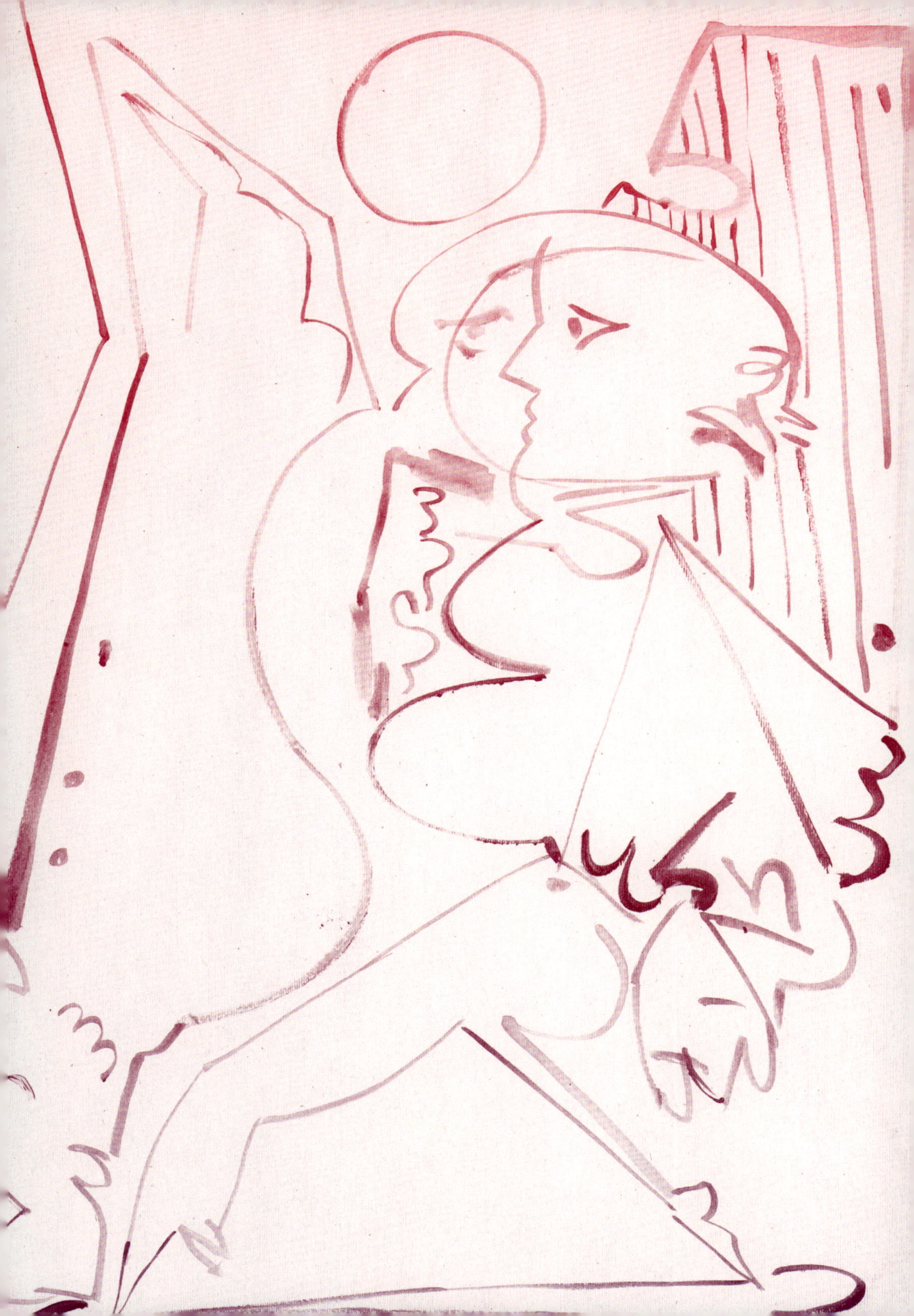

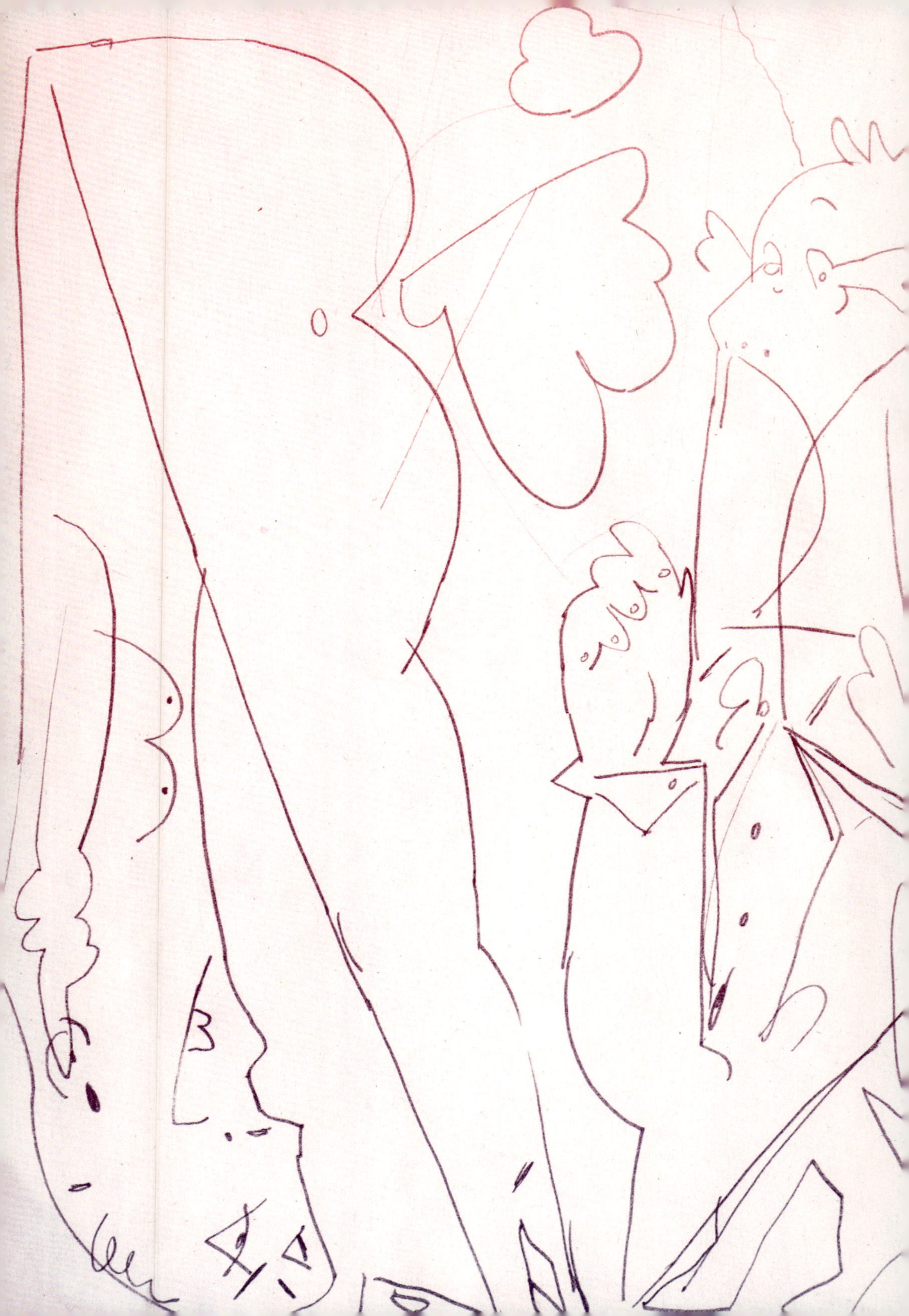

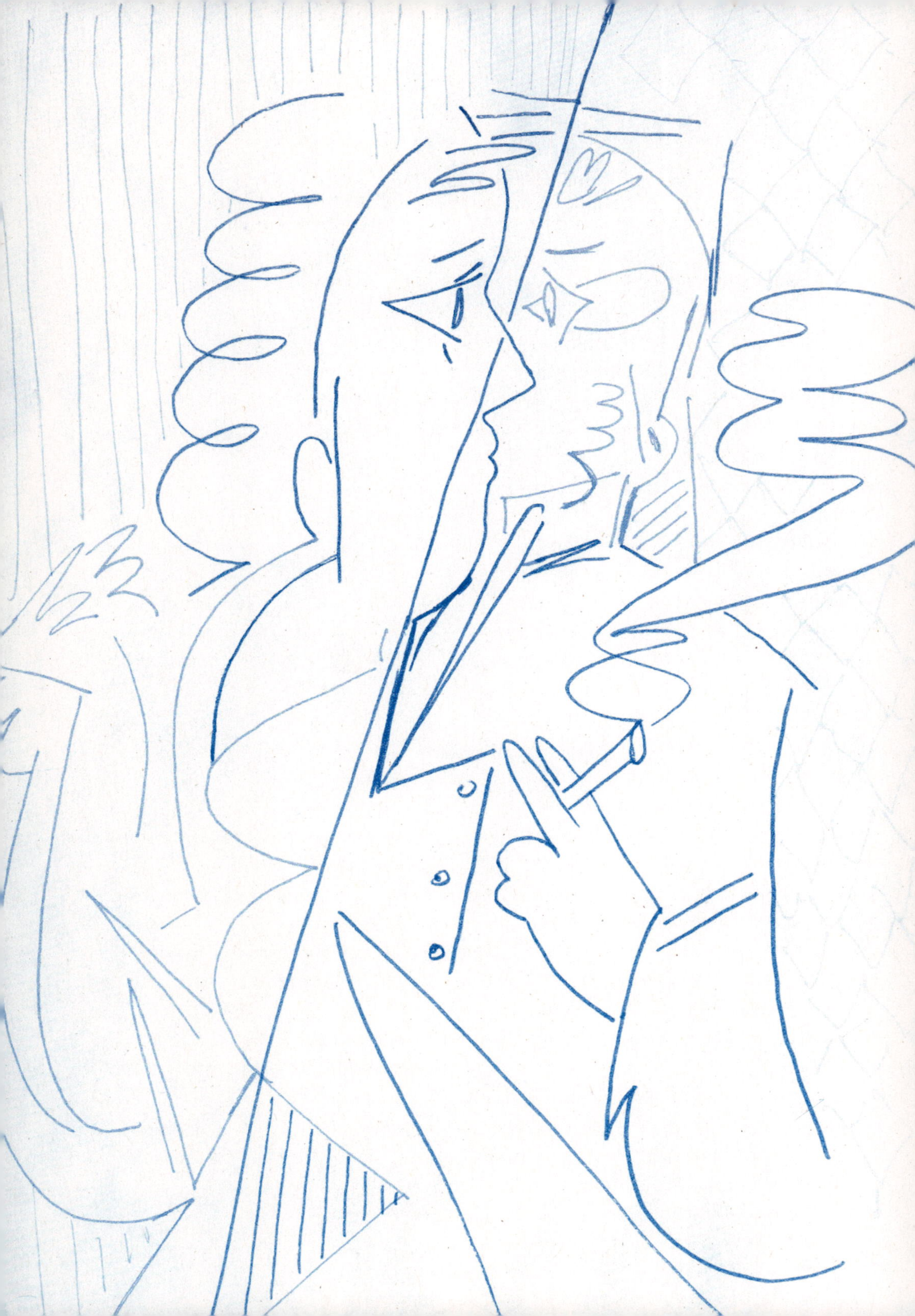

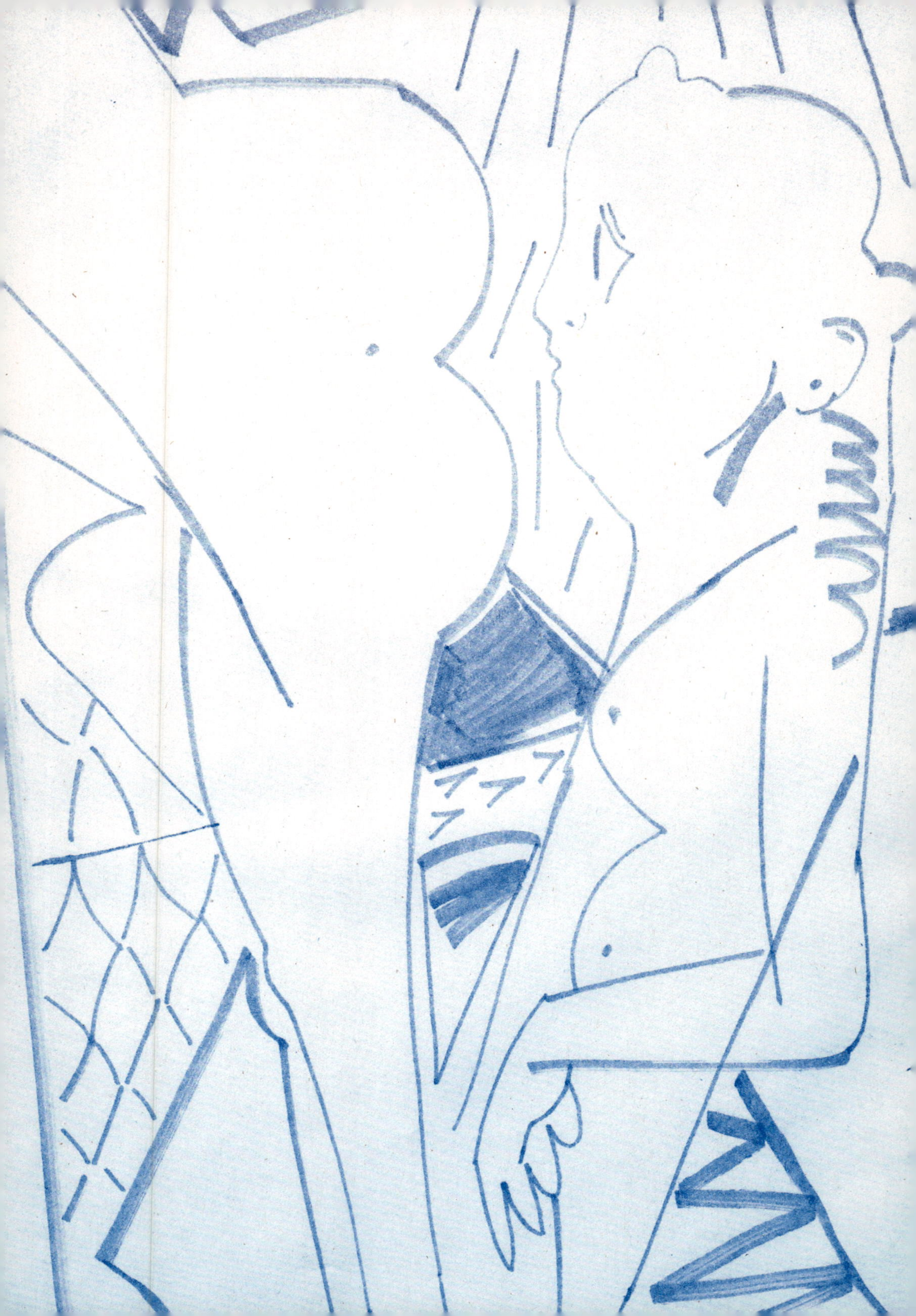

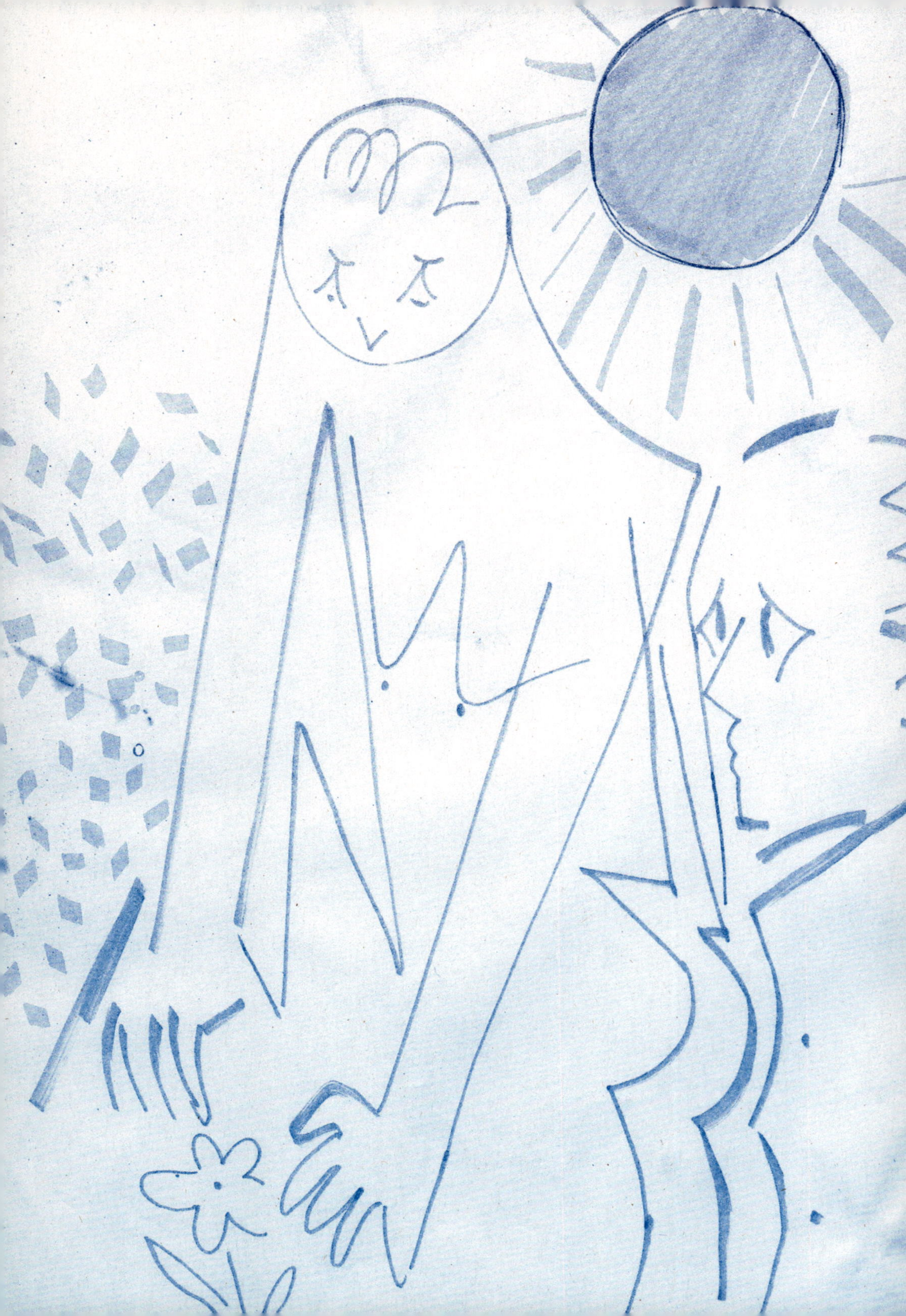

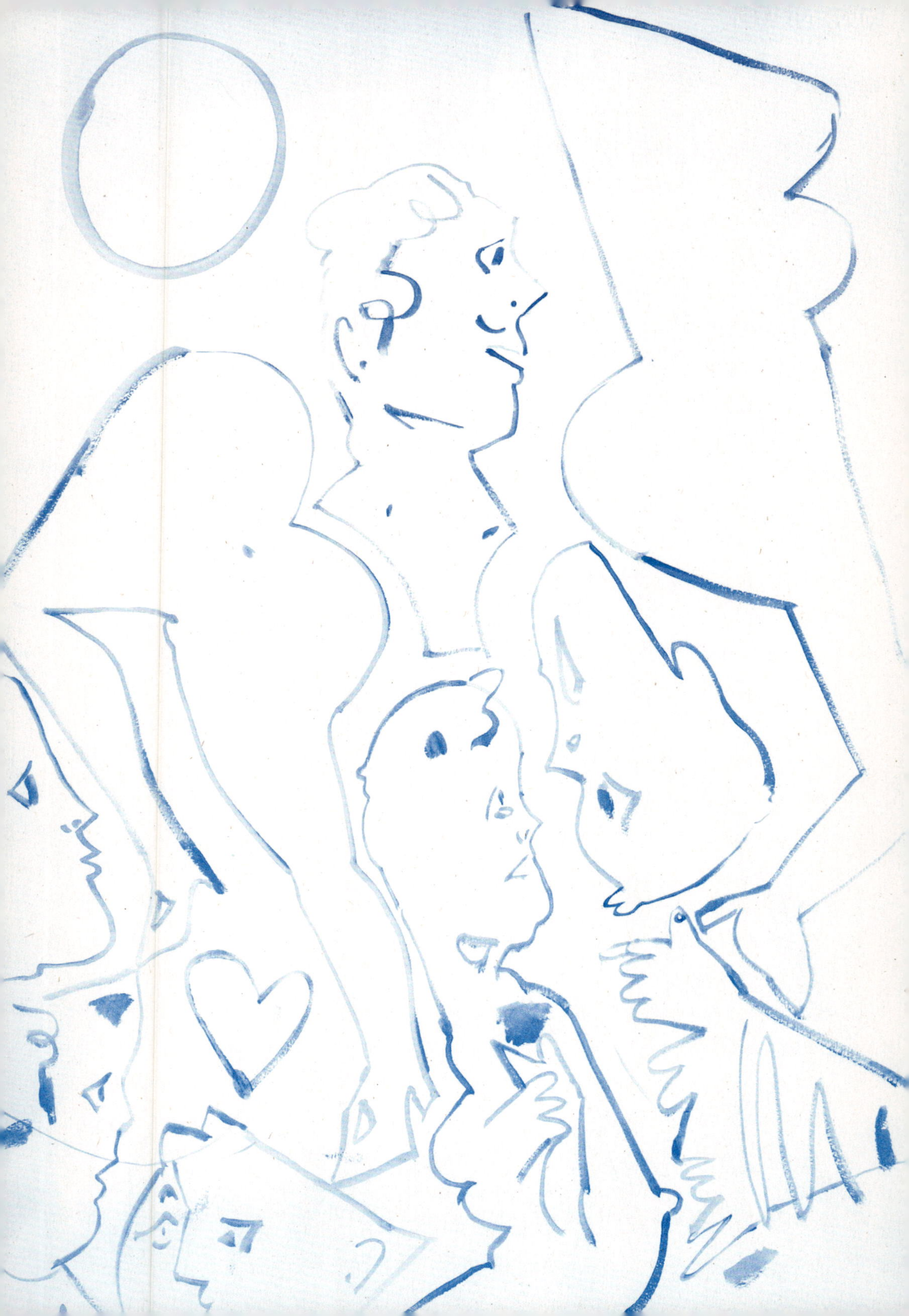

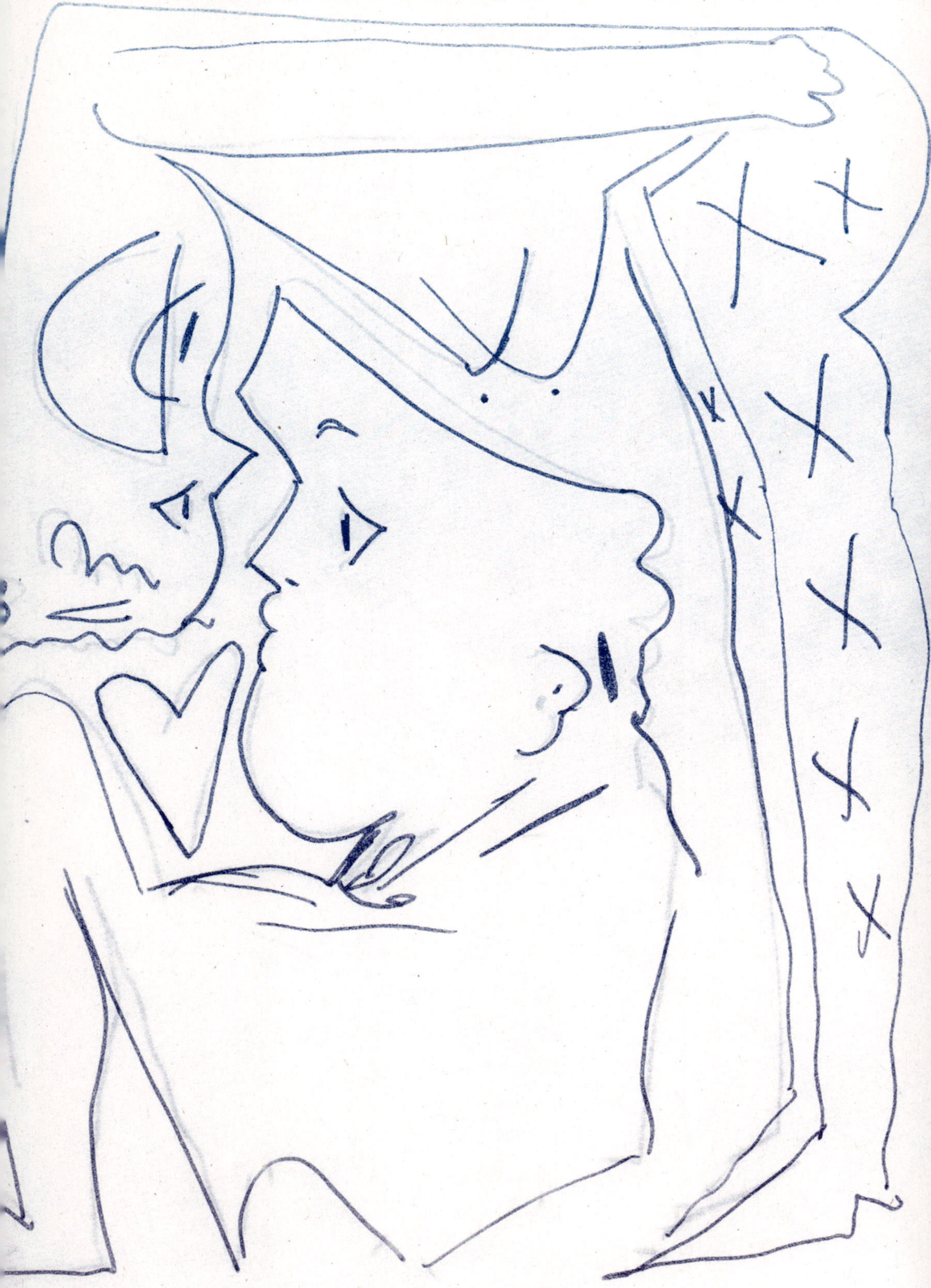

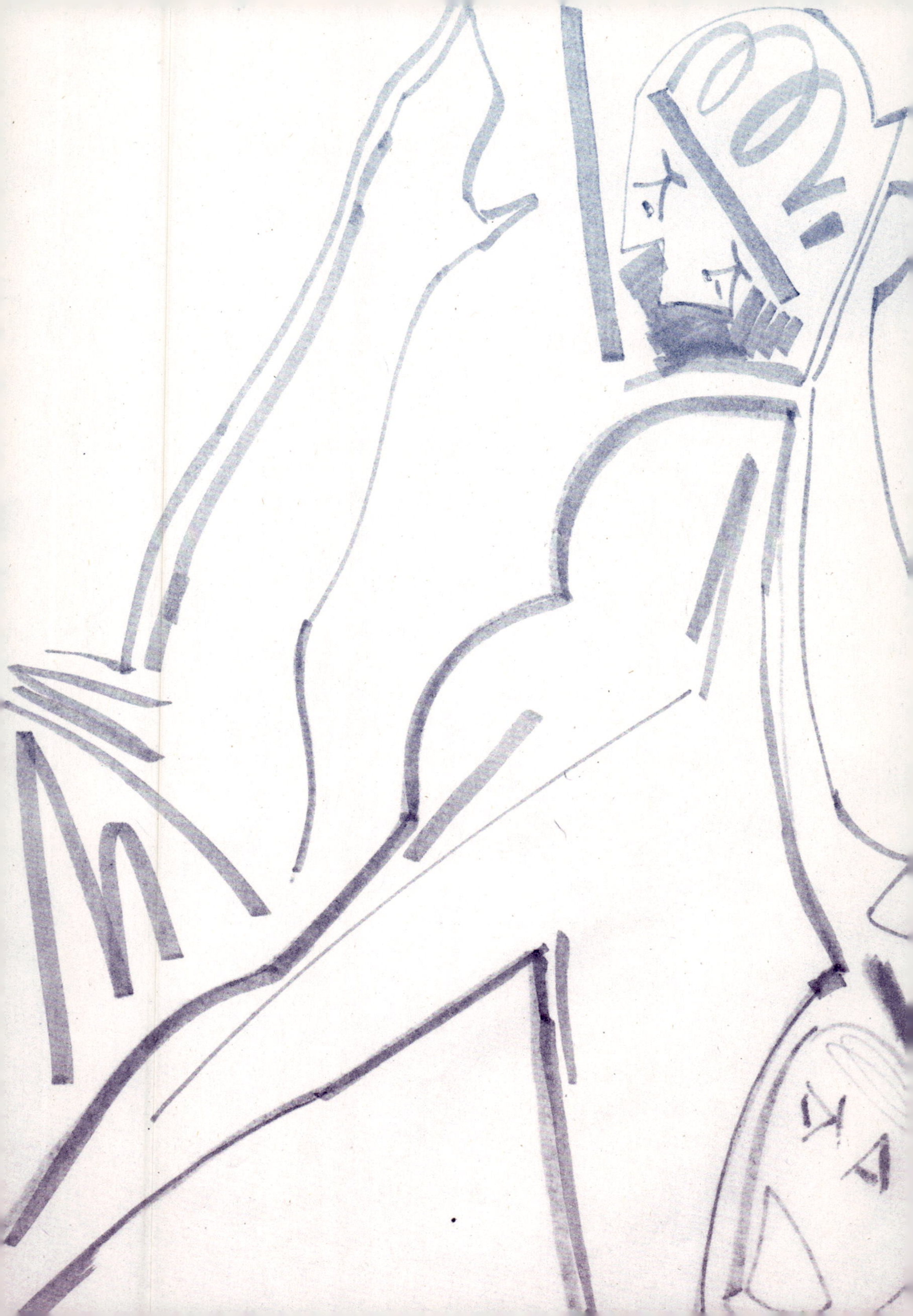

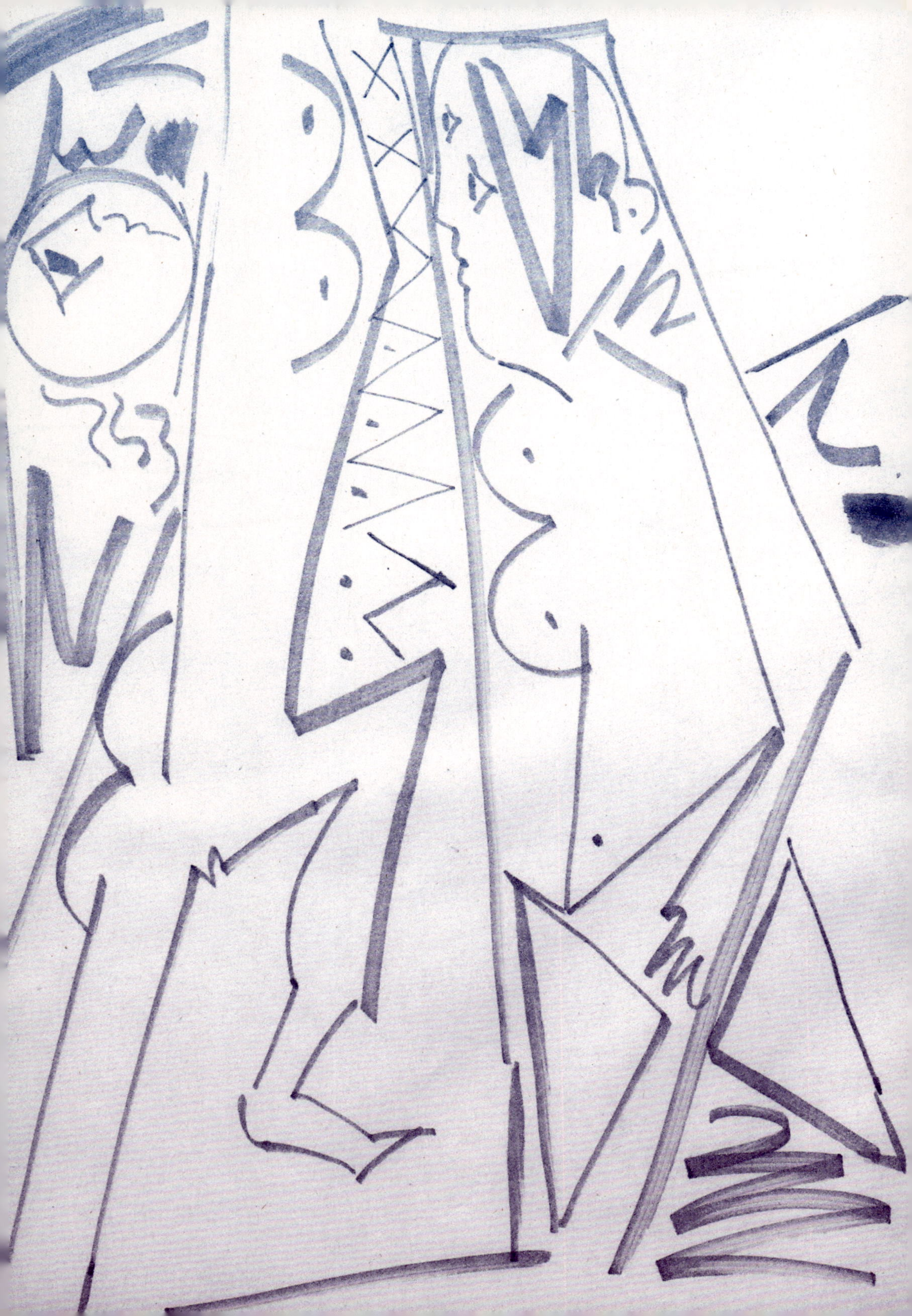

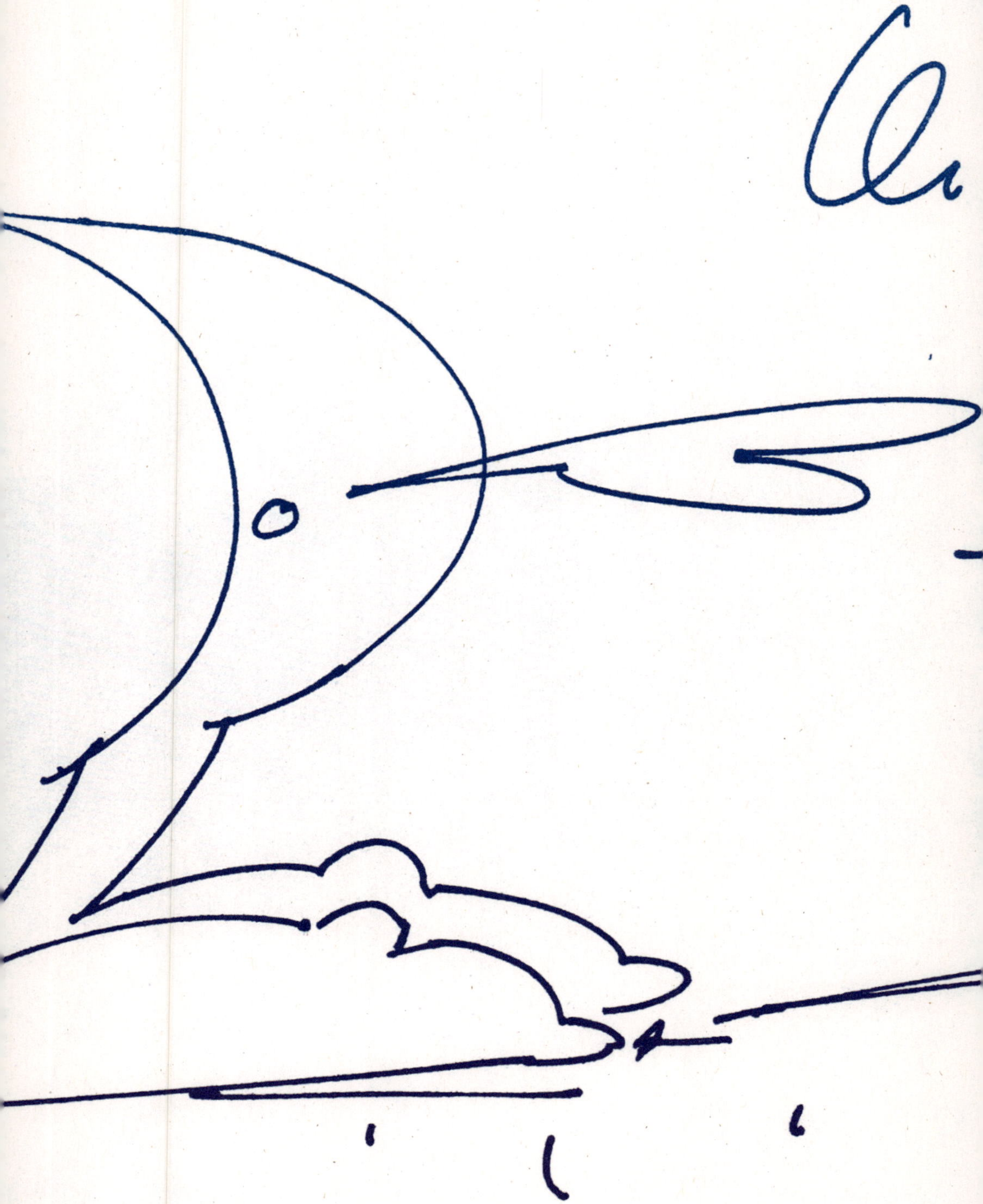

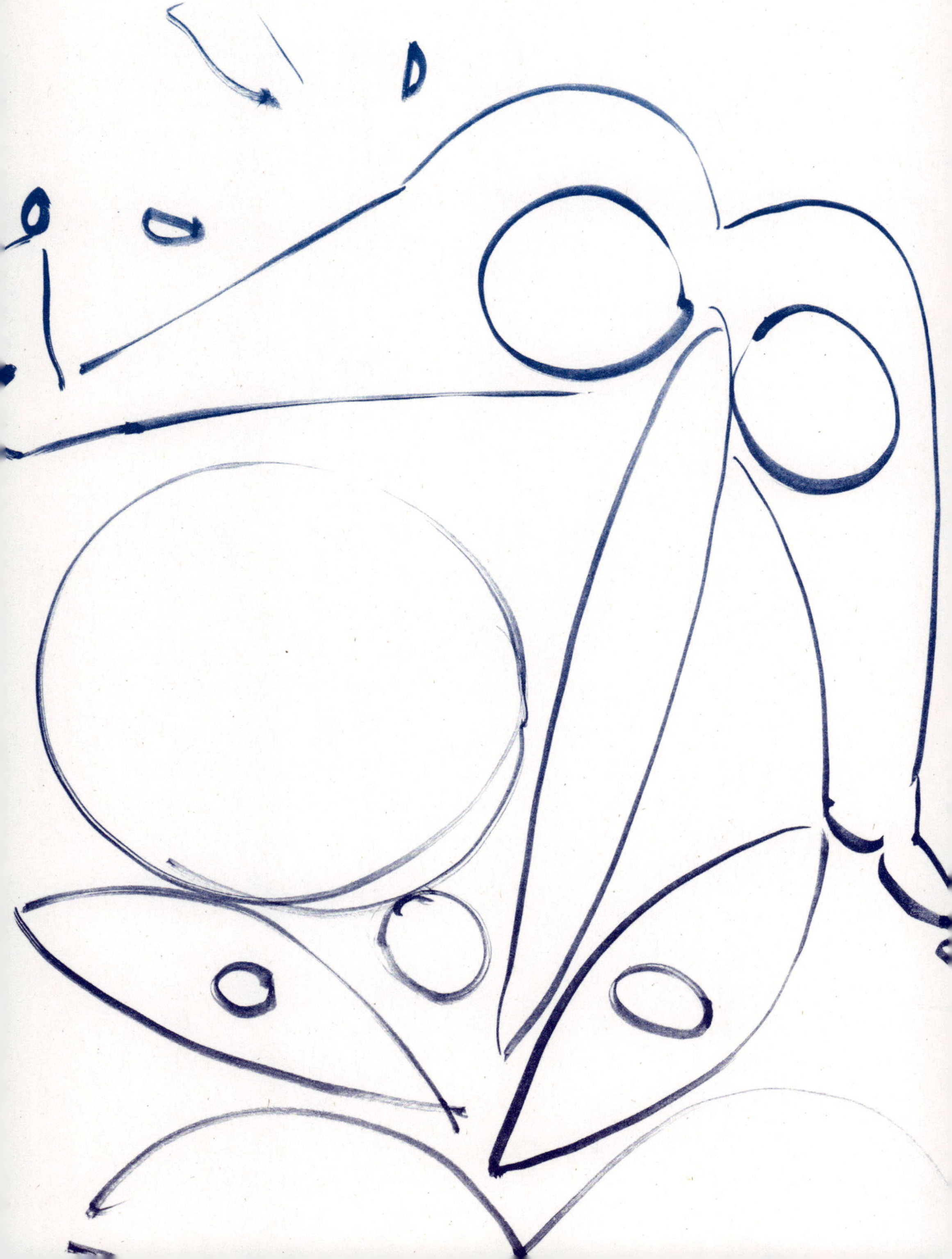

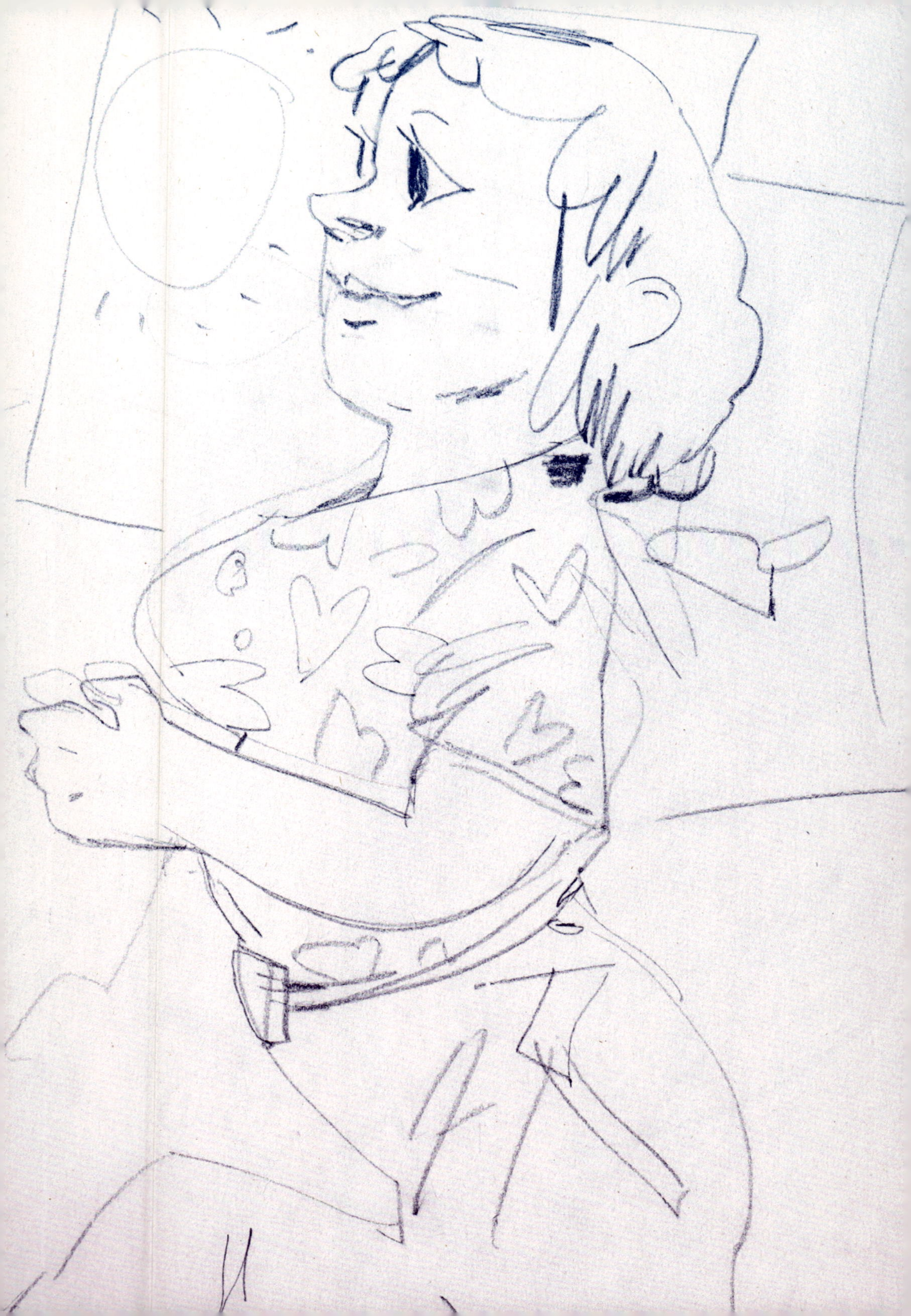

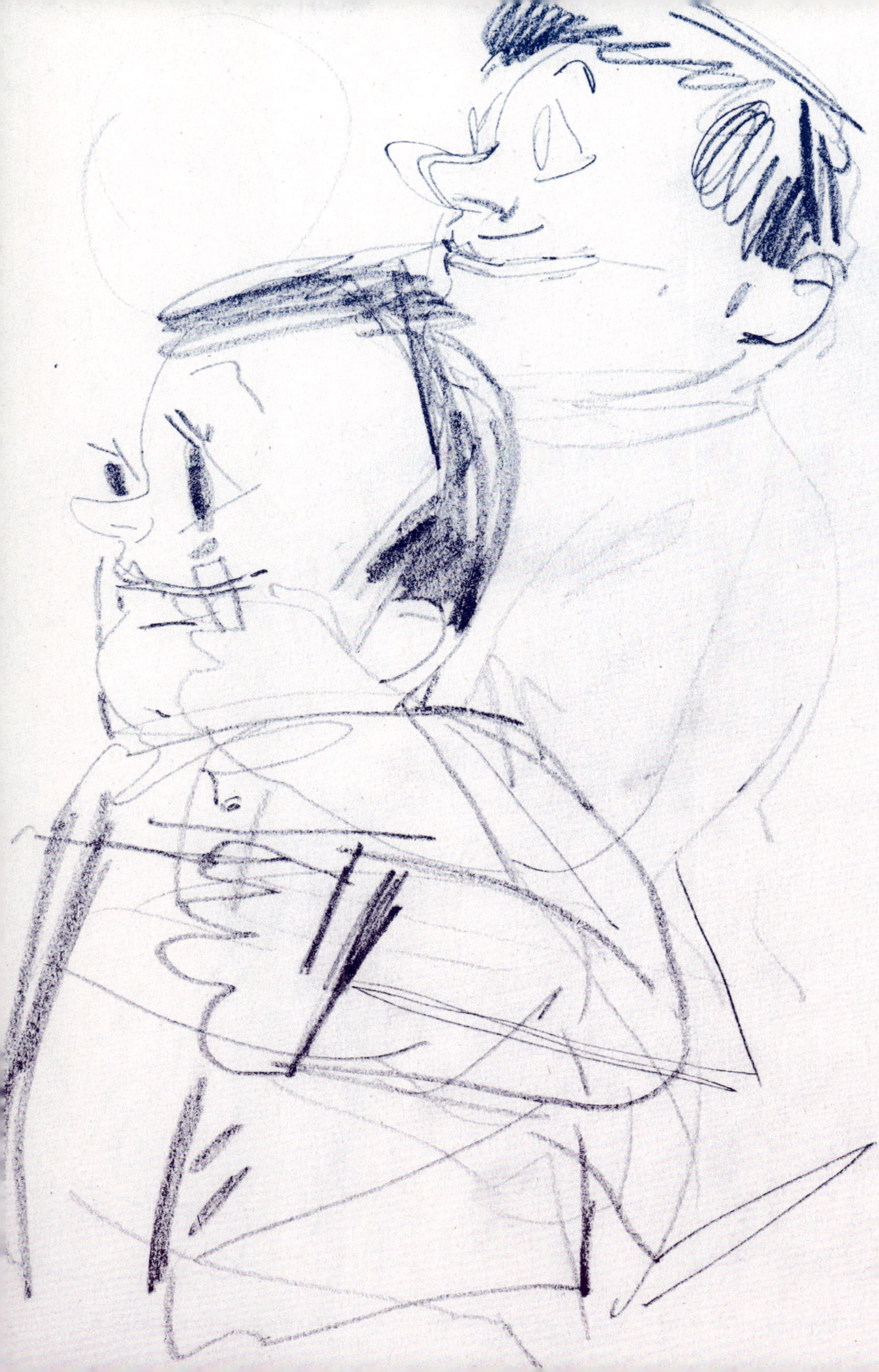

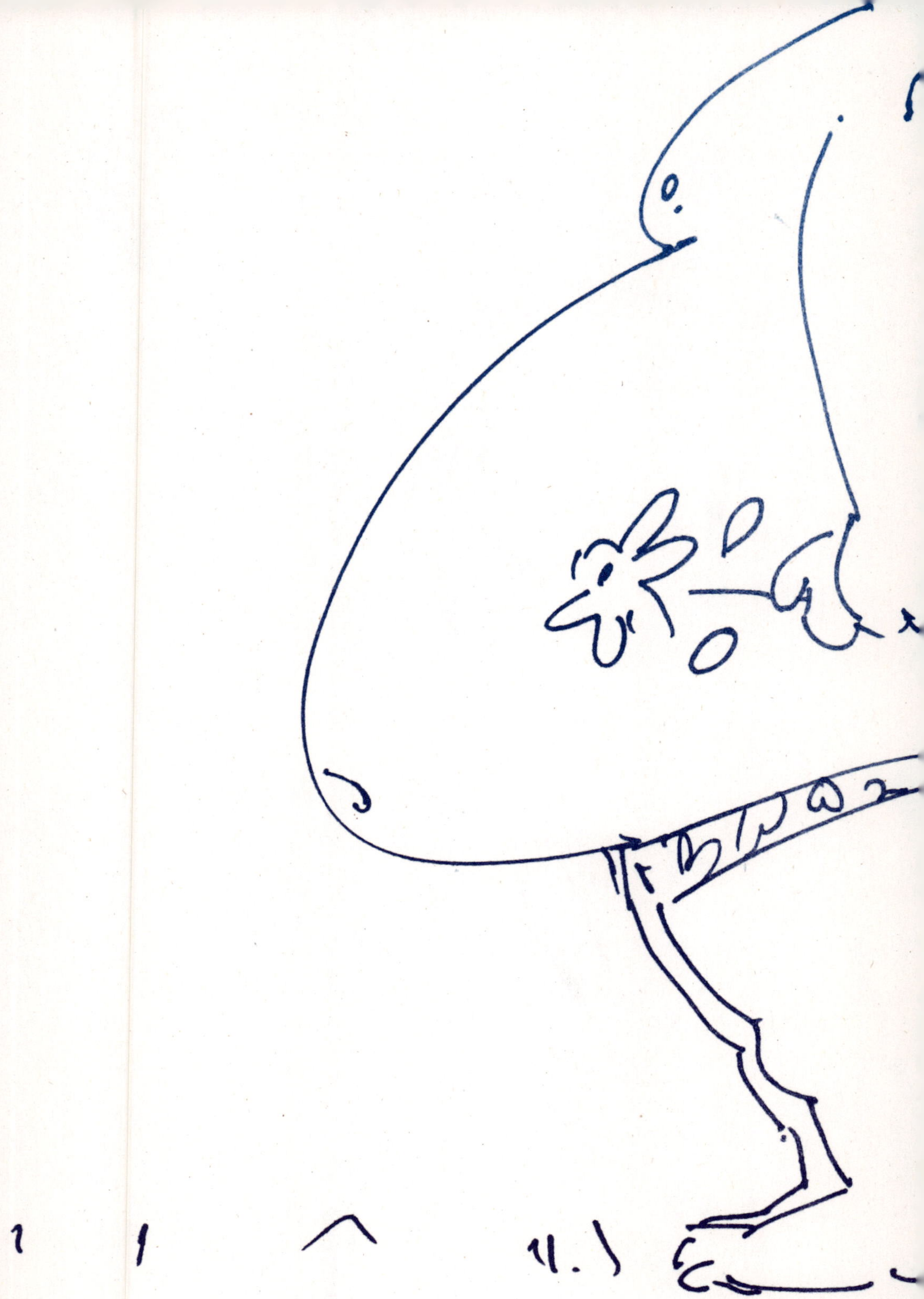

From pages 116 to 140: series of 24 individual sketches and drawings made with ink and pencil on paper.
Courtesy of the artist. Photo: Artist Studio

# Les ombres qu'ils projettent

Lillian Davies

« Au début, j'aime cacher ma nationalité », m'a récemment confié Hoda Kashiha. Celle-ci est née à Téhéran dans les dernières années de la guerre Iran-Irak, un conflit qui a débuté par l'invasion de l'Iran par l'Irak et qui s'est terminé par la mort de plus d'un demi-million d'Iraniens. La France et les États-Unis ont officiellement soutenu l'Irak, malgré les soupçons d'utilisation d'armes chimiques par l'armée irakienne. Au cours de l'été 1987, un an après la naissance de Kashiha, je me souviens d'avoir vu un homme à la coupe de cheveux courte et rasée et portant un treillis kaki sur les télévisions du sud des États-Unis. Il s'agissait du lieutenant-colonel Oliver North, du Conseil de sécurité nationale des États-Unis, qui faisait l'objet d'une enquête pour avoir orchestré, malgré l'embargo américain, des ventes d'armes à l'Iran afin de financer les Contras contre-révolutionnaires du Nicaragua. Enfants, de part et d'autre d'un fossé politique et idéologique de plus en plus profond, Kashiha et moi témoignons de flashs d'un même récit dangereusement fragmenté. Kashiha, elle, consacre son travail d'artiste à l'étude de ces fragments et des ombres qu'ils projettent.

Kashiha grandit dans la capitale iranienne, où elle participe à des programmes extrascolaires à l'Institut pour le développement intellectuel des enfants et des jeunes adultes. Appelés « Kanoon », abréviation du nom en farsi, ces programmes ont été lancés dans les années 1960, lorsque l'impératrice Farah Diba a aidé son amie Lily Amir-Arjomand à créer une bibliothèque à destination des plus jeunes. Les rayonnages se sont remplis de livres internationaux pour enfants, traduits en farsi, et Kanoon a rapidement commencé à publier des histoires iraniennes et à organiser pour les jeunes des ateliers d'écriture, de théâtre et de cinéma. « Kanoon est devenu une sorte d'incubateur pour certains des artistes les plus célèbres du pays[1] » et fonctionne encore aujourd'hui, dans une moindre mesure.

Enfant, Kashiha se rend souvent au Musée d'Art contemporain de Téhéran, conçu par Kamran Diba et inauguré en 1977. L'été suivant, la première foire d'art en plein air d'Iran se déroule dans les jardins du musée. L'État commence à subventionner les arts dans les années 1950 et la première Biennale de Téhéran attire des

1
« Institute for the Intellectual Development of Children and Young Adults », *Bidoun*, Winter 2009, https://www.bidoun.org/articles/institute-for-the-intellectual-development-of-children-young-adults.

foules du monde entier au printemps 1958. L'Office des beaux-arts, qui deviendra plus tard le Ministère de la Culture, permet d'accéder à des emplois dans le secteur culturel, à des commandes artistiques et à des relations avec une classe de collectionneurs en plein essor[2]. Le soutien public et privé aux arts étant en place, une première génération d'artistes modernes apparaît, dont Bahman Mohasses (1931-2010), auteur de peintures et de sculptures « surréalistes et iconoclastes[3] », est peut-être le plus connu. Bedjat Sadr (1924-2009), contemporaine de Mohasses, est une référence essentielle pour Kashiha. Les déclarations de Sadr quant à ses collages de photos sont limpides : « Nous devons utiliser et prendre tout ce qui peut exprimer les sentiments de notre époque, déchirer les pages de magazines, les coller et trouver encore de nouveaux outils[4] ». La photographe Shadi Ghadirian (née en 1974), qui a bénéficié du mentorat de Bahman Jalali, est l'une des artistes les plus célèbres de la deuxième génération iranienne, qui s'est développée après que la République islamique ait renversé le shah et coupé de nombreux liens internationaux.

À l'instar des peintres Sam Samiee (né en 1988) et Ala Dehghan (née en 1982), Kashiha appartient à la troisième génération d'artistes qui émerge après le 11 septembre 2001 et l'installation des maisons de vente aux enchères dans la région, dont Christie's qui inaugure sa première vente à Dubaï en 2006. C'est à cette époque qu'il est redevenu courant pour les artistes iraniens d'étudier et d'exposer à l'étranger. S'il y a un événement historique qui définirait la quatrième génération qui émerge actuellement dans le pays, m'explique Kashiha, cela serait l'émergence du réseau social Instagram.

Kashiha fréquente Narjes, une école privée pour filles du centre de Téhéran, avant d'étudier les beaux-arts à l'université de Téhéran, où elle obtient une licence. À la bibliothèque centrale de l'université, la nudité dans les livres de peinture européenne est systématiquement expurgée. Cet acte de censure transforme les images reproduites – imaginez *La Naissance de Vénus* d'Alessandro Botticelli (1485-1486) sous la forme de larges marques noires émergeant d'un paysage aquatique – et insinue une interdiction générale

2
Voir Media Farzin, « A Short History of Art Exhibitions in Iran, 1946–78 », in *Iran Modern*, New York, edité par Fereshteh Daftari et Layla S. Diba, Asia Society Museum, 2013, p. 67-71.

3
Morad Montazami, « Moderne et contemporain : usages et enjeux en historiographiques compares », conférence du projet ARVIMM, l'Unité d'arabe de l'Université de Genève, de l'Institut d'étude de l'Islam et des sociétés du monde musulman et l'École normale supérieure, Centre Pompidou et EHESS, Paris, 2018.

4
Behdjat Sadr au sujet de ces photocollages, 1995, cité dans le communiqué de presse de l'exposition Behjat Sadr de Cyrus Goberville et Daniele Balice (5 avril - 1er juin 2019), Galerie Balice Hertling, Paris.

de la peinture de style européen. Lorsque Kashiha poursuit ses études à l'université de Boston quelques années plus tard, elle produit essentiellement des dessins – ce qui n'est peut-être pas surprenant, étant donné le parcours de l'artiste et de son goût pour l'humour noir. L'artiste américaine Amy Sillman fait d'ailleurs remarquer que tous les grands peintres pop sont des dessinateurs dans l'âme[5]. À Boston, Dana Frankfort, professeur de Kashiha[6], la pousse à utiliser la toile comme support. La confiance de la jeune artiste grandit grâce à cette nouvelle possibilité et à cette échelle élargie. Alors que Kashiha travaille à l'obtention de sa maîtrise en peinture, elle inaugure sa première exposition personnelle à la galerie Etemad[7] à Téhéran.

Après ses études aux États-Unis, Kashiha retourne à Téhéran en 2016, à un moment où les sanctions se multiplient envers l'Iran et où l'agitation politique s'intensifit. En guise de répit et de méthode pour atteindre l'équilibre et la sérénité qu'elle recherche dans son travail à l'atelier, elle commence à pratiquer quotidiennement le yoga et à nager régulièrement. Dans sa toile *((Swimming and Melting))* (2017), Kashiha joue avec l'immersion et l'effacement d'une figure fragmentée, mobilisant des techniques du mouvement Dada. Elle vient ainsi perturber un paysage numérique semblable à un écran, infusé d'images de dessins animés. L'année suivante, Kashiha expose à Paris sa toile *Dream Makes Cloud* (2018), une juxtaposition de deux visages de poupée à travers des bandes de spray bleu qui évoquent des éclats de verre. Cette peinture est montrée dans « The Oil of Pardis », faisant clairement référence à l'industrie pétrolière du golfe Persique, un événement organisé par Hormoz Hematian, fondateur de Dastan's Basement. La toile de Kashiha est présentée aux côtés d'œuvres de Mohasses, Samiee et Parvaneh Etemadie (née en 1948) à la Galerie Balice Hertling. Lors d'une visite en Iran organisée par la Fondation Pejman l'année précédente, le galeriste parisien Daniele Balice avait rencontré Kashiha dans son atelier de Téhéran ainsi que Hematian.

Au début de la pandémie de Covid-19, Kashiha quitte Téhéran pour s'installer dans une propriété située à une heure du centre-ville. C'est dans un ancien entrepôt

5
Amy Sillman, *Faux Pas : Selected Writings and Drawings*, After 8 Books, Paris, 2020, p. 207.

6
Frankfort « était si perspicace », indiquait Kashiha avec admiration lors d'une conversation avec l'autrice le 14 juin 2024.

7
Historiquement marchand d'art islamique, Etemad a été le premier galeriste iranien à ouvrir une succursale à Dubaï, ville qui constitue un véritable moteur (notamment depuis la première édition d'Art Dubaï en 2007) dans le développement international du monde de l'art du Golfe.

réhabilité, assez grand pour accueillir un court de tennis, que Kashiha installe son atelier. L'espace, avec ses évocations du sport et de la discipline, lui convient parfaitement : « Je considère la peinture comme une façon de penser. J'essaie de me créer un terrain de jeu[8] ».

Inaugurée à l'été 2020 à la Galerie Nathalie Obadia à Bruxelles, lors d'une brève interruption des restrictions imposées par la Belgique en cas de pandémie, Kashiha ouvre sa première exposition personnelle en Europe, « Dear St. Agatha I am witness of your tears In the land of Tulips », en référence à la sainte patronne des martyrs et des victimes de viols. Dans l'œuvre éponyme, une figure féminine torturée, apparemment observée par une paire d'yeux géants, entre en collision avec une étendue de tulipes vermillon. Originaires d'Iran, les tulipes sont la fleur nationale du pays. La légende veut qu'une tulipe rouge pousse à chaque endroit où meurt un soldat patriote.

Peu après, l'artiste accélère la « destruction de la narration linéaire[9] » qu'elle visait, en fixant chacune des huit peintures de grand format qui constituent l'installation *In Appreciation of Blinking* (2020-2021) à son propre support métallique sur roulettes. Pour cette œuvre, Kashiha s'approprie *L'Incrédulité de saint Thomas* (vers 1601-1602) du Caravage et élabore une progression par sauts d'images collées recouvertes d'un lavis d'acrylique noir qui s'étend progressivement plus bas sur chaque toile. Dans le dernier tableau, *Back as Black*, toute la composition initiale est plongée dans l'obscurité. Son « monochrome de minuit » rappelle le *Carré noir* (1915) de Kasimir Malevitch tout autant que l'utilisation récurrente de la peinture à l'huile noire de Sadr, que le conservateur Fabrice Hergott expliquait comme un symbole de « l'immense tache [. . .] que cette huile représente dans l'histoire de l'Iran[10] ». Le carré noir fait également écho à la réponse des réseaux sociaux aux soulèvements politiques de l'Iran à la fin de 2017, ainsi qu'au « Blackout Tuesday », organisé à la suite des meurtres de Breonna Taylor et de George Floyd par la police aux États-Unis.

Lors de la résidence de Kashiha en hiver 2022 à Brest, en France, le directeur de Passerelle Centre d'art contemporain, Loïc Le Gall, lui suggère de considérer le

8
Echange d'emails avec l'autrice, mars 2022

9
*Ibid*.

10
Fabrice Hergott, « Spirals », *Behdjat Sadr : Traces*, Paris, Zamân Books, 2014, p. 8.

11
Clarice Lispector, *Água Viva*, New York, New Directions, 1973, p. 11. Je pourrais tout aussi bien citer ici Junichiro Tanizaki, *Éloge d'ombre* (1933), tant les deux écrivains élaborent une ode au pouvoir créatif de l'ombre et de l'obscurité.

métal, comme l'avait fait Sadr, non seulement comme un support, mais aussi comme un médium. L'incorporation de ce matériau industriel par l'artiste est logique. Les géométries que Kashiha façonne dans le métal trouvé reprennent les formes découpées au pochoir qui structurent bon nombre de ses compositions. Mais surtout, les sculptures de Kashiha projettent des ombres. Et l'ombre, comme le *duende* de Gabriel García Lorca, incarne un espace créatif richement nuancé. Cet usage m'évoque une phrase de Clarice Lispector dans Água *Viva* (1973) : « Pour me refaire et te refaire, je retourne à mon état de jardin et d'ombre, de réalité froide[11] ».

Kashiha expose également son travail vidéo pour la première fois à Brest, révélant son processus créatif d'expérimentations. Elle conçoit des compositions animées avant de les placer sur la toile. Le film d'animation qu'elle réalise pendant le confinement lors de la pandémie de Covid-19, *The Eyes Fill with Brightness Slip Over to the Black Shades* (2021), est une autre source cruciale de l'obscurité tombante de la série de peintures *In Appreciation of Blinking*.

Récemment, Kashiha a planté des tournesols à l'extérieur de son atelier. Elle aime cette fleur et les représentations solaires que Vincent van Gogh en a fait dans ses grandes toiles qu'il a peintes à la Maison Jaune, dans le sud de la France. Dans *Another world is waiting for us* (2023), l'exposition la plus récente de Kashiha en Europe – à la galerie Nathalie Obadia à Bruxelles –, l'artiste continue à utiliser le motif de la fleur, soulignant la violence de l'amour, la cueillette envieuse de quelque chose de précieux. Incluse dans ce corpus, la toile composite de Kashiha *Don't Push to the Left! Keep a Move On* (2023) fait appel à la dynamique de la sculpture et représente une forme féminine abstraite en chute libre dans un dangereux déséquilibre. Dernièrement, Kashiha a commencé à recouvrir ses toiles d'un motif d'ombres pâles. Créées à l'aide de projecteurs obscurcis par des découpes de vinyle en forme de main, ces silhouettes coupées et tendues s'emparent de la violence de la beauté.

# Images et bonheur : conversation entre Hoda Kashiha et Loïc Le Gall

LL : Tu as suivi une double formation artistique : tu as étudié l'art en Iran de manière assez traditionnelle, puis tu as achevé tes études à Boston. Comment cette association de deux cultures a-t-elle influencé ta pratique de la peinture ? 

HD : L'école en Iran où j'ai obtenu ma licence des beaux-arts était conservatrice et très traditionnelle. J'aime faire référence aux dessins animés et aux caricatures dans mes œuvres, et j'apprécie particulièrement les couleurs vives. Mais dans cette école, nos professeurs expliquaient que je ne pouvais pas introduire de telles choses, sinon mes œuvres auraient l'air de cartoons ou d'illustrations. J'ai donc dû m'autocensurer car j'estimais que cela était nécessaire à ce moment-là. Lorsque je suis arrivée aux États-Unis et que j'ai vu une telle profusion de typologies d'œuvres d'art, j'ai pensé que je pouvais tout intégrer dans mes œuvres, tout ce que j'aimais, peu importe que cela soit de l'ordre de la carricature ou non. Il était possible de tout mélanger ! J'ai eu envie de réapprendre à peindre sur la toile. Même si mon école d'art à Boston était relativement classique pour le contexte américain, les artistes invités, ainsi que mes camarades de classe, ont eu un effet considérable sur ma pratique et la compréhension de ce qui était permis ou non.

LL : Je pense que ton travail est très progressiste, tant au niveau du concept que de la manière dont il est peint. Tu déclares être très influencée par les dessins animés, les cartoons et les bandes dessinées. Peux-tu m'en dire plus ?

HD : D'où cela me vient ? Je ne sais pas réellement. Quand j'étais enfant, j'achetais beaucoup de magazines avec des caricatures – je voulais devenir une caricaturiste célèbre. Je ne sais pas pourquoi. J'ai toujours fait beaucoup de portraits de ma famille et de mes amis. J'ai longtemps utilisé le style cartoon dans mes œuvres. Je pensais que c'était un bon moyen, subtil, une bonne approche, pour évoquer ce qui se passe en Iran. Les fictions et les contenus sur les réseaux sociaux – et je fais le lien avec la culture du dessin animé et de la caricature – permettent une énorme liberté, et j'aime m'en inspirer. Sur le net, les contenus sont créés presque immédiatement et rediffusés à l'infini. Il y a un effet viral. Dans une dimension où cela est difficile de tout contrôler, ces contenus peuvent colporter des histoires alternatives ou de l'humour noir. Mais lorsqu'on se réfère trop littéralement à la noirceur du monde, les œuvres deviennent de simples drames, et je ne souhaite pas m'inscrire dans une posture dramatique.

LL : La situation et le contexte iraniens influencent certainement ta peinture. Ils t'accompagnent au quotidien. C'était sans doute différent lors de ton expérience aux États-Unis ?

HD : Tu sais, chaque jour, l'actualité est saisissante dans mon pays, et il faut donc se concentrer sur soi-même, ouvrir son horizon. Les sujets que je traite reflètent également cette réalité. C'est en partie pour cela que j'ai quitté les États-Unis. La vie quotidienne y exige peut-être moins de remises en question qu'en Iran. J'ai l'impression que tout cela sous-tend mon travail. Lorsque je suis à l'atelier, mes histoires personnelles se mêlent à celles du pays dans son ensemble, et plus encore à ce qui se passe au niveau international. Ici [en Iran], chaque jour, il se passe quelque chose qui m'inspire, mais je ne désire pas en parler directement. En fin de compte, lorsque je regarde mon travail, je ne pense pas qu'il soit iranien, ni même politique. Je pense qu'il s'échappe des frontières politiques ou culturelles.

LL : C'est vrai, il est impossible de réduire ton travail au contexte iranien. Certes, il y a des formes et des motifs typiques qui peuvent rappeler l'histoire de l'art de la région, mais en fin de compte, je ne pourrais pas dire, en regardant simplement l'œuvre, si son autrice est d'origine chinoise, iranienne ou encore mexicaine. Néanmoins, il y a quelque chose que je remarque chez toi et chez d'autres artistes originaires d'Iran, comme Tala Madani (née en 1981) par exemple, à savoir une capacité à manier l'absurde.

HD : Je ne suis pas sûre que cela soit si courant actuellement. Cela fait probablement davantage partie de notre histoire.

LL : J'aimerais évoquer une œuvre importante que tu as exposée pour la première fois dans ta galerie de Téhéran, Dastan Gallery. Puis qui a été diffusée en Europe à Passerelle Centre d'art contemporain, à la galerie Nathalie Obadia à Paris et lors d'Art Basel Unlimited. Elle s'intitule *In Appreciation of Blinking* (2021). C'est une œuvre vraiment différente. Il ne s'agit pas seulement d'une peinture, mais aussi d'une installation, voire d'une sculpture. Je souhaite évoquer ici de nouvelles façons de montrer les peintures et la manière dont ce médium peut être renouvelé encore et encore. Pour cette installation, tu as choisi de placer les peintures sur des socles mobiles que l'on peut disposer à sa guise dans l'espace d'exposition. Pourquoi ce choix original ?

HD : Installer des peintures au mur, c'est tellement évident et une idée inébranlable en apparence. La plupart du temps, j'ai l'impression que cela invite juste les gens à regarder l'œuvre et à penser basiquement : « ok, j'aime ou je n'aime pas ». Le spectateur devient alors très passif. Je voulais rendre le scénario de lecture plus ludique en donnant aux visiteurs la possibilité de jouer avec les peintures. Il s'agit d'une action, d'une interaction. De plus en plus souvent, je pense non seulement à la peinture sur laquelle je travaille, mais aussi à l'espace d'exposition qui la contient. Lorsque j'installe mes toiles dans un espace, j'envisage l'atmosphère et la manière dont les publics seront activement impliqués.

LL : J'ai la nette impression que ton désir d'inclure le public apporte une certaine joie au travail. Lors de ton exposition « I'm Here, I'm not Here » en 2022 à Passerelle Centre d'art contemporain à Brest, tu as porté un regard particulier sur la manière dont les visiteurs interagissent avec ton travail. Tu as réalisé de nouvelles œuvres sculpturales et d'autres incorporant de la lumière, que je trouve très ludiques. Comment ton travail évolue-t-il aujourd'hui ? Développes-tu davantage d'installations et de displays spécifiques à chaque exposition ?

HD : En ce moment, j'ai envie de jouer avec des tissus et des toiles et de les mêler. Même dans mes peintures, je m'engage dans différentes directions. Je travaille actuellement sur trois projets différents, sans lien entre eux. L'un d'eux s'inspire de la peinture miniature indienne. L'autre est inspiré par les dessins animés de la Panthère rose. Enfin, le dernier projet est plus de l'ordre de la poésie.

J'ai récemment passé du temps à New York, et mon studio était petit. J'ai dû m'adapter à la taille du lieu. Une fois de plus, j'ai produit quelque chose qui sort, a priori, de mon style habituel. J'essaie généralement de refuser d'avoir une signature, une patte reconnaissable. Lorsqu'un artiste est coincé dans une spirale de répétition, je trouve cela très triste, même si l'œuvre fait preuve d'une grande maîtrise ou d'une grande technique. Parfois, je suis très satisfaite de ce que j'ai pu faire dans un tableau et j'en suis surprise, mais je ne veux pas le reproduire, alors je pars dans la direction opposée pour l'œuvre suivante. Je déteste avoir des certitudes dans mon travail, et pour moi c'est ainsi que l'art conserve son caractère ludique.

LL : J'aime la façon dont tu tentes de brouiller les pistes ! Tu as parlé d'une nouvelle série sur le personnage iconique de la Panthère rose. Je suis particulièrement intrigué car lors de ton exposition à Brest, tu as montré pour la première fois tes courts métrages d'animation. Ces courtes vidéos sont des points de départ pour de nouvelles peintures, n'est-ce pas ?

HD : Il m'arrive de faire des croquis sur mon iPad, qui prennent la forme, en effet, d'une courte vidéo, et de commencer ensuite une peinture sur le même principe.

LL : Tu crées des images animées, puis elles deviennent fixes. Je trouve cette relation avec les vidéos et les dessins animés assez magique et belle, parce qu'elle ouvre à une culture populaire que beaucoup de gens connaissent et peuvent apprécier. Pour en revenir à l'installation *In Appreciation of Blinking*, la première fois que tu l'as exposée, c'était à Téhéran ; et tu as dû recouvrir une partie de la peinture. Je présume qu'il y a une quelconque censure derrière cela ?

HD : Je n'ai pas été autorisée à montrer une partie de l'œuvre représentant un homme avec une langue. J'ai dû la recouvrir. Finalement, c'était intéressant parce que j'ai recouvert la langue d'un autocollant. À cette époque, je développais une autre série, *I Am Here, I Am Not Here* (2020), qui questionnait la censure. Cette série traite de la manière dont nous pouvons être supprimés, ignorés ou effacés, par le pouvoir ou par la mort. J'ai répété le même sujet sur plusieurs de mes peintures : un corps est tantôt couvert d'une marque rouge ou d'une forme noire, tantôt il est déformé. Dans certains pays, la censure en vient à faire recouvrir de formes noires les corps jugés « impudiques », ou témoignant de thèmes contestataires. J'ai tenté de trouver ce qu'il reste de nous après la mort et notre disparition, lorsque notre regard s'éteint.

LL : Cela me fait penser aux livres qui sont expurgés en Iran.

HD : Lorsque j'étais à l'école, beaucoup de livres étaient censurés, avec des passages noircis. Je m'interrogeais : « est-ce que c'est caché par magie ? ». Les nus et certaines figures disparaissaient. C'était intriguant car cela créait un nouveau type d'esthétique. On savait qu'il y avait un corps nu, mais on ne le voyait pas. Cela permettait à nos imaginations de phosphorer. Que se cache-t-il derrière tout cela ? Parfois, une nouvelle version d'un tableau est « curatée » par le gouvernement. Ces actions suscitent d'autres réflexions, par exemple : si vous mourez ou si vous êtes effacé par le pouvoir, existez-vous encore ? J'ai donc réalisé la série *I Am Here, I Am Not Here*, puis *In Appreciation of Blinking*, et l'œuvre a été censurée. J'ai eu l'impression d'une certaine manière que la boucle était bouclée.

LL : Les images de femmes sont au cœur de ton travail. Et ce que tu expliques, c'est que le pouvoir réprime les corps dans l'espace public, en particulier le corps des femmes. Cherches-tu des stratagèmes pour les montrer tout de même ? Car dans certaines de tes peintures, tu utilises des styles particuliers qui masquent ou modifient les formes et donc la lecture, comme le cubisme par exemple. Je pense en particulier à *Looking at the Mirror* (2021).

HD : Les corps sont très importants dans mon travail. Ils le façonnent. Quand je conçois une peinture abstraite, elle vient du corps, qui est si abstrait lui-même. Et le spectateur ne peut pas forcément le comprendre, c'est ce point qui m'intéresse toujours. En ce moment, c'est au cœur de mes recherches sur les miniatures persanes et indiennes. Je tente des combinaisons de cubisme, de peintures indiennes et de miniatures iraniennes. Encore une fois, le corps d'une femme est impliqué dans son environnement quotidien. Cette idée s'est imposée dans mon travail après « Femme, Vie, Liberté[1] ». Je suis devenue plus curieuse de la représentation des cheveux, et j'ai commencé à regarder les peintures indiennes. Celles-ci montrent beaucoup de cheveux et de corps féminins, qui sont alignées avec la nature, avec les fleurs. J'ai également commencé à travailler avec un tour de potier qui amène un rapport très direct avec la peau et la chair. Les vases et autres céramiques que j'ai fabriqués évoquaient cette fois intentionnellement des corps féminins.

LL : Tu trouves des stratégies évasives et originales pour montrer les corps. Tu as mentionné le fait de changer délibérément de style pour ne pas t'enliser dans une monotonie et une facilité, mais la représentation des corps est restée un fil rouge dans ton œuvre. Je pense qu'il y a différents niveaux de compréhension et de lecture dans ta manière de changer constamment de style. Je sais que tu regardes beaucoup les réseaux sociaux, qui sont une fenêtre sur un catalogue d'infinité d'images. Lorsque l'on regarde les contenus artistiques, quand on lit les magazines d'art contemporain, on découvre qu'il y a des milliers de styles différents. Quand on est sur les réseaux sociaux, on a accès au monde entier, et c'est sûrement la beauté de ces outils. Tes peintures sont souvent liées aux événements ou à des trends diffusés sur réseaux sociaux. Par exemple, lors des grandes manifestations en Iran il y a quelques années, certains ont posté des carrés noirs sur Instagram en signe de solidarité et de protestation. Et tu as repris ce symbole dans l'une de tes peintures, *My Sincere Love to Kazimir Malevich, Black on Black* (2020). C'était juste avant le mouvement Black Lives Matter, qui a également utilisé le carré noir comme

1
« Femme, Vie, Liberté » est un slogan qui a vu le jour au sein des mouvements kurdes dirigés par des femmes, avant de transcender son contexte initial et d'acquérir une reconnaissance mondiale à la suite des manifestations de 2022 en Iran, déclenchées par la mort de Mahsa Amini. La Police de la moralité du gouvernement iranien, avait arrêté Amini parce qu'elle ne portait pas le hijab conformément aux normes gouvernementales.

signe sur les réseaux sociaux. Inclus-tu souvent des éléments signifiant de ce type dans ton travail ?

HD : Oui, mais pas toujours. Je ne m'impose pas de le faire, mais si je vois quelque chose au hasard et que j'établis une relation entre mon travail et cette idée, cela me préoccupe. Je suis libre de le faire, c'est-à-dire de les intégrer à mon travail. Je pense que ma peinture est comme un réceptacle à rebuts. Pour moi, la peinture est comme ça. Mes idées viennent des médias sociaux, des dessins animés, de l'actualité, puis je les mêle, toutes ensemble. Je les peins et je peux me lancer dans une autre expérience. En ce qui concerne la peinture que tu viens de mentionner, je pensais alors à la question du noir à cause des manifestations lorsque les gens partageaient des carrés noirs sur leur Instagram. Et puis j'ai recommencé à étudier en détail l'idée du noir. J'étais également tellement obsédée par Malevitch à cette époque que j'ai trouvé comment les regrouper dans cette œuvre.

LL : Il est étonnant que tu te sois obsédée par le noir, car ton travail était alors tout à fait à l'opposé, tout en couleurs.

HD : Les gens disent que le noir n'attire pas et ne se vend pas. Mon travail était si coloré que j'avais peut-être peur de peindre en noir. J'ai donc délibérément essayé de me mettre au défi de cette manière. Je réfléchissais au concept du noir et je voulais faire quelque chose de stimulant pour moi.

LL : Parler du sombre et de l'obscurité m'amène à vouloir parler de son antithèse : l'humour dans ton travail. Il y a énormément de blagues et de choses amusantes dans tes peintures, n'est-ce pas ?

HD : J'aime vraiment créer un moment suspendu dans l'exposition où les publics peuvent venir observer mon travail, rire ou pleurer avec lui, puis repartir. Lorsque les œuvres sont simplement drôles, les gens ne les prennent pas au sérieux. J'aime parler de la vie. Après la révolution en Iran il y a dix ans, j'avais une vingtaine d'années, et lorsque je visitais des galeries ou d'autres expositions d'art à Téhéran, je voyais beaucoup de peintures inspirées par Lucian Freud et Francis Bacon. Il y avait tant de mauvaises peintures représentant des corps fragmentés. C'était tellement laid. Je ne pense pas que nous devrions tous parler uniquement de bonheur, mais il ne s'agissait pas d'esthétique et de forme, il s'agissait simplement d'inviter les gens à la laideur. C'était comme un prestige, une vantardise intellectuelle ou une annonce dépressive. La raison pour laquelle j'apprécie introduire des choses drôles dans mes œuvres est que je veux inviter les gens à voir des points spécifiques, des choses dures qui sont en même temps drôles ou intéressantes. Je ne souhaite pas montrer uniquement la laideur de la vie.

LL : Ta peinture célèbre la vie et le fait d'être en vie. Et c'est beau, surtout actuellement où le monde est ravagé par des politiques destructrices. Tes œuvres sont telles des bouffées d'air frais, mais si l'on désire approfondir leur signification derrière le vernis, il faut observer la marche du monde aujourd'hui. Il y a tellement de niveaux pour comprendre ton travail, c'est sérieux tout en étant dérisoire.

HD : Tu viens de préciser un objectif important de ma pratique : c'est sérieux, tout en étant léger. La peinture est comme un puzzle. Tu t'aventures dans diverses directions, puis tu tentes de trouver les différentes pièces complémentaires et de les assembler.

LL : Le puzzle est une belle métaphore.

HD : *In Appreciation of Blinking* était pour moi une allégorie sur la vie et la mort par exemple. La fragilité de la vie est importante, parce que la vie est si tragique.

LL : La tragédie dans une série ! J'ai une dernière question sur ta manière d'envisager ton corpus d'œuvres : as-tu toujours travaillé en série ?

HD : Je n'ai pas toujours été une artiste qui pense en séries, mais je le suis de plus en plus. Peut-être parce que mon esprit se concentre aujourd'hui sur la narration. J'aime raconter des histoires. Oui, c'est la raison. Mon travail s'oriente de plus en plus vers les séries parce que j'ai besoin de déployer des histoires !

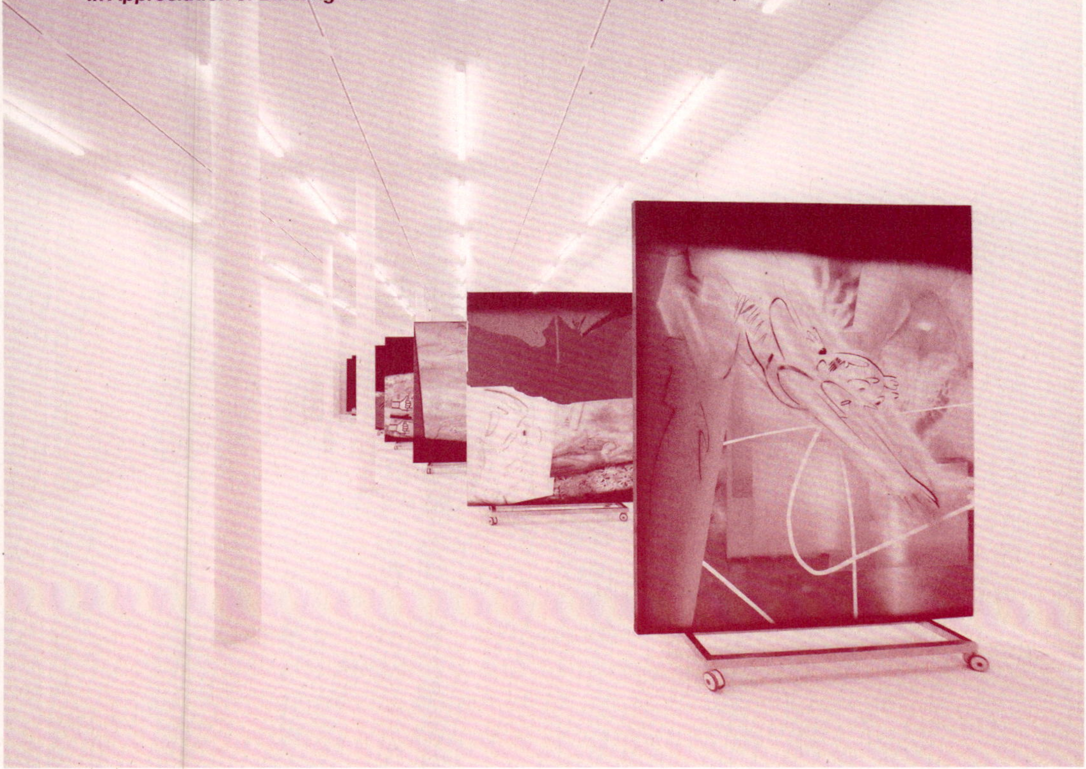

*In Appreciation of Blinking* installation view at Parallel Circuit, Tehran, 2021. Photo: Matin Jameie

*In Appreciation of Blinking* installation view at Galerie Nathalie Obadia, Paris, 2022. Photo: Aurélien Mole

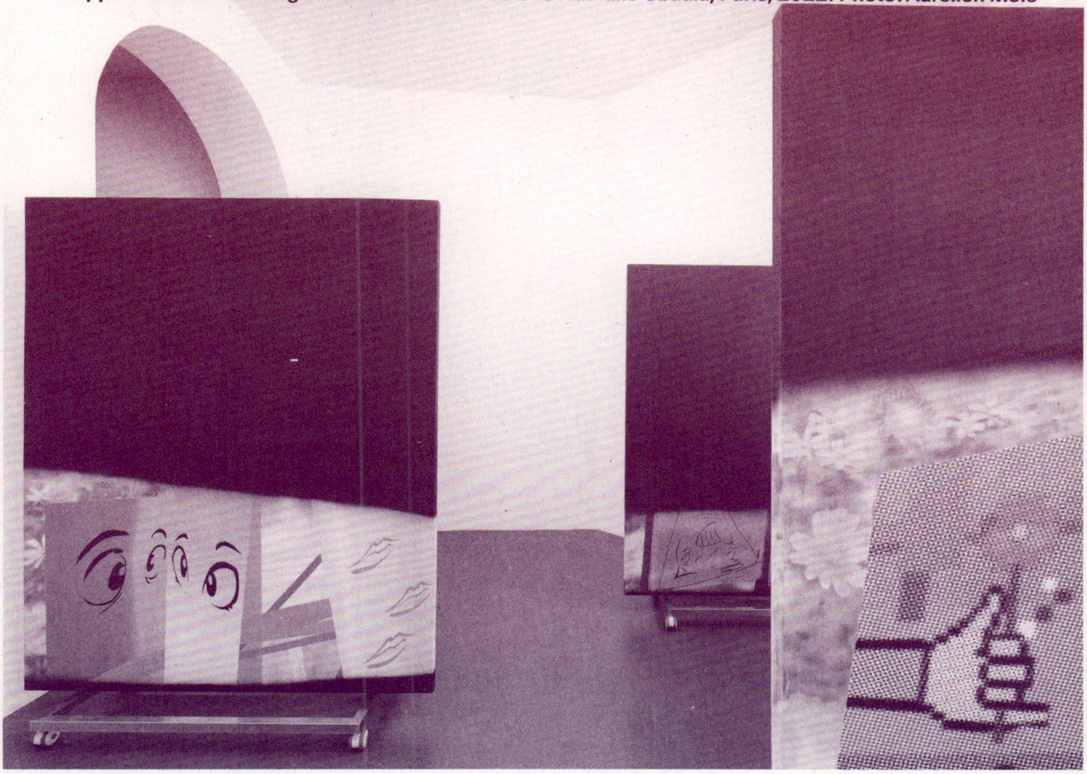

*Another world is waiting for us* installation view at Galerie Nathalie Obadia, Brussels, 2023.
Photo: We Document Art

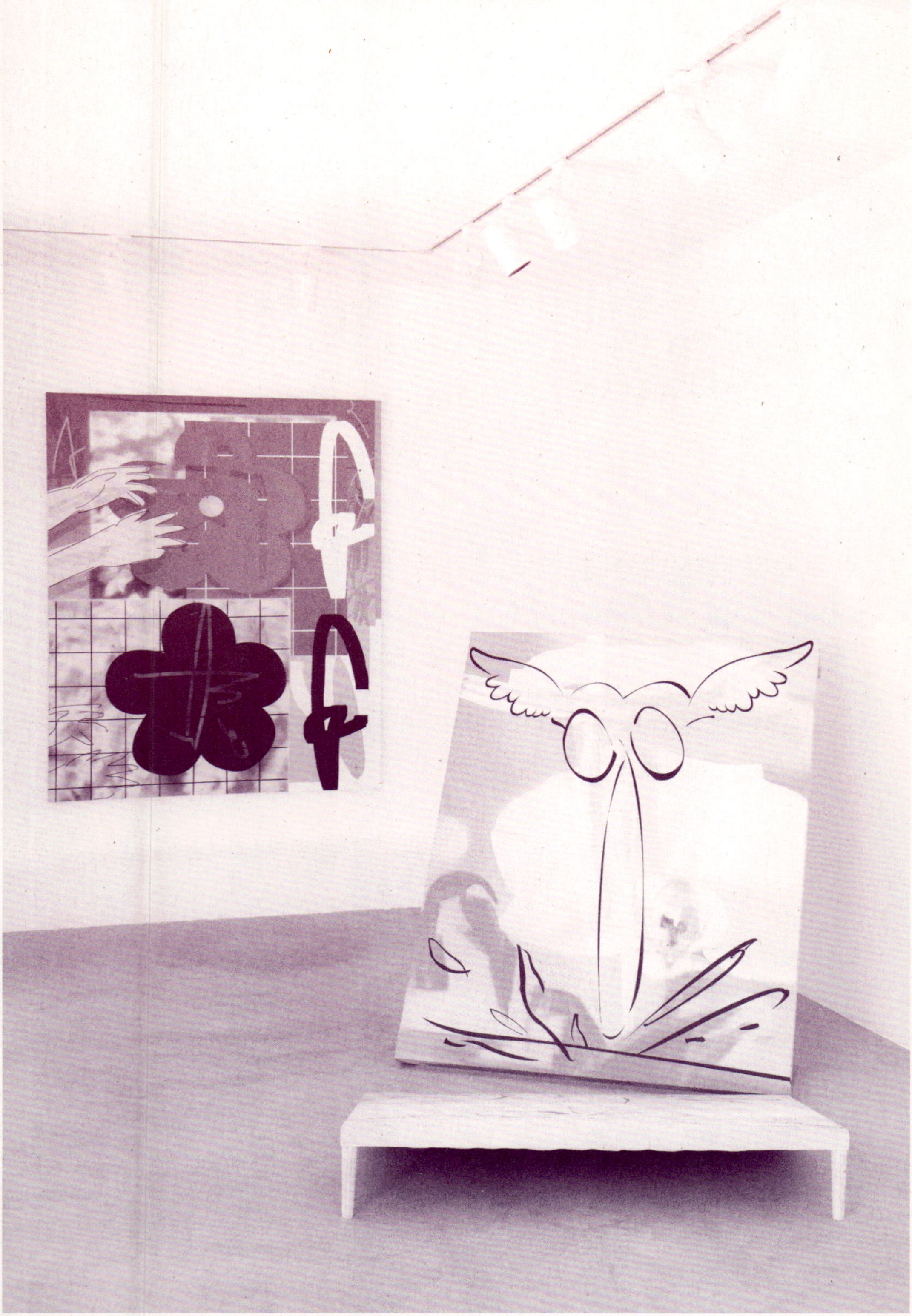

*Another world is waiting for us* installation view at Galerie Nathalie Obadia, Brussels, 2023. Photo: We Document Art

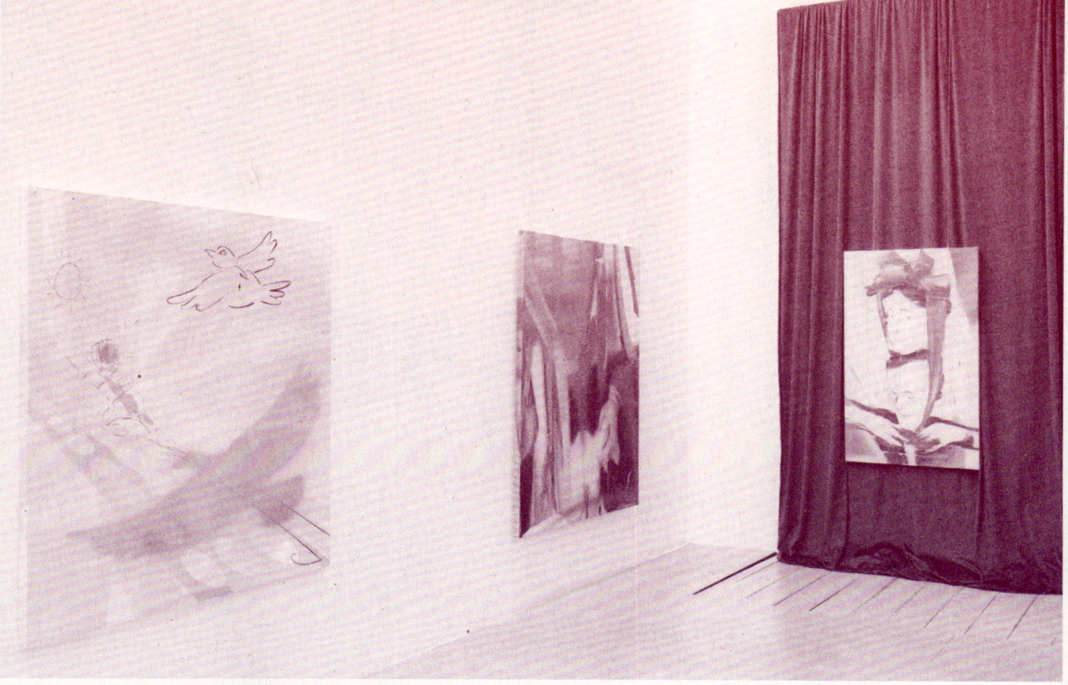

*Dear St. Agatha I Am Witness of Your Tears, in the Land of Tulips* installation view at Galerie Nathalie Obadia, Brussels, 2020. Photo: We Document Art

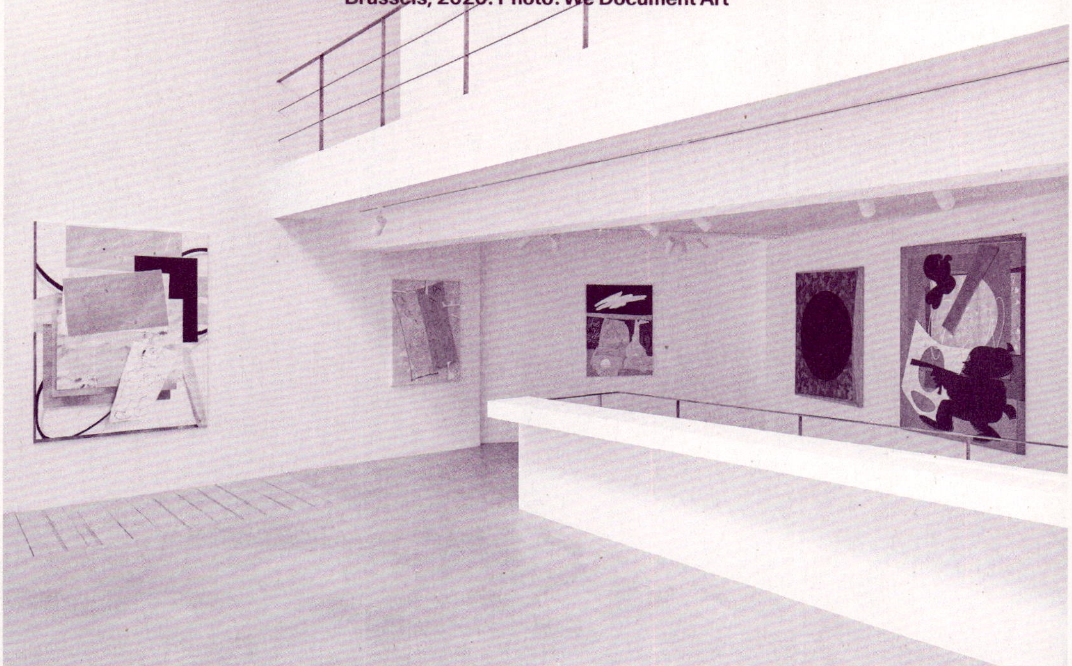

*I'm Here, I'm not Here* installation view at Passerelle Centre d'art contemporain, Brest, 2022.
Photo: Aurélien Mole

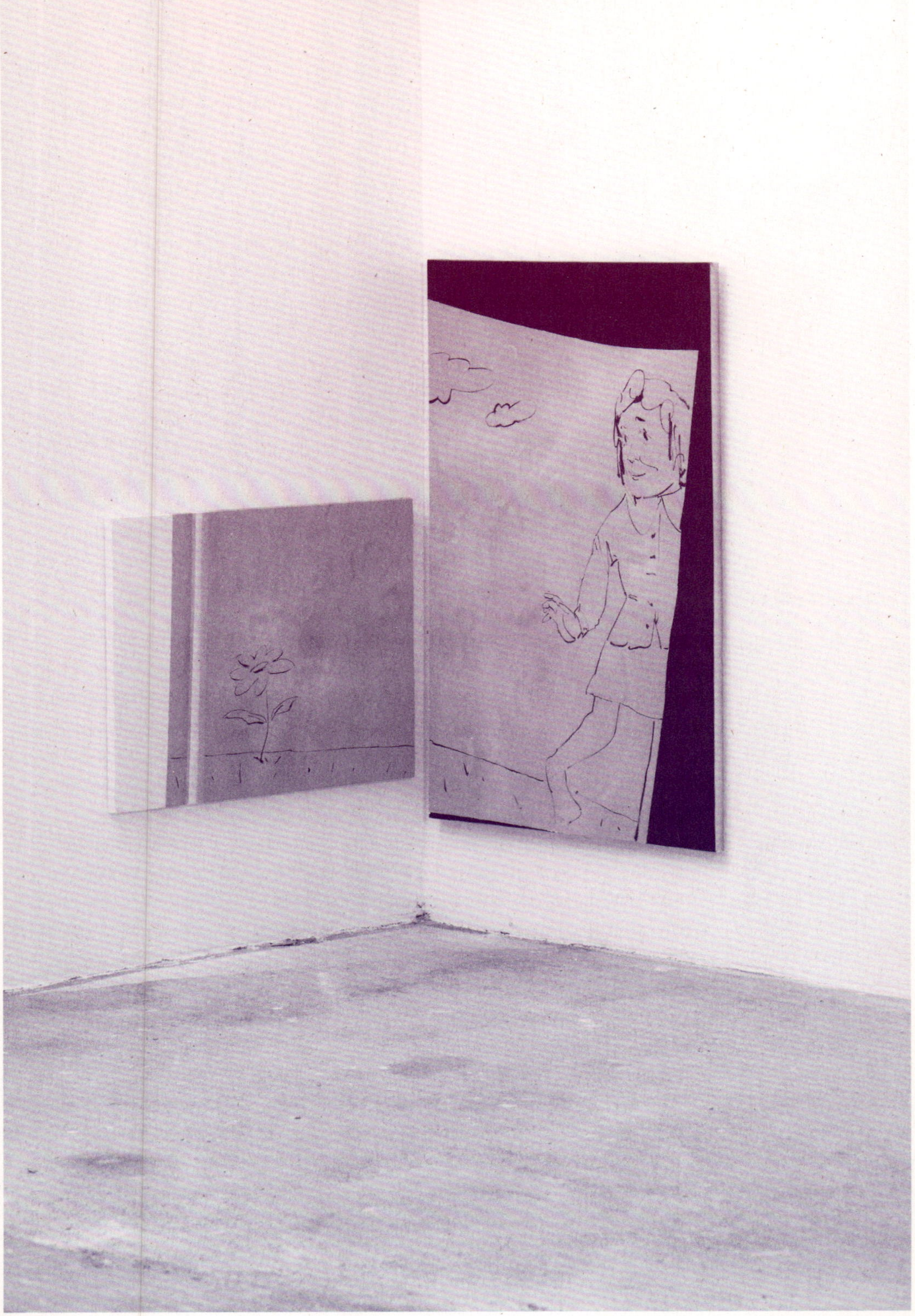

*I'm Here, I'm not Here* installation view at Passerelle Centre d'art contemporain, Brest, 2022.
Photo: Aurélien Mole

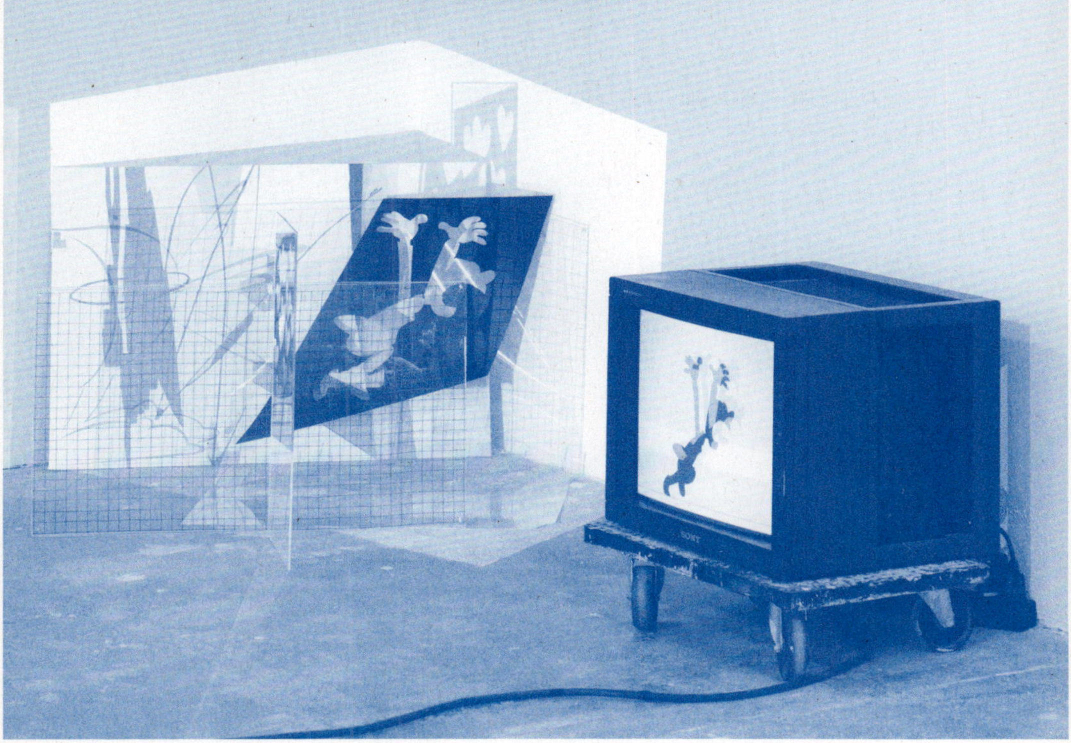

*Prospect* installation view at Parallel Circuit, Tehran, 2023. Photo: Matin Jameie

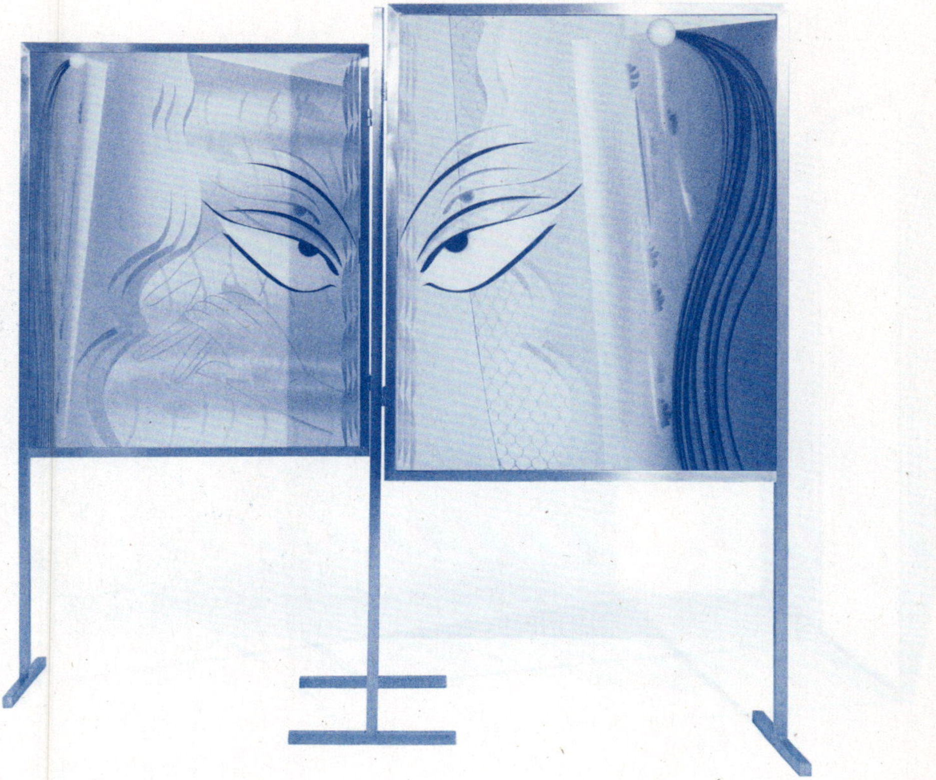

*Farewell to My Shadow*, 2023. Steel, 150 × 120 cm. Photo: Matin Jameie

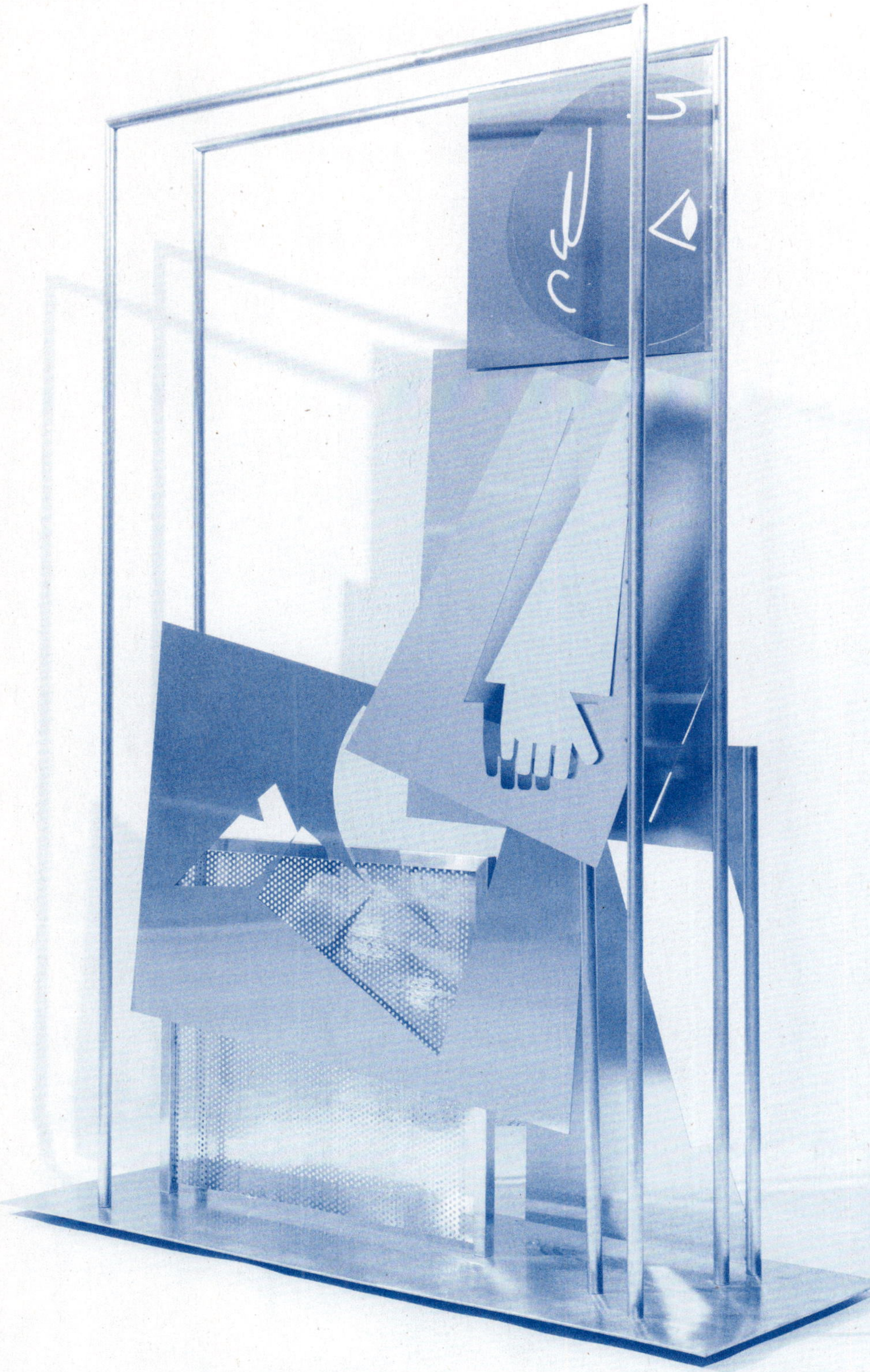

Artist Studio, 2021. Photo: Hoda Kashiha

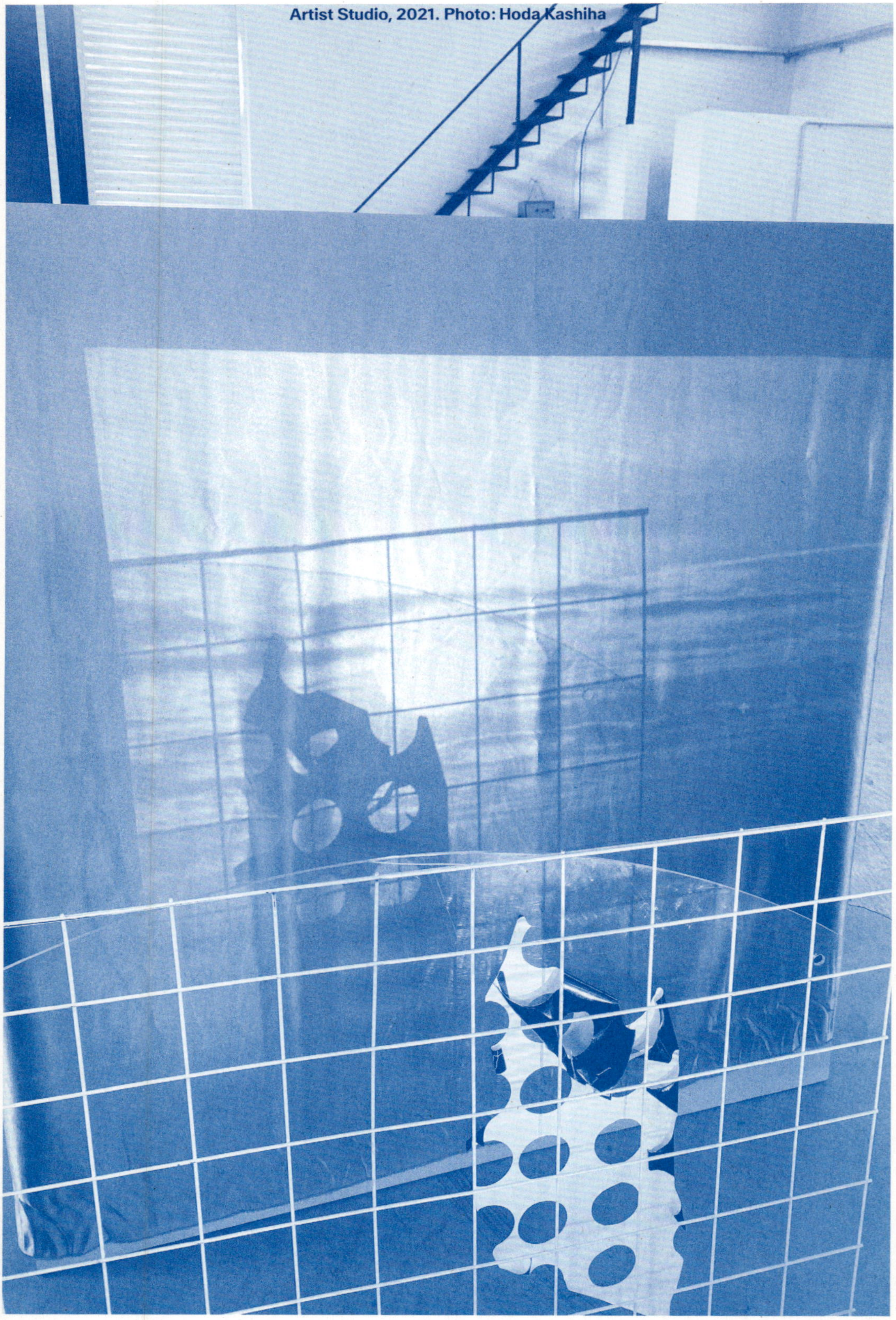

Artist Studio, 2023. Photo: Hoda Kashiha

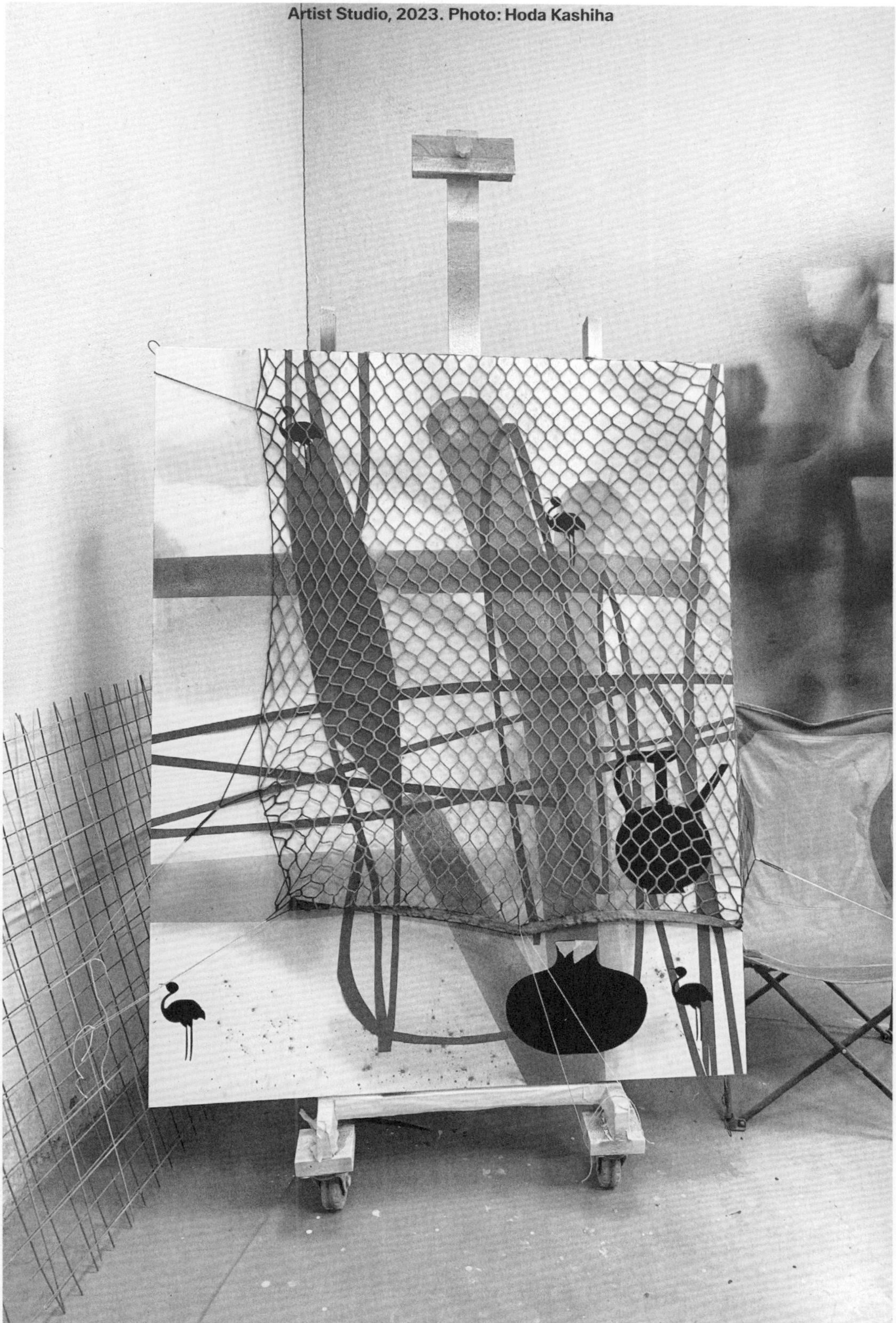

*Two Methods for Separating Sun from Flower*, 2022, *100 years*, seventh annual group exhibition in collaboration between Jeffrey Deitch and Gagosian, Miami, 2022. Photo: Sebastiano Pellion di Parsano

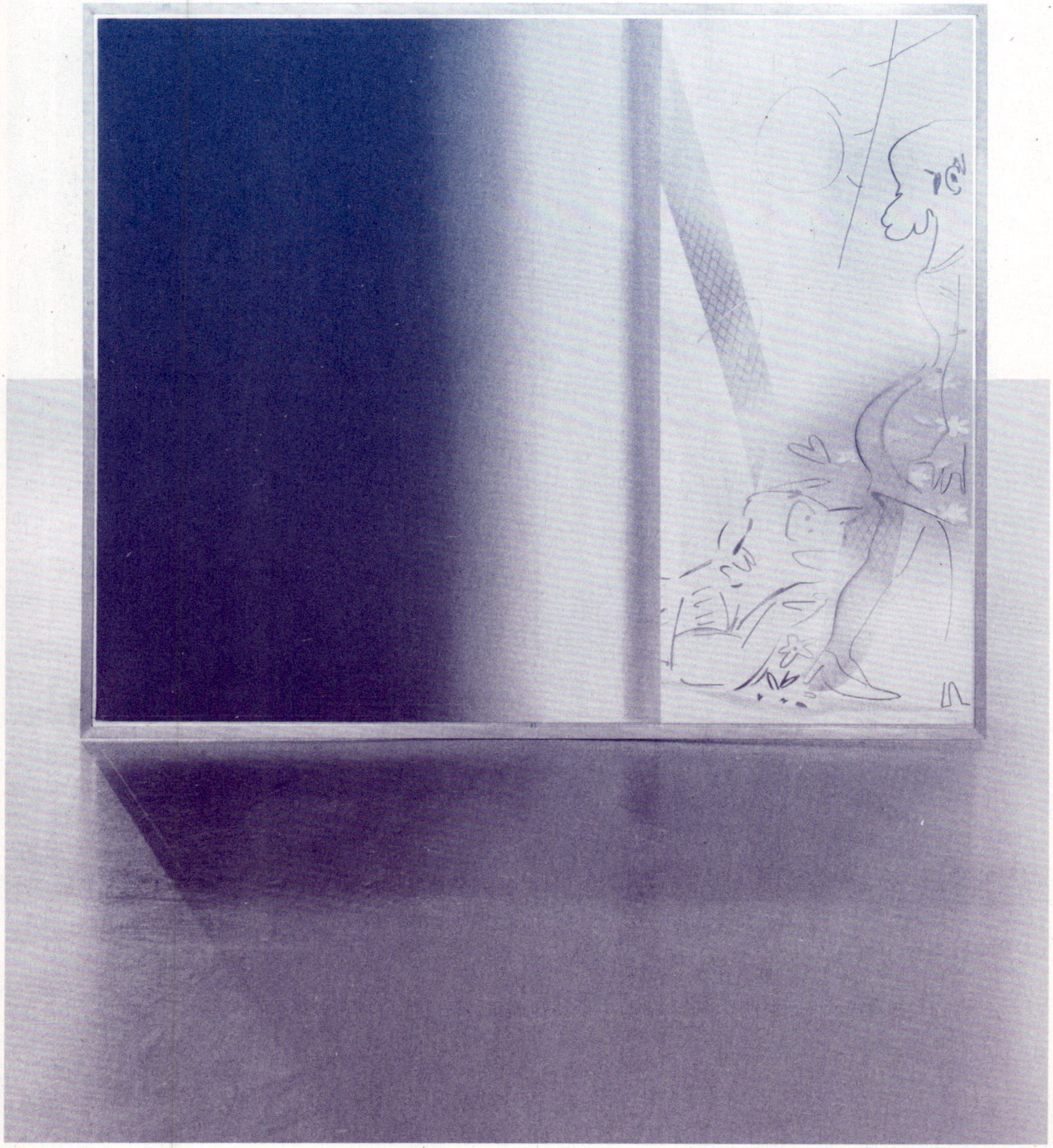

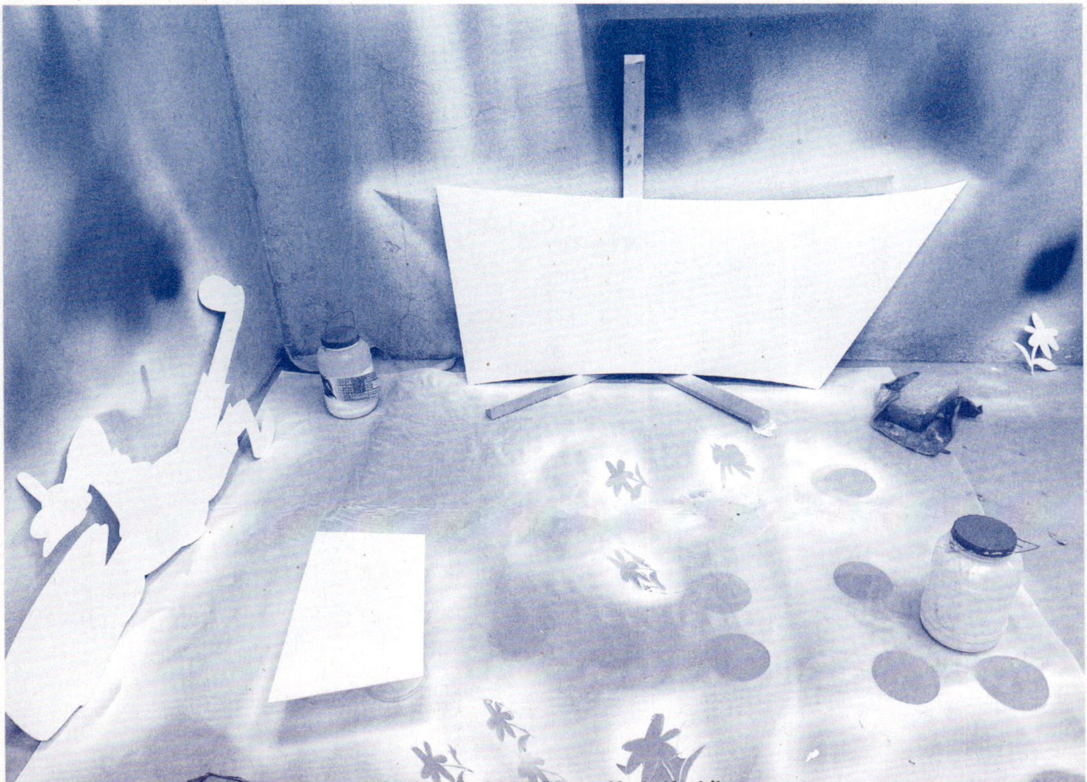

Artist Studio, 2021. Photo: Hoda Kashiha

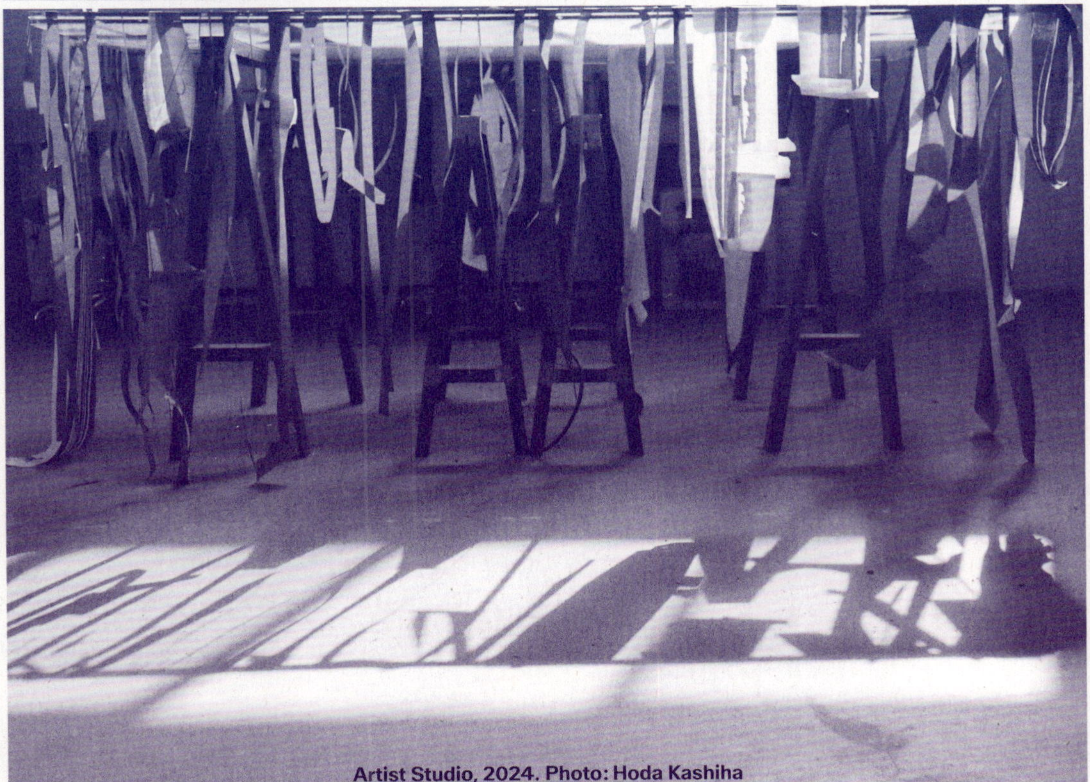

Artist Studio, 2024. Photo: Hoda Kashiha

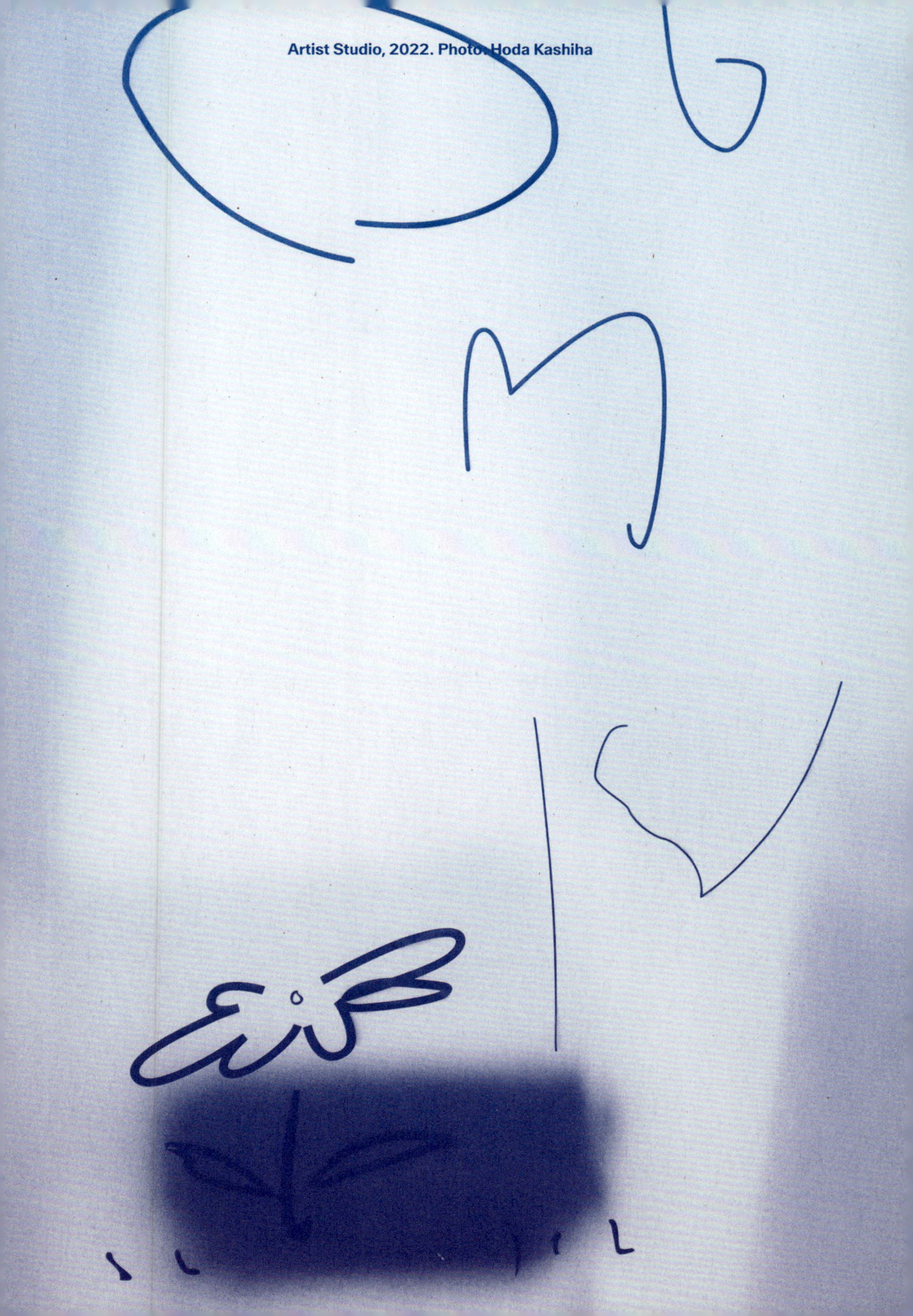

Artist Studio, 2022. Photo: Hoda Kashiha

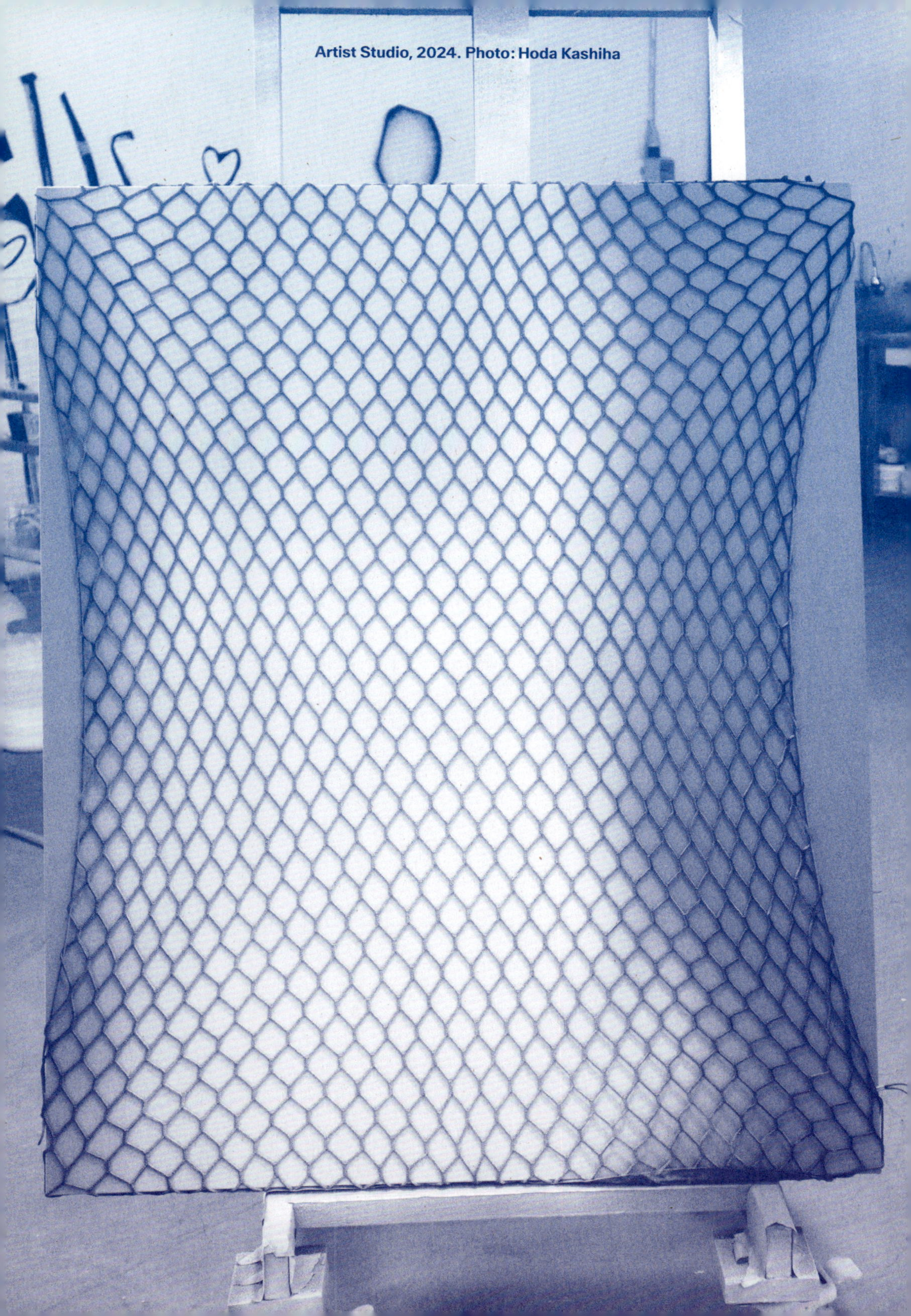

Artist Studio, 2024. Photo: Hoda Kashiha

Artist Studio, 2023. Photo: Hoda Kashiha

Artist Studio, 2023. Photo: Hoda Kashiha

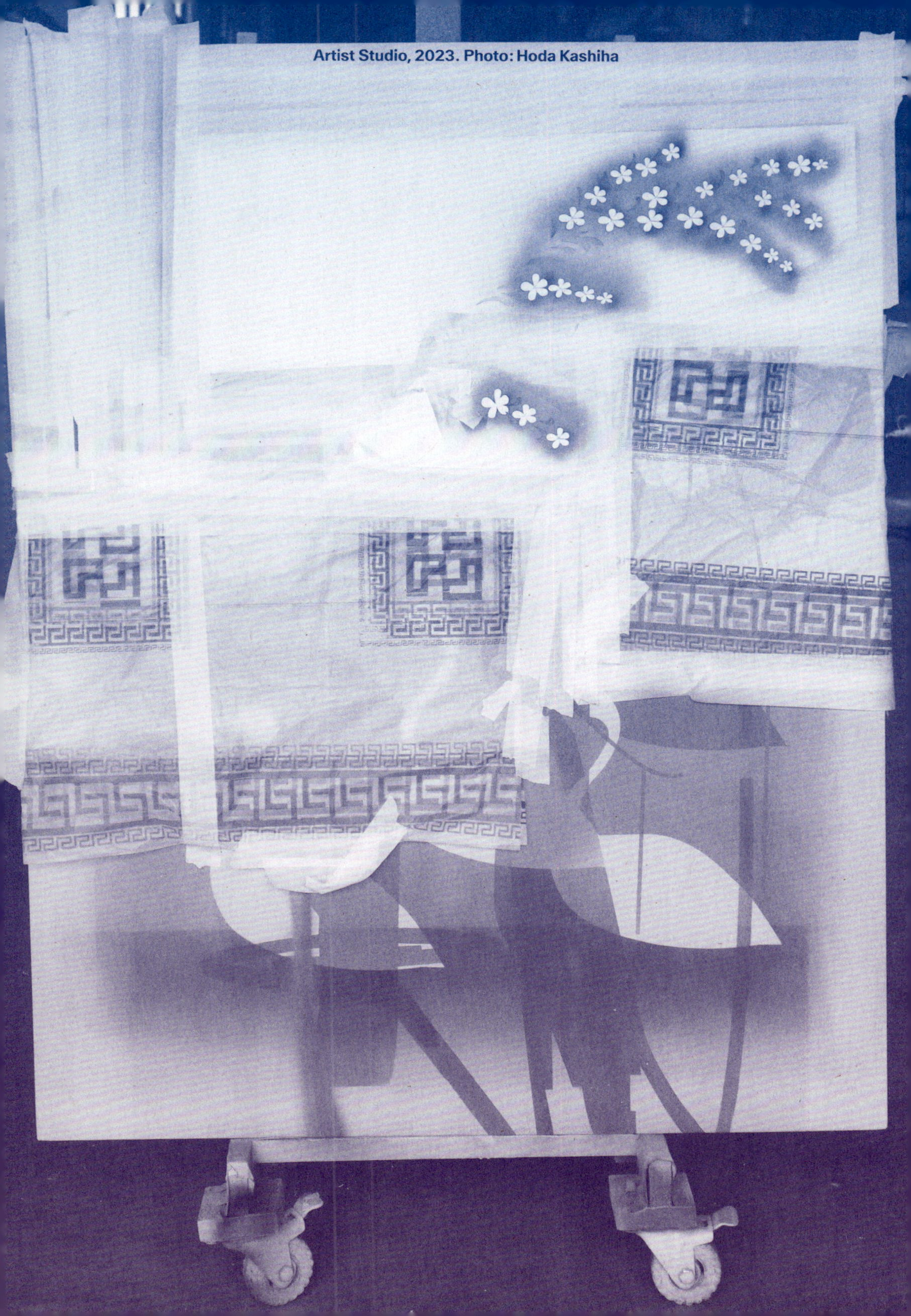

# آن سایه هایی که می افکنند

لیلیان دیویس

همین تازگی‌ها هدی کاشی‌ها به من گفت «دراوایل [برخوردها] دوست دارم ملیتم را پنهان کنم». کاشی‌ها در تهران و در سال‌های پایانی جنگ ایران و عراق به دنیا آمد، جنگی که با حمله‌ی عراق به ایران آغاز شد و با بیش از نیم میلیون کشته در ایران به پایان رسید. فرانسه و آمریکا به طور رسمی از عراق حمایت می‌کردند، با این که سوء ظن‌هایی مبنی بر استفاده‌ی عراق از تسلیحات شیمیایی وجود داشت. در تابستان ۱۹۸۷، یک سال پس از تولد کاشی‌ها، یادم هست که در تلویزیون مردی با موهای کوتاه و لباس ارتشی زیتونی دیدم که در جایی در جنوب آمریکا بود. این مرد سرهنگ دوم، الیور نورث از شورای امنیت ملی ایالات متحده بود که تحت تحقیقات قرار داشت؛ به اتهام طراحی و اجرای روشی برای فروش اسلحه به ایران برای تأمین مالی کنتراهای ضد انقلابی نیکاراگوئه، در شرایطی که تحریم‌های آمریکا برقرار بود. کاشی‌ها و من، که کودکانی در دو سوی یک شکاف فزاینده‌ی سیاسی و ایدئولوژیک بودیم، هردو شاهد لحظاتی از یک روایت خطرناک تکه‌تکه شده بودیم. کاشی‌ها کار هنری خود را به مطالعه‌ی این تکه‌ها و سایه‌هایی که می‌افکنند اختصاص داده است.

کاشی‌ها در پایتخت ایران بزرگ شده. او ، در کلاس‌های فوق برنامه‌ی کانون پرورش فکری کودکان و نوجوانان شرکت می‌کرد. شروع این برنامه‌ها که به «کانون» معروف شد، به دهه‌ی ۱۹۶۰ و کمک‌های فرح دیبا به دوستش لیلی امیر ارجمند برای تأسیس کتابخانه‌ای برای کودکان برمی‌گردد. قفسه‌های این کتابخانه پر شد از کتاب‌های کودکان که از خارج از کشور آمده و به فارسی ترجمه شده بودند، و خیلی زود کانون شروع به انتشار داستان‌های ایرانی و برگزاری کارگاه‌هایی مخصوص کودکان و نوجوانان برای نویسندگی خلاق، تئاتر و سینما کرد «کانون به محلی برای رشد برخی از شناخته شده‌ترین هنرمندان کشور تبدیل شد » و هنوز، هرچند با ظرفیت کمتر، به فعالیت خود ادامه میدهد.
۱

کاشی‌ها در کودکی اغلب از موزه‌ی هنرهای معاصر تهران دیدن می‌کرد؛ موزه‌ای که معماری آن‌را کامران دیبا طراحی کرده و در سال ۱۹۷۷ افتتاح شد. تابستان سال بعد از گشایش این موزه، اولین نمایش هنری فضای باز ایران در باغ‌های موزه برگزار شد. در ایران، حمایت دولتی از هنر در دهه‌ی ۱۹۵۰ آغاز شده بود و اولین دوسالانه‌ی تهران در بهار ۱۹۵۸ مخاطبین بین‌المللی را به خود جذب کرد. اداره‌ی کل هنرهای زیبای کشور (که بعداً به وزارت فرهنگ تبدیل شد) باعث شد تا مشاغلی در بخش فرهنگ و هنر شکل بگیرد، سفارش آثار هنری ممکن شود و ارتباط با طیف‌های روبه‌رشد مجموعه‌داران فراهم شود.۲
با افزایش حمایت بخش‌های دولتی و خصوصی از هنر، نسل اول هنرمندان مدرن ظهور کرد؛ از میان آن‌ها شاید بهمن محصص (۱۹۳۱ - ۲۰۱۰) با نقاشی‌ها و مجسمه‌های «سورئالیستی،

شمایل‌شکنانه» بیش‌تر از همه شناخته‌شده باشد.۳ بهجت صدر (۲۰۰۹–۱۹۲۴)، از معاصران محصص، مرجع و منبع الهامی مهم برای کاشی‌ها محسوب میشود. صدر در مورد کلاژهای عکس خود به صراحت می‌گفت: «ما باید از هر چیزی که می‌تواند احساسات زمان ما را بیان کند استفاده کنیم و وام بگیریم، صفحات مجلات را پاره کنیم، آن‌ها را به هم بچسبانیم و دوباره ابزارهای جدیدی پیدا کنیم.»۴ شادی قدیریان (م. ۱۹۷۴)، که زیر نظر بهمن جلالی آموزش دیده، یکی از شناخته‌شده‌ترین هنرمندان نسل دوم ایران است، نسلی که پس از سرنگونی شاه توسط جمهوری اسلامی و قطع بسیاری از روابط بین‌المللی شکل گرفت.

کاشی‌ها هم مثل نقاشانی چون سام سمیعی (م. ۱۹۸۸) و آلا دهقان (م. ۱۹۸۲)، متعلق به نسل سوم هنرمندانی است که پس از ۱۱ سپتامبر و پس از ورود حراجی‌ها به منطقه ظهور کردند. (کریستیز اولین حراج دبی خود را در سال ۲۰۰۶ افتتاح کرد.) در همین دوران بود که تحصیل در دانشگاه‌های خارجی و برگزاری نمایش‌های بین‌المللی دوباره بین هنرمندان ایرانی رایج شد. این‌طور که کاشی‌ها به من می‌گوید، اگر یک رویداد تاریخی باشد که بتوان با آن نسل چهارم هنرمندان کشور را تعریف کرد، ظهور اینستاگرام است.

کاشی‌ها پیش از تحصیل در دوره‌ی کارشناسی هنرهای زیبا در دانشگاه تهران، در دبیرستان غیردولتی دخترانه‌ی نرجس در مرکز شهر تهران درس می‌خواند. در کتابخانه ی مرکزی دانشگاه، تصاویر برهنه در کتابهای نقاشی اروپایی به صورت سیستماتیک سانسور میشوند. این سانسور، تصویرها را تغییر می‌دهد؛ «تولد ونوس» (۸۶-۱۴۸۵) اثر ساندرو بوتیچلی را در نظر بگیرید و تصور کنید که به شکل مستطیل‌های سیاه‌رنگی درآمده که روی یک منظره قرار گرفته‌اند. چنین سانسوری بر نوعی ممنوعیت کلی بر نقاشی به سبک اروپایی دلالت دارد. چند سال بعد که کاشی‌ها در بوستون شروع به تحصیل کرد، بیش‌تر مشغول طراحی بود؛ که شاید با توجه به پیشینه‌ی او و همچنین مهارتش در طنز سیاه، جای تعجب نداشته باشد. (ایمی سیل‌من، نقاش آمریکایی، معتقد است که همه‌ی نقاشان بزرگ کمیک ، در ذات خود طراح هستند.)۵ دانا فرانکفورت، استاد کاشی‌ها در بوستون، او را تشویق کرد که روی بوم نقاشی کند.۶ به مرور زمان، اعتماد به نفس این هنرمند جوان در این رسانه‌ی جدید بالاتر رفت و مقیاس کارهایش بزرگتر شد. کاشی‌ها حین تحصیل در دوره‌ی کارشناسی ارشد هنرهای زیبا در رشته‌ی نقاشی، اولین نمایش انفرادی خود را در گالری اعتماد در تهران برگزار کرد.۷

کاشی‌ها در سال ۲۰۱۶ پس از اتمام تحصیلاتش در آمریکا به تهران بازگشت. این دوره همزمان با گسترش تحریم‌های بین‌المللی

و افزایش ناآرامی‌های سیاسی بود. او برای دستیابی به توازن و جریان‌یافتن نوعی تعادل در کار هنری‌اش شروع به تمرین روزانه‌ی یوگا و شنای منظم کرد. کاشی‌ها در نقاشی «شناکردن و ((ذوب‌شدن))» (۲۰۱۷)، با غوطه‌ورکردن و پاک‌کردن یک فیگور تکه‌تکه شده بازی کرده و از تکنیک‌های دادائیستی برای مختل‌کردن یک منظره‌ی دیجیتالی صفحه‌مانند که مملو از تصاویر کارتونی آماده است، استفاده می‌کند. سال بعد، در گالری بلیچه هرتلینگ در پاریس، نقاشی «رؤیا ابر می‌سازد» (۲۰۱۸) را به نمایش گذاشت که تقابل دو چهره‌ی عروسکی را در میان لکه‌های اسپری آبی نشان می‌دهد، لکه‌هایی که شبیه تکه‌های شیشه هستند.

دنیله بلیچه، گالری‌دار ساکن پاریس، در سفری به ایران که توسط بنیاد پژمان ترتیب داده شده بود به استودیوی هدی کاشی‌ها آمد و با او و هرمز همتیان، گالری‌دار جوان که مؤسس زیرزمین دستان است، آشنا شد. بلیچه از همتیان دعوت کرد تا نمایشی را در پاریس برگزار کند. نتیجه‌ی این دعوت، نمایش «نفت پردیس» بود که ارجاعی آشکار به صنعت نفت در خلیج فارس داشت. در این نمایش، نقاشی «رؤیا ابر می‌سازد» اثر کاشی‌ها در کنار آثاری از اردشیر محصص، سام سمیعی و پروانه اعتمادی (م. ۱۹۴۸) قرار گرفت.

در ابتدای همه‌گیری کرونا، کاشی‌ها از تهران به خانه‌ای در حاشیه‌ی شهر نقل مکان کرد که حدود یک ساعت با مرکز شهر فاصله دارد. او از آن زمان تاکنون در این خانه مستقر بوده است. کاشی‌ها یک انبار بزرگ را به استودیوی خود تبدیل کرد، فضایی که به بزرگی یک زمین تنیس است. این فضا یادآور سازوکارهای ورزش و نظم است و با او سازگاری خوبی دارد: «من نقاشی را راهی برای فکرکردن می‌دانم. سعی می‌کنم یک زمین بازی برای خودم ایجاد کنم».۸

در تابستان ۲۰۲۰، همزمان با وقفه‌ای کوتاه در محدودیت‌های کرونایی بلژیک، نخستین نمایش انفرادی هدی کاشیها در اروپا با عنوان «ای سنت آگاتای عزیز، من شاهد اشک‌هایت در سرزمین لاله‌ها هستم» در گالری ناتالی اوبادیا در بروکسل برگزار شد؛ عنوانی که به قدیس حامی شهیدان و قربانیان تجاوز اشاره دارد. در اثری با همین نام، فیگور یک زن شکنجه‌شده، که ظاهراً زیر نظر یک جفت چشم غول‌پیکر انیمه‌ای است، با دسته‌ی بزرگی از لاله‌های قرمز رنگ مواجه شده. گل لاله بومی ایران و گل ملی این کشور است. افسانه‌ای وجود دارد که می‌گوید هرجا یک سرباز وطن کشته می‌شود، یک گل لاله‌ی قرمز می‌روید.

اندکی پس از این نمایش، هنرمند روندِ «تخریب روایت خطی» مورد نظر خود را شتاب بخشید و در نمایش «در ستایش

پلک‌زدن» (۲۰۲۰-۲۰۲۱)، هر یک از هشت نقاشی بزرگ مجموعه را روی پایه‌های فلزی چرخدار نصب کرد.۹ کاشی‌ها در این نمایش از «ناباوری سنت توماس» (۲-۱۶۰۱) اثر کاراواجو اقتباس کرده؛ او یک توالی از تصاویر کلاژشده که با لکه‌های اکریلیک سیاه پوشیده شده می‌سازد و رنگ سیاه به تدریج در هریک از نقاشی‌ها فضای کادر را از بالا به پایین بیش‌تر می‌پوشاند. در آخرین نقاشی، «بازگشت به سیاهی»، کل ترکیب در تاریکی غرق شده است. رنگ سیاه این کارهای او، نقاشی «مربع سیاه» (۱۹۱۵) کازیمیر مالویچ و همچنین استفاده گسترده‌ی [بهجت] صدر از رنگ روغنی سیاه را یادآوری می‌کند. فابریس هرگوت، کیوریتور، این کار صدر را اشاره‌ی می‌داند به «لکه‌ی عظیمی که نفت در تاریخ ایران به دوش می‌کشد.»۱۰ همچنین، مربع سیاه یادآور فعالیت‌هایی است که در شبکه‌های اجتماعی پس از اعتراض های سیاسی آبان ۱۳۹۸ در ایران و همچنین «سه‌شنبه‌ی خاموشی» پس از قتل بریانا تیلور و جورج فلوید توسط پلیس در ایالات متحده، سازماندهی شده بود.

در زمان حضور کاشی ها در زمستان ۲۰۲۲ در برنامه رزیدنسی شهر برست فرانسه، لوییک لو گال، کیوریتور مرکز هنر معاصر پاسرل، پیشنهاد کرد که او هم مانند صدر از فلز نه فقط به عنوان یک ساختار، بلکه به عنوان یک رسانه استفاده کند که استفاده از این ماده‌ی صنعتی و گنجاندن آن در ساختار کارهایش، منطقی است. شمایل هندسی‌ای که کاشی‌ها با قطعات فلزی یافت شده می‌سازد، یادآور شابلون‌هایی است که در بسیاری از کارهایش استفاده می‌کند. شاید مهم‌ترین نکته این باشد که مجسمه‌های کاشی‌ها سایه می‌افکنند. و سایه، همانند «دوئنده»ی گابریل گارسیا لورکا، تجسم یک فضای خلاقانه و پر از ظرافت است. همانطور که کلاریس لیسپکتور در «آگوا ویوا» (۱۹۷۳) می‌نویسد، «برای بازساختن خودم و بازساختن تو، به حالت باغ و سایه و واقعیت بی‌تنش بازمی‌گردم.»۱۱

همچنین کاشی‌ها در برست برای اولین بار آثار ویدیویی خود را به نمایش گذاشت و روند آزمایش‌هایش در ترکیب‌بندی روی سطح دیجیتال را پیش از اجرا روی بوم نشان داد. «چشم‌ها پر از درخشش می‌شوند و به سایه‌های سیاه می‌لغزند» (۲۰۲۱)، فیلم انیمیشنی که او در طول قرنطینه ساخته، منبع مهم دیگری برای نمایش تاریکی فزاینده‌ای است که در توالی نقاشی‌های «در ستایش پلک‌زدن» می‌بینیم.

کاشی‌ها به تازگی بیرون استودیوی خود گل آفتابگردان کاشته است. او عاشق این گل است،همچنین شیفته ی نقاشیهای ونسان ونگوگ از شکوفه های درخشان آن روی بومهای بزرگیست که در خانه ی زرد جنوب فرانسه کار شده اند. در «دنیای دیگری در

انتظار ماست» (۲۰۲۳) که جدیدترین نمایش هدی کاشی‌ها در اروپا بود، هنرمند به استفاده از نقوش گل ادامه داده و به خشونت عشق و چیدن حریصانه‌ی یک شکوفه‌ی کمیاب اشاره کرده است. نقاشی دوتکه‌ی «به چپ فشار نده! به حرکت خود ادامه بده» (۲۰۲۳) که بخشی از این مجموعه‌ی آثار است، از نوع پویایی مجسمه‌گونه بهره گرفته و تصویری انتزاعی‌شده از یک فرم زنانه که در حال سقوط است و درعدم توازنی خطرناک قرار گرفته را نمایش می‌دهد. تازگی‌ها، کاشی‌ها شروع به پوشاندن بوم‌های خود با نقش‌های کم‌رنگ سایه‌شکل کرده است. او این سایه‌ها را با استفاده از نورافکن‌هایی طراحی می‌کند که بخشی از آن‌ها را با برش‌هایی از جنس وینیل با شکلی شبیه به دست می‌پوشاند. این شبح‌های بریده‌شده و کشیده‌شده، خشونت زیبایی را می‌کاوند.

۱. نگاه کنید به
"Institute for the Intellectual Development of Children and Young Adults," *Bidoun*, Winter 2009, https://www.bidoun.org/articles/institute-for-the-intellectual-development-of-children-young-adults.

۲. نگاه کنید به
Media Farzin, "A Short History of Art Exhibitions in Iran, 1946–78," in *Iran Modern*, ed. Fereshteh Daftari and Layla S. Diba (New York: Asia Society Museum, 2013), 67–71.

۳. به نقل از
Morad Montazami, "Moderne et contemporain: usages et enjeux en historiographiques compares," lecture at ARVIMM, l'Unité d'arabe de l'Université de Genève, de l'Institut d'étude de l'Islam et des sociétés du monde musulman et l'École normale supérieure, Centre Pompidou and EHESS, Paris, 2018.

۴. بهجت صدر در مورد کلاژهای عکس خود، ۱۹۹۵، به نقل از
Behjat Sadr: Press Release by Cyrus Goberville and Daniele Balice (April 5- June 1, 2019), Balice Hertling Galerie, Paris.

۵. نگاه کنید به
Amy Sillman, *Faux Pas: Selected Writings and Drawings* (Paris: After 8 Books, 2020), 207.

۶. کاشی‌ها در گفتگویی با نویسنده در ۱۴ ژوئن ۲۰۲۴ با لحنی تحسین‌برانگیز درباره‌ی فرانکفورت گفت که «خیلی تیزبین بود».

۷. اعتماد که پیشینه‌ای به عنوان فروشنده‌ی آثار هنر اسلامی داشت، اولین گالری ایرانی‌ای بود که شعبه‌ای در دبی افتتاح کرد، شهری که به ویژه پس از اولین دوره‌ی آرت‌دبی در سال ۲۰۰۷ به

یک موتور واقعی در توسعه‌ی بین‌المللی دنیای هنر حوزه‌ی خلیج فارسی تبدیل شده است.
۸. ایمیل به نویسنده، آوریل ۲۰۲۲.
۹. ایمیل به نویسنده، آوریل ۲۰۲۲.
۱۰. نقل قول کامل:
"The immense stain, the indelible oil slick like a gob that this oil represents in the history of Iran, through which this country was restored to the rank of producer, eliciting covetousness and the darkest passions of the human soul." Fabrice Hergott, "Spirals," in *Behdjat Sadr: Traces* (Paris: Zamân Books, 2014), 8.
۱۱. نگاه کنید به
Clarice Lispector, *Água Viva*, trans. Benjamin Moser (New York: New Directions, 1973)
البته در اینجا می‌توانستم از جونیچیرو تانیزاکی هم نقل قول کنم، خصوصاً چون هر دو نویسنده به زیبایی در ستایش قدرت خلاقانه‌ی سایه و تاریکی نوشته‌اند:
Junichiro Tanizaki, *In Praise of Shadows* (1933)

# شعف در نشانه: گفت‌وگوی هدی کاشی‌ها و لوکا لو پینتو

لوییک لو گال: تو پیشینه‌ای دوگانه داری؛ در ایران به روشی نسبتاً متعارف و متکی بر سنت، هنر خواندی و بعد از آن تحصیلاتت را در بوستون ادامه دادی. ترکیب این دو فرهنگ چه تأثیری بر روند نقاشی تو گذاشته است؟

هدی کاشی‌ها: در دوره‌ی کارشناسی در ایران در دانشکده‌ای تحصیل می‌کردم که محافظه‌کار و بسیار متکی بر سنت بود. معمولاً دوست دارم در کارهایم از ویژگی‌های کارتونی و کاریکاتور استفاده کنم و عاشق رنگ‌های تند هستم. اما در دانشکده، استادان ما اعتقاد داشتند که نباید چنین چیزهایی را وارد کارم کنم، وگرنه کارهایم بیش‌تر به عنوان کاریکاتور یا تصویرسازی طبقه‌بندی خواهند شد. به همین دلیل، سعی می‌کردم خودم را سانسور کنم. فکر می‌کردم که این کار، امری ضروری است. وقتی به ایالات متحده آمدم و طیف وسیع‌تری از انواع هنر را دیدم، احساس کردم که می‌توانم هر چیزی را که دوست دارم وارد آثارم کنم؛ بدون توجه به این که عناصر تصویرسازی و کاریکاتور داشته باشد یا خیر. می‌توانستم همه‌ی آن‌ها را با هم ترکیب کنم! تصور کردم که می‌خواهم دوباره از نو نقاشی کردن روی بوم را یاد بگیرم. اگرچه دانشگاهی که در بوستون در آن تحصیل می‌کردم نسبت به فضای کلی دانشگاه‌های هنری آمریکا محافظه‌کار محسوب می‌شد، اما با این وجود، هنرمندانی که به آنجا دعوت می‌شدند و همچنین همکلاسی‌هایم تأثیر زیادی بر کار من می‌گذاشتند و خصوصاً گستره‌ی کارهایم از این نظر که چه چیزهایی ممکن و مجاز بود را توسعه می‌دادند.

لوییک: فکر می‌کنم کار تو خیلی پیشرو است؛ هم در مفهوم و هم در شیوه‌ی نقاشی. خیلی تحت تأثیر کاریکاتور و کمیک هستی. ممکن است بیش‌تر در مورد این موضوع بگویی؟

هدی: این که این تأثیر از کجا سرچشمه گرفته را نمی‌دانم. وقتی بچه بودم، مجلات کاریکاتور زیادی می‌خریدم. می‌خواستم یک کاریکاتوریست معروف شوم. نمی‌دانم چرا. همیشه پرتره‌های زیادی از افراد خانواده و دوستانم می‌کشیدم. خیلی وقت است که در کارهایم از کاریکاتور و تصویرسازی استفاده می‌کنم. فکر می‌کردم که این شیوه‌ای مناسب و ظریف، و رویکردی خوب برای بیان چیزهایی است که در ایران می‌گذرد. مشاهده‌ی هر داستان و محتوایی که در شبکه‌های اجتماعی دیده می‌شود برای من آزادی فکری زیاد فراهم می‌کند و دوست دارم از آن‌ها الهام بگیرم. این نوع محتوا برای من ارتباط و تناظری عمیق با فرهنگ طنز، کاریکاتور و تصویرسازی دارد. در شبکه‌های آنلاین، محتوا تقریباً بلافاصله ایجاد و هم‌رسانی و به سرعت تکثیر و به اصطلاح وایرال می‌شود. از آن‌جا که کنترل فضای مجازی بسیار دشوار است، محتواهای آلترناتیو و غریب ی طنز سیاه به وفور پیدا

می‌شود. وقتی [در بیان هنری] مستقیماً به سیاهی و تاریکی و تلخی اشاره کنیم، آثار شبیه یک درام می‌شوند. دوست ندارم کار دراماتیک بسازم.

لوییک: مطمئناً وضعیت و شرایط ایران بر کارت تأثیر می‌گذارد. این چیزها همیشه همراه تو هستند. احتمال می‌دهم که این تأثیر در مدتی که در آمریکا زندگی می‌کردی تفاوت داشته.

هدی: در کشور من هر روز چیز جدیدی اتفاق می‌افتد و باید دائماً درباره‌ی خودتان، در مورد هر آن‌چه می‌خواهید فکر کنید. موضوعاتی که به آن‌ها می‌پردازم نیز این مسئله و دغدغه را منعکس می‌کند. یکی از دلایلی که باعث شد از آمریکا بازگردم تا حدی به همین مسئله برمی‌گردد. در آمریکا، شاید زندگی روزمره نیاز به پرسش‌های مداوم کمتری نسبت به ایران داشته باشد. اما در تصور من، تمام پرسش‌های روزمره، زیربنای کارم هستند. وقتی در استودیو هستم، داستان‌های شخصی‌ام با داستان‌های جاری در کل کشور، و حتی فراتر از آن، با آنچه در سطح بین‌المللی در جریان است در هم آمیخته می‌شوند. هر روز چیزی اتفاق می‌افتد و من از آن الهام می‌گیرم، اما دوست ندارم مستقیماً در مورد آن صحبت کنم. هرچند در نهایت وقتی به کارم نگاه می‌کنم، فکر نمی‌کنم ایرانی باشد، یا حتی سیاسی. فکر می‌کنم فاقد مرزهای سیاسی یا فرهنگی است.

لوییک: درست است. تقلیل‌دادن کارت به مرزهای فرهنگی، سیاسی یا اجتماعی ایران غیرممکن است. مطمئناً اشکال و الگوهایی در کارهایت هست که یادآور تاریخ منطقه باشند اما در نهایت، نمی‌توانم صرفاً با نگاه‌کردن به اثر، بگویم که سازنده‌ی آن از پیشینه چینی، ایرانی یا مکزیکی آمده است. با این وجود، چیز مشترکی در کار تو و سایر هنرمندان ایرانی، مثل طلا مدنی، می‌بینم و به نظر من این چیز، توانایی تو در پرداختن به امر پوچ است.

هدی: مطمئن نیستم که این موضوع در حال حاضر امر رایجی باشد. احتمالاً بیش‌تر در تاریخ ما دیده می‌شود.

لوییک: می‌خواهم درباره‌ی یکی از آثار مهم تو صحبت کنم که نخستین بار در گالری دستان در تهران به نمایش درآمد. سپس این اثر در اروپا هم به نمایش گذاشته شد: در مرکز هنر معاصر "پاسرل" (Passerelle)، در گالری ناتالی اوبدیا (Nathalie Obadia) در پاریس و همچنین در بخش نامحدود آرت بازل (Art Basel Unlimited). این اثر با عنوان در ستایش پلک زدن (۲۰۲۱) شناخته می‌شود. اثری واقعاً متفاوت است. فقط یک نقاشی نیست، بلکه یک چیدمان، حتی یک مجسمه است. می‌خواهم در مورد راه‌های جدید نمایش نقاشی‌ها و این که چگونه این رسانه

می‌تواند بارها و بارها تجدید و به‌روز شود، با تو صحبت کنم. برای آن چیدمان تصمیم گرفتی که نقاشی‌ها را روی پایه‌های متحرک قرار دهی تا به شکل مورد نظرت در فضای نمایشگاه چیده شوند. چرا چنین انتخاب غیرمعمولی کردی؟

هدی: به نظرم نصب‌کردن کارها روی دیوار، نمایی خیلی محکم و سفت و سخت دارد. بیش‌تر وقت‌ها احساس می‌کنم در چیدمان‌های روی دیوار، انگار فقط از مردم دعوت شده که بیایند و به کارها نگاه کنند، فکر کنند که آن را دوست دارند یا نه. در چنین شرایطی، به بیننده نقشی منفعل داده می‌شود. می‌خواستم با چیدمانی که گفتی، فرصتی به بازدیدکننده‌ها بدهم تا با روحیه‌ای بازیگوشانه با کارها رابطه برقرار کنند؛ نوعی عمل و تعامل. هرچه بیش‌تر در مسیر کارم پیش می‌روم در کنار فکر کردن به خود نقاشی، به فضا هم فکر می‌کنم. وقتی نقاشی‌ها را در یک فضا نصب می‌کنم، به فضاسازی، به جوی که ایجاد می‌شود، به این که چه‌طور ممکن است بازدیدکننده‌ها فعالانه با کارها و فضا تعامل کنند فکر می‌کنم.

لوییک: تصور می‌کنم که این تمایلی که برای درگیرکردن مخاطب با کارها و نمایش داری، منجر به نوعی شور و شعف می‌شود. در «من اینجا هستم، من اینجا نیستم»، نمایشی که در ۲۰۲۲ در مرکز هنر معاصر پاسرل در شهر برست داشتی، دوباره نگاهی ویژه به نحوه‌ی دیدن و تعامل بازدیدکنندگان با کارها نشان دادی. آثار سه‌بعدی تو و کارهایی که شامل نور بودند از نظر من وجهی بازیگوشانه داشتند. در حال حاضر کارت از چه نظر در حال تکامل است؟ آیا چیدمان‌های این‌چنینی و ویژه در کار تو بیش‌تر خواهد شد؟

هدی: در حال حاضر دلم می‌خواهد با پارچه‌ها و بوم‌های مختلف بازی کنم و ترکیب‌های جدید به دست بیاورم. در نقاشی‌هایم هم مسیرهای مختلفی را امتحان می‌کنم. در حال حاضر مشغول کار روی سه پروژه‌ی مختلف و غیرمرتبط هستم. یکی از آن‌ها از برخی نقاشی‌های مینیاتور هندی الهام گرفته است. یکی از آن‌ها ملهم از کارتون‌های پلنگ صورتی، و دیگری شامل آثاری شاعرانه‌تر است. چند وقت پیش، مدتی در نیویورک اقامت داشتم و در استودیوی کوچکی کار می‌کردم. مجبور شدم خودم را با مقیاس آنجا تطبیق دهم. این طور شد که مسیر جدیدی رفتم و کارهای متفاوتی هم تولید کردم. معمولاً سعی می‌کنم از یک سبک متمایز و قابل تشخیص خودداری کنم. وقتی هنرمند در یک مارپیچ تکرار گیر می‌کند خیلی ناراحت می‌شوم، حتی اگر کار نشانگر تسلط عمیق یا تکنیک قوی او باشد. گاهی اوقات وقتی در یک نقاشی کار جدیدی انجام می‌دهم حس رضایت به من دست می‌دهد و حتی شگفت‌زده می‌شوم، اما نمی‌خواهم آن را تکرار کنم. بر همین اساس، در کار بعدی مسیر مخالف یا متفاوتی را انتخاب می‌کنم. از

قطعیت در کارم متنفرم و تصور می‌کنم همین مسئله باعث می‌شود تا کار بازیگوشی خود را حفظ کند.

لوییک: تلاش تو برای پوشاندن ردپایت را دوست دارم! به مجموعه‌ی جدیدی اشاره کردی که از پلنگ صورتی الهام گرفته. ممکن است بیش‌تر در موردش توضیح بدهی؟ کنجکاوی من به خصوص به خاطر انیمیشن‌های کوتاهی است که در نمایش برست ارائه کرده بودی. این فیلم‌های کوتاه، نقطه‌ی شروعی برای نقاشی‌های جدیدت محسوب می‌شود، درست است؟

هدی: گاهی اوقات طرح‌هایی را روی آی‌پد می‌کشم که شبیه یک ویدیوی کوتاه می‌شوند و بعد نقاشی را در همان راستا شروع می‌کنم.

لوییک: اول تصاویر متحرک می‌سازی و بعد به به تصاویر ثابت برمی‌گردی. به نظر من این رابطه با تصویر متحرک و کارتون جادویی و زیباست چون یادآور فرهنگ عامه است، چیزی که بیشتر مردم با آن آشنا هستند و می‌توانند با آن ارتباط برقرار کنند و از آن لذت ببرند. اینجا بد نیست برگردیم به «در ستایش پلک‌زدن». اولین باری که این مجموعه را نمایش دادی در تهران بود و مجبور شدی بخشی از نقاشی را بپوشانی. آیا دلیل این کار، مقررات سانسور بود؟

هدی: اجازه نداشتم یک بخش از اثر را نمایش بدهم؛ یک مرد و زبانش. مجبور شدم آن را بپوشانم. در نهایت، موضوع جالبی بود زیرا زبان را با یک برچسب پوشاندم. همان موقع مشغول کار روی مجموعه‌ی دیگری بودم، «من اینجا هستم، من اینجا نیستم» (۲۰۲۰)، که به نوعی راجع به سانسور بود. این مجموعه در مورد این موضوع است که چگونه می‌توانیم توسط قدرت یا مرگ سرکوب شویم، نادیده گرفته شویم، نابود یا ناپدید شویم. در اینجا همان موضوع را مانند نقاشی‌هایم تکرار کردم. بدن با یک علامت قرمز یا یک شکل سیاه پوشیده شده یا تغییر شکل یافته. در برخی از کشورها، سانسور آمده تا بدن‌هایی را که «ناشایست» تلقی می‌شوند یا مضامین اعتراضی را نشان می‌دهند با شکل‌های سیاه بپوشاند. سعی کردم آنچه را پیدا کنم که پس از مرگ و ناپدید شدن از ما باقی می‌ماند، یعنی وقتی دیگر نگاهمان تاریک شده.

لوییک: مرا به یاد کتاب‌هایی می‌اندازد که بخشی‌هایی از آن‌ها در ایران سانسور می‌شود.

هدی: در دوران تحصیلم می‌دیدم که بسیاری از کتاب‌ها به شکل سانسورشده به دست ما می‌رسید و بخش‌هایی از آن‌ها سیاه می‌شد. همیشه تعجب می‌کردم: آیا این‌ها به وسیله‌ی جادو پنهان شده؟ برهنگی‌ها و چهره‌های خاصی ناپدید شده بودند. موضوع جالبی بود

چرا که یک جور زیبایی‌شناسی مختص خود ایجاد می‌کرد. مشخص بود که زیر سیاهی، یک بدن برهنه وجود دارد اما نمی‌توانستی آن را ببینی. باعث می‌شد قوه‌ی تخیل فعال شود؛ فکر می‌کردم که پشت این‌ها چیست؟ گاهی اوقات، دولت تصمیم گرفته بود نسخه‌ی جدیدی از یک نقاشی را ارائه کند. این چیزها پرسش‌های زیادی ایجاد می‌کنند. مثلاً، اگر چیزی بمیرد یا توسط قدرت پاک شود، آیا هنوز وجود دارد؟ «من اینجا هستم، من اینجا نیستم» و «در ستایش پلک‌زدن» را با توجه به چنین موضوع‌هایی ساختم، و دومی سانسور شد. احساس می‌کردم که این به نوعی نقطه‌ی اوج تمام آن ایده‌هاست.

لوییک: غالباً تصویر زن در مرکز کارت است و این‌طور که توضیح می‌دهی، قدرت، بدن، به خصوص بدن زنان را در فضا و محیط عمومی سرکوب می‌کند. آیا سعی داری این را در کارت به نمایش بگذاری؟ در برخی از نقاشی‌ها از سبک‌های خاصی استفاده می‌کنی که فرم‌ها را پنهان می‌کنند یا تغییر می‌دهند، مثل جاهایی که متأثر از کوبیسم هستی؛ منظورم آثاری مثل «نگاه کردن به آینه» (۲۰۲۱) است.

هدی: بدن‌ها در کار من بسیار مهم هستند. در واقع کار را شکل می‌دهند. حتی وقتی یک نقاشی انتزاعی می‌کشم، از بدن می‌آید، که بسیار انتزاعی است، و بیننده نمی‌تواند این موضوع را به خوبی متوجه شود. من هنوز به این موضوع علاقه‌ی زیادی دارم. در حال حاضر، این مسئله یکی از موضوعات کلیدی در پژوهش‌هایی است که در مورد مینیاتورهای ایرانی و هندی می‌کنم. در تصور من، ترکیبی از کوبیسم، نقاشی‌های هندی و نقاشی‌های مینیاتور ایرانی شکل می‌گیرد. باز می‌بینیم که بدن زن با محیط درگیر می‌شود. این فکر پس از «زن، زندگی، آزادی*» بیش از پیش در کارم شکل گرفت. مثلاً حالا نسبت به مو کنجکاوتر شده‌ام، و بعد که بیش‌تر به نقاشی‌های هندی نگاه کردم دیدم که مو و فرم‌های بدن زنانه در آن‌ها زیاد دیده می‌شود، به طوری که با طبیعت، با گل‌ها همسو و همراه هستند. شروع به تجربه‌کردن با چرخ سفالگری کردم. گلدان‌ها و سایر سرامیک‌هایی که ساختم عمداً بدن‌های زنانه را تداعی می‌کردند. بنابراین، بله، بدن همواره در کارم درون‌مایه‌ای تکرارشونده است.

لوییک: تو راهکارهایی گول‌زننده و نوآورانه برای نمایش بدن پیدا می‌کنی. اشاره کردی که سبک خودت را دائماً تغییر می‌دهی تا در یک فرآیند یکنواخت تجاری گرفتار نشوی، اما هم‌زمان راهی پیدا کرده‌ای که بدن را در کارهایت حفظ کنی. وقتی نقاشی می‌کنی، درجه‌های مختلفی برای درک‌کردن تغییرات دائمی‌ای که در سبک ایجاد می‌شود وجود دارد. می‌دانم که به محتوایی که در شبکه‌های اجتماعی می‌بینی، دقت زیادی می‌کنی. این فضاها پنجره‌ای به بی‌نهایت تصویر هستند. وقتی به محتواهای هنری نگاه می‌کنی،

* «زن، زندگی، آزادی» شعاری است که ریشه در جنبش‌های کُردی تحت رهبری زنان داشت؛ اما بعدتر از زمینه‌ی اولیه‌اش فراتر رفت و پس از اعتراضات سال ۲۰۲۲ در ایران که به دنبال مرگ مهسا امینی آغاز شد، شهرت جهانی پیدا کرد. گشت ارشاد امینی را به اتهام عدم رعایت حجابِ موردنظرِ حکومت دستگیر کرده بود.

وقتی مجلات هنر معاصر را می‌خوانی، می‌بینی که هزاران سبک مختلف وجود دارد. وقتی در شبکه‌های اجتماعی هستی، به کل جهان دسترسی داری، و این مسئله گویای لذت استفاده از این ابزارهاست. نقاشی‌های تو اغلب به شبکه‌های اجتماعی مرتبط هستند. در جریان تظاهرات در ایران، برخی از مردم مربع‌هایی سیاه را در اینستاگرام به عنوان نشانه همبستگی در اعتراض منتشر می‌کردند. تو از این نماد در یکی از نقاشی‌هایت استفاده کردی؛ «تقدیم با عشق به کازیمیر مالویچ، سیاه روی سیاه» (۲۰۲۰). درست قبل از جنبش «جان سیاهان مهم است» بود، که در طول آن نیز از مربع سیاه به عنوان یک نشانه در شبکه‌های اجتماعی استفاده می‌شد. زیاد پیش می‌آید که از عناصری از این دست در نقاشی‌هایت استفاده کنی؟

هدی: بله، اما نه همیشه. خودم را مجبور نمی‌کنم که این کار را انجام دهم، اما اگر به طور تصادفی چیزی را ببینم و بین آثارم و آن موضوع ارتباط برقرار کنم، وارد دغدغه‌هایم می‌شود. از چنین موضوعی استقبال می‌کنم؛ از این که این‌ها را به کارم وارد کنم. فکر می‌کنم کارم مانند یک سطل زباله است. برای من نقاشی این‌طور است. ایده‌هایم از رسانه‌های اجتماعی، از چیزهای کارتونی، از اخبار می‌آیند، و سپس همه‌ی آن‌ها را با هم ادغام می‌کنم. آن‌ها را نقاشی می‌کنم، و سپس به سراغ تجربه‌ی دیگری می‌روم. در مورد نقاشی‌ای که به آن اشاره کردی، به سیاه فکر می‌کردم، به خاطر تظاهرات، و این که مردم مربع‌هایی سیاه را در اینستاگرام به اشتراک می‌گذاشتند. این‌طور بود که عمیق‌تر به سیاه فکر کردم. در آن دوره خیلی به مالویچ فکر می‌کردم و ارتباطات زیادی بین همه‌ی این ایده‌ها پیدا کردم.

لوییک: خیلی عجیب است که می‌گویی توجه زیادی به سیاه داشتی، اما برعکس این مسئله، کارت پر از رنگ بود.

هدی: گفته می‌شود که رنگ سیاه جذاب نیست یا فروش نمی‌رود. کار من خیلی رنگارنگ بود، و شاید از این که با رنگ سیاه نقاشی کنم می‌ترسیدم. این‌طور شد که سعی کردم خودم را به این شکل به چالش بکشم. در مورد مفهوم سیاه فکر می‌کردم، و می‌خواستم کاری انجام دهم که برایم چالش‌برانگیز باشد.

لوییک: ممکن است در مورد طنز در کار تو صحبت کنیم؟ شوخی‌ها و چیزهای سرگرم‌کننده‌ای که در نقاشی‌هایت دیده می‌شود.

هدی: واقعاً دوست دارم لحظه‌ای را در گالری یا در فضا یا هر جایی ایجاد کنم که مردم بتوانند بیایند و به کارهای من نگاه کنند و با آنها بخندند یا گریه کنند؛ پیش از این که آنجا را ترک کنند. وقتی آثار فقط خنده‌دار هستند، کسی آن‌ها را جدی نمی‌گیرد. عاشق

صحبت کردن در مورد زندگی هستم. در دوران پس از انقلاب ایران، حدود ده سال پیش که در دهه‌ی بیست‌سالگی بودم، وقتی از گالری‌ها یا سایر نمایشگاه‌های هنری در تهران بازدید می‌کردم، نقاشی‌های زیادی را می‌دیدم که از کارهای لوسین فروید و فرانسیس بیکن الهام گرفته بودند. نقاشی‌های بد زیادی می‌دیدم که در مورد بدن‌های تکه‌تکه شده بودند. واقعاً زشت بود. منظورم این نیست که همه‌ی ما باید دائما و فقط در مورد شادی حرف بزنیم، اما در اینجا منظورم زیبایی‌شناسی هم نیست، فرم هم نیست؛ موضوع دعوت مردم به زشتی بود. این رویکرد انگار حاکی از نوعی پرستیژ یا یک جور لاف روشن‌فکری بود؛ این که اعلام کنیم «احساس بدی به زندگی دارم». دلیلی که دوست دارم در کارهایم به چیزهای بپردازم که بامزه یا ظریف هستند، این است که می‌خواهم از مردم دعوت کنم که نکات به‌خصوصی را ببینند؛ چیزهایی تاریک که در عین حال خنده‌دار یا جالب هستند. من نمی‌خواهم فقط زشتی زندگی را نشان دهم.

لوییک: کار تو زندگی و حقیقتِ زنده‌بودن را جشن می‌گیرد. و کارت زیباست، به ویژه امروز که جهان زیر سلطه‌ی سیاست‌های مخرب ویران می‌شود. نقاشی‌های تو مثل تنفس هوای تازه هستند، اما اگر بخواهی در آن‌ها عمیق‌تر شوی، باید به آنچه امروز در جهان می‌گذرد هم توجه کنی. در کار تو، سطح‌های زیادی برای درک و استنباط وجود دارد. جدی است، اما در عین حال جدی نیست.

هدی: هدفی که در کارم دارم را به خوبی بیان کردی؛ جدی است اما جدی نیست. نقاشی‌کردن مثل یک پازل است. در جهت‌های مختلف پیش می‌روی و بعد سعی می‌کنی قطعات مختلف را پیدا کنی و آن‌ها را کنار هم قرار دهی.

لوییک: پازل استعاره‌ی زیبایی است.

هدی: «در ستایش پلک‌زدن» برای من مجموعه‌ای درباره‌ی زندگی و مرگ بود. شکنندگی زندگی مهم است، زیرا زندگی خیلی تراژیک است.

لوییک: تراژدی در یک مجموعه! آیا همیشه در چارچوب مجموعه کار کرده‌ای؟

هدی: این طور نبوده که همیشه در چارچوب مجموعه فکر کنم، اما اخیراً بیش‌تر شده. شاید به این دلیل باشد که ذهنم این روزها روی روایت‌ها متمرکز است. ذهنم دوست دارد داستان بگوید. بله، دلیلش همین است. کار من بیش‌تر و بیش‌تر به سمت مجموعه پیش می‌رود زیرا می‌خواهد داستان بگوید.

*Where Is the Flower Gone?* (detail), 2019. Acrylic on canvas, 150 × 100 cm
Courtesy of the artist and Galerie Nathalie Obadia Paris/Brussels. Photo: We Document Art

*How to Make Vertical Sky* (detail), 2021. Acrylic and modeling paste on canvas, 150 × 120 cm
Private collection. Photo: Matin Jameie

*I Died but I still Love You* (detail), 2019. Acrylic on canvas, 139 × 107 cm
Courtesy of the artist and Galerie Nathalie Obadia Paris/Brussels. Photo: We Document Art

*The Darkness Reveals the Eyes* (detail), 2020. Acrylic on canvas, 180 × 150 cm
Courtesy of the artist and Dastan Gallery. Photo: Matin Jameie

*Flowers Are Picked One by One...* (detail), 2022. Acrylic on canvas, 170 × 200 cm
Courtesy of the artist and Galerie Nathalie Obadia Paris/Brussels. Photo: Matin Jameie

*Untitled* (detail), 2019. Acrylic on suede canvas, 100 × 70 cm
Courtesy of the artist and Galerie Nathalie Obadia Paris/Brussels. Photo: We Document Art

*Dear St. Agatha I Am Witness of Your Tears, In the Land of Tulips* (detail), 2020. Acrylic on canvas, 150 × 130 cm
Fonds Erard de Becker, Belgium. Photo: Matin Jameie

*The Love Fire* (detail), 2021. Acrylic on canvas, 180 × 150 cm
Private collection, Tehran. Photo: Artist Studio

*The Chill Fighter Can Scatter the Eyes* (detail), 2021. Acrylic on canvas, 150 × 180 cm
Courtesy of the artist and Dastan Gallery. Photo: Artist Studio

*There Is a Brick Wall, Bricks Are Broken and She Falls, So Happy Birthday to All* (detail), 2021. Acrylic on canvas, 210 × 175 cm
Courtesy of the artist and Galerie Nathalie Obadia Paris/Brussels. Photo: Matin Jameie

*I Am Here, I Am Not Here* (detail), 2021. Acrylic and wood glue on canvas, 150 × 120 cm
Courtesy of the artist and Galerie Nathalie Obadia Paris/Brussels. Photo: Aurélien Mole

*Tantalus Punishment* (detail), 2021. Acrylic and silkscreen print on canvas, 210 × 175 cm
Courtesy of the artist and Galerie Nathalie Obadia Paris/Brussels. Photo: Matin Jameie

*Purple Is Healing the Wound Between Sword and Neck* (detail), 2022. Acrylic on canvas, 180 × 150 cm
Éric Jacquet collection, Lyon. Photo: We Document Art

*Oh! Butterflies* (detail), 2023. Acrylic on canvas, 210 × 175 cm
Courtesy of the artist and Dastan Gallery. Photo: Artist Studio

*All Beautiful Lives Start Floating when Dark Falls, Maybe I Am Somewhere Else Above Skies* (detail), 2019. Acrylic on canvas, 185 × 151 cm
Private collection, Belgium. We Document Art

*Black as Black*, 2021. Acrylic on canvas, 210 × 175 cm
Courtesy of the artist and Galerie Nathalie Obadia Paris/Brussels. Photo: Matin Jameie

*Last Sunset, Last Dive*, 2021. Acrylic on canvas, 210 × 175 cm
Courtesy of the artist and Galerie Nathalie Obadia Paris/Brussels. Photo: Matin Jameie

*The Top Secret*, 2021. Acrylic on canvas, 210 × 175 cm
Courtesy of the artist and Galerie Nathalie Obadia Paris/Brussels. Photo: Matin Jameie

*Along Evening*, 2021. Acrylic on canvas, 210 × 175 cm
Courtesy of the artist and Galerie Nathalie Obadia Paris/Brussels. Photo: Matin Jameie

*Tantalus Punishment*, 2021. Acrylic and silkscreen print on canvas, 210 × 175 cm
Courtesy of the artist and Galerie Nathalie Obadia Paris/Brussels. Photo: Matin Jameie

*Oh, no, no, no, no... Don't Let Him Gooo...!*, 2021. Acrylic on canvas, 210 × 175 cm
Courtesy of the artist and Galerie Nathalie Obadia Paris/Brussels. Photo: Matin Jameie

*The Curiosity of St. Thomas Made the Hole, as the Holes Make the Eyeholes*, 2021. Acrylic and wood glue on canvas, 210 × 175 cm
Courtesy of the artist and Galerie Nathalie Obadia Paris/Brussels. Photo: Matin Jameie

*There Is a Brick Wall, Bricks Are Broken and She Falls, So Happy Birthday to All*, 2021. Acrylic on canvas, 210 × 175 cm
Courtesy of the artist and Galerie Nathalie Obadia Paris/Brussels. Photo: Matin Jameie

*In Appreciation of Blinking*, 2021, installation view at Unlimited/Art Basel, 2023. Acrylics, silkscreen, and wood glue on canvas, set of 8 paintings: 210 × 175 cm (each)
Courtesy of the artist and Galerie Nathalie Obadia Paris/Brussels. Photo: Dawn Blackman

*I Am Here, I Am Not Here* (diptych), 2020. Acrylic on canvas, 150 × 120 cm (each)
Private collection. Photo: Aurélien Mole

*I Am Here, I Am Not Here* (diptych), 2020. Acrylic on canvas, 150 × 120 cm (each)
Private collection. Photo: Aurélien Mole

*I Am Here, I Am Not Here*, 2021. Acrylic and wood glue on canvas, 150 × 120 cm
Courtesy of the artist and Galerie Nathalie Obadia Paris/Brussels. Photo: Aurélien Mole

*I Am Here, I Am Not Here*, 2021. Acrylic and wood glue on canvas, 150 × 120 cm
Courtesy of the artist and Galerie Nathalie Obadia Paris/Brussels. Photo: Aurélien Mole

*I Am Here, I Am Not Here*, 2021. Acrylic, modeling paste, and Plexiglas on printed canvas, 150 × 120 cm
Courtesy of the artist and Galerie Nathalie Obadia Paris/Brussels. Photo: Aurélien Mole

*The Chill Fighter Can Scatter the Eyes*, 2021. Acrylic on canvas, 150 × 180 cm
Courtesy of the artist and Dastan Gallery.
Photo: Artist Studio

*Untitled*, 2021. Acrylic on canvas, 100 × 70 cm
Private collection. Photo: Artist Studio

*Between Lips and Lipstick*, 2022. Acrylic and wood Glue on canvas, 70 × 50 cm
Courtesy of the artist and Dastan Gallery.
Photo: Artist Studio

*The Love Fire*, 2021. Acrylic on canvas, 180 × 150 cm
Private collection. Photo: Artist Studio

*Everlasting Wait for Blue*, 2021. Acrylic on canvas, 180 × 150 cm
Private collection. Photo: Artist Studio

*Everyone is a Hunter in a Hunting Ground*, 2020. Acrylic on canvas, 180 × 150 cm
Private collection. Photo: Matin Jameie

*Apollo Pursuing Daphne* (diptych), 2020. Acrylic on canvas, 140 × 90 cm, 150 × 120 cm
Private collection. Photo: We Document Art

*I Am Walkin While I Am Walkin*, 2019. Acrylic on canvas, 150 × 130 cm
Private collection. Photo: Artist Studio

*Erasing the World*, 2021. Acrylic on canvas, 130 × 150 cm
Private collection. Photo: Artist Studio

*Orange Like Fire Burns Us into the Sunset. Yes! This Is the Beginning of Summer, Hot Summer*, 2022. Acrylic and silicon powder on canvas, variable dimensions Courtesy of the artist and Galerie Nathalie Obadia Paris/Brussels. Photo: Aurélien Mole

*After Blue Is Yellow*, 2019. Acrylic on canvas, 100 × 70 cm
Private collection. Photo: Artist Studio

*Bird Sings from Orange Which Is About Majesty*, 2019. Acrylic on canvas, 150 × 180 cm
Private collection. Photo: Artist Studio

*Dear St. Agatha I Am Witness of Your Tears, In the Land of Tulips* (detail), 2020. Acrylic on canvas, 150 × 130 cm
Fonds Erard de Becker, Belgium. Photo: Matin Jameie

*The Time He Left His Shadow*, 2021. Acrylic on canvas, 180 × 150 cm
Private collection, Nanjing. Photo: Aurélien Mole

*Eyes Never Stop Seeing All Things*, 2020. Acrylic on canvas, 180 × 150 cm
Depla-Lantsoght collection, Belgium.
Photo: We Document Art

*How to Choose a Right Perfume in a Suspended World?*, 2019. Acrylic on canvas, 120 × 100 cm
Private collection, Paris. Photo: We Document Art

*Rainfall after Smoke*, 2020. Acrylic, acrylic gel, and sand on canvas, 150 × 120 cm
Courtesy of the artist and Galerie Nathalie Obadia Paris/Brussels. Photo: We Document Art

*Full Cycle*, 2021. Acrylic on canvas, 130 ×150 cm
Courtesy of the artist and Galerie Nathalie Obadia Paris/Brussels. Photo: Matin Jameie

*Untitled*, 2019. Acrylic on canvas, 100 × 70 cm
Courtesy of the artist and Galerie Nathalie Obadia Paris/Brussels. Photo: We Document Art

*Rabbiting in the Hunting Ground*, 2020. Acrylic on canvas, 180 × 150 cm
Courtesy of the artist and Galerie Nathalie Obadia Paris/Brussels. Photo: We Document Art

*Everything Started from the Day, Earth Turned and Turned, and One Bird Pooped on My Head*, 2023. Acrylic on canvas, rotating base 50 × 50 cm, 100 × 70 cm, 150 × 90 cm Ø 75 cm
Courtesy of the artist and Galerie Nathalie Obadia Paris/Brussels. Photo: We Document Art

*Where Is the Flower Gone?*, 2019. Acrylic on canvas, 150 × 100 cm
Courtesy of the artist and Galerie Nathalie Obadia Paris/Brussels. Photo: We Document Art

*All Beautiful Lives Start Floating When Dark Falls, Maybe I Am Somewhere Else Above Skies*, 2019. Acrylic on canvas, 185 × 151 cm
Private collection, Belgium. Photo: We Document Art

*I Died but I Still Love You*, 2019. Acrylic on canvas, 139 × 107 cm
Courtesy of the artist and Galerie Nathalie Obadia Paris/Brussels. Photo: We Document Art

*The Banished Sun*, 2021. Acrylic on canvas, 150 × 120 cm
NBB collection, Geneva. Photo: Matin Jameie

*Return Sun Melts Bodies into One*, 2021. Acrylic on canvas, 150 × 120 cm
Private collection, Nanjing. Photo: Aurélien Mole

*Look at the Mirror*, 2021. Acrylic on canvas, 150 × 130 cm
Depla-Lantsoght collection, Belgium. Photo: Aurélien Mole

*The Long Days of Summer Melt Thirsty Bodies into Water*, 2022. Acrylic on canvas, 150 × 120 cm
Private collection, Paris. Photo: Aurélien Mole

*Getting Caught Between East and West*, 2022. Acrylic and silicon powder on canvas, 120 × 150 cm
Private collection, Paris. Photo: Aurélien Mole

*Two Methods for Separating Sun from Flower*, 2021. Acrylic on wood panel rotated in metal frame, 120 × 150 cm. Installation view *100 years*, seventh annual group exhibition in collaboration between Jeffrey Deitch and Gagosian, Miami, 2022. Private collection. Photo: Sebastiano Pellion di Parsano

*Everything Vanished Except Lipstick Traces on Skin*, 2022. Acrylic on canvas, 120 × 150 cm
Private collection, Hong Kong. Photo: We Document Art

*The Eye, The Eyehole, The Hole*, 2021. Acrylic and wood glue on canvas, 120 × 100 cm
Courtesy of the artist and Galerie Nathalie Obadia Paris/Brussels. Photo: Aurélien Mole

*Untitled*, 2019. Acrylic on suede canvas, 100 × 70 cm
Courtesy of the artist and Galerie Nathalie Obadia Paris/Brussels. Photo: We Document Art

*Red Ribbon*, 2022. Oil on canvas, 150 × 90 cm
Private collection, Belgium. Photo: We Document Art

*The Final Point*, 2022. Acrylic on canvas, 150 × 95 cm
Courtesy of the artist and Galerie Nathalie Obadia Paris/Brussels. Photo: Matin Jameie

*I Am Angry, but Everything Is Fine*, 2022. Acrylic on canvas, 120 × 100 cm
Courtesy of the artist and Galerie Nathalie Obadia Paris/Brussels. Photo: Matin Jameie

*Flowers Are Picked One by One...*, 2022. Acrylic on canvas, 170 × 200 cm. Photo: Matin Jameie

*Even the Last Red One...*, 2022. Acrylic on canvas, 180 × 150 cm
Courtesy of the artist and Galerie Nathalie Obadia Paris/Brussels. Photo: Matin Jameie

*Loop the Loop*, 2022. Acrylic on canvas, 150 × 150 cm
Courtesy of the artist and Galerie Nathalie Obadia Paris/Brussels. Photo: Matin Jameie

*The Wrong Shadow*, 2022. Acrylic on canvas, 158 × 150 cm
Private collection, Paris. Photo: Matin Jameie

*The Bardo*, 2022. Acrylic on canvas, 150 × 120 cm
Private collection, Hong Kong. Photo: Matin Jameie

*Purple is Healing the Wound between Sword and Neck*, 2022. Acrylic on canvas, 180 × 150 cm
Éric Jacquet collection, Lyon. Photo: We Document Art

*Farewell to my shadow*, 2023, steel, 150 × 120 cm. Monlibert collection, Paris. *The Bardo*, 2022, Acrylic on canvas, 150 × 120 cm; *Just for a second / Heaven unveiled itself / The sun returned to flowers / And the bright guilty word was invented: Sunflower*, 2022, Embroidery on printed velvet, 150 × 120 cm.

Installation view *Another world is waiting for us* at Galerie Nathalie Obadia, Brussels, 2023.
Courtesy of the artist and Galerie Natalie Obadia.
Photo: We Document Art

*Water Like Mirror / Hugged My Profile Face in the Red Hot Sky and Now/ My Full Portrait Is Unveiled / in the Soaked Chilled Sky*, 2023. Acrylic on canvas, each canvas 120 × 100 cm
Courtesy of the artist and Dastan Gallery. Photo: Matin Jameie

*Left over Memories*, 2023. Soft pastel and acrylic on canvas, 150 × 120 cm
Private collection. Photo: Artist Studio

*The Milk and Iris*, 2023. Acrylic on canvas, 150 × 120 cm
Courtesy of the artist and Dastan Gallery. Photo: Artist Studio

*Woman Holding the Vase / The Vase Holding the Flower / The Lips / The Eyes / The Vase / Fit Water and Light in Herself*, 2023. Soft pastel and acrylic on canvas, 150 × 120 cm
Private collection. Photo: Artist Studio

*Rainy Day*, 2023. Soft pastel and acrylic on canvas, 150 × 120 cm
Courtesy of the artist. Photo: Artist Studio

*Spread Your Soul on The Vermilion Soil*, 2023. Acrylic on canvas, 150 × 120 cm
Private collection. Photo: Artist Studio

*Moonlight*, 2023. Acrylic on canvas, 150 × 150 cm
Courtesy of the artist and Dastan Gallery. Photo: Artist Studio

*Float in Green*, 2023. Acrylic and silicon powder on canvas, 150 × 120 cm
Courtesy of the artist. Photo: Artist Studio

*Shahrivar Like a Tear Drop Decided to Fall This is Liberation Time for All*, 2023. Acrylic on canvas, 150 × 120 cm
Private collection. Photo: Artist Studio

*Don't Push to the Left! Keep Move On*, 2022. Acrylic on canvas, wooden table, and metal, 180 × 150 cm
Courtesy of the artist and Galerie Nathalie Obadia Paris/Brussels. Photo: Matin Jameie

*The Narcissist Awoke and He Faced Broken Bed*, 2023. Acrylic on canvas, 150 × 120 cm, 75 × 120 cm
Courtesy of the artist and Galerie Nathalie Obadia Paris/Brussels. Photo: Matin Jameie

*Oh! Butterflies*, 2021. Acrylic on canvas, 210 × 175 cm
Courtesy of the artist and Dastan Gallery. Photo: Artist Studio

This publication is published on the occasion of the exhibition *I'm Here, I'm not Here*
Hoda Kashiha

18 Feb—14 May 2022
Passerelle Centre d'art contemporain
41, rue Charles Berthelot
29200 Brest
France
cac-passerelle.com

Passerelle Centre d'art contemporain:
Emmanuelle Baleydier, Thibault Brébant, Jean-Christophe Deprez-Deperiers, Camille Guihard, Loïc Le Gall, Maël Le Gall, Jean-Christophe Primel, Marine Soler

Acknowledgments

Galerie Nathalie Obadia Paris/Brussels
Nathalie Obadia, Jérôme Menasché, Valérie Wille, Marie Chappaz

Dastan Gallery, Tehran/Toronto
Hormoz Hematian, Sam Roknivand

Soroosh Noorbakhsh,
Réza Salami
Pierre Le Saint
Maïwenn Thominot

The lenders and all the collectors who wish to remain anonymous.

Catalogue
Hoda Kashiha: Slipping on Fragmented Shapes

Edited by
Hoda Kashiha

Publishing Editor
Agnese Cantelmi, Mousse

Graphic Design
Gloria Favaro, Mousse

Texts
Lillian Davis, Loïc Le Gall

Translations
Loïc Le Gall from English to French
Ashkan Zahraei from English to Farsi

Copyediting and Proofreading
Lindsey Westbrook, Marie Chappaz

GALERIE NATHALIE OBADIA
PARIS BRUXELLES

DASTAN



Published and distributed by
Mousse Publishing – Contrappunto s.r.l.
via Piercandido Decembrio 28
20137, Milan–Italy
moussemagazine.it

First Edition
2025

Printed by Grafiche Antiga

ISBN 978-88-6749-641-9

27 € / 30 $

Hoda Kashiha is represented by
Galerie Nathalie Obadia Paris/Brussels
Dastan Gallery Tehran/Toronto